Salud!

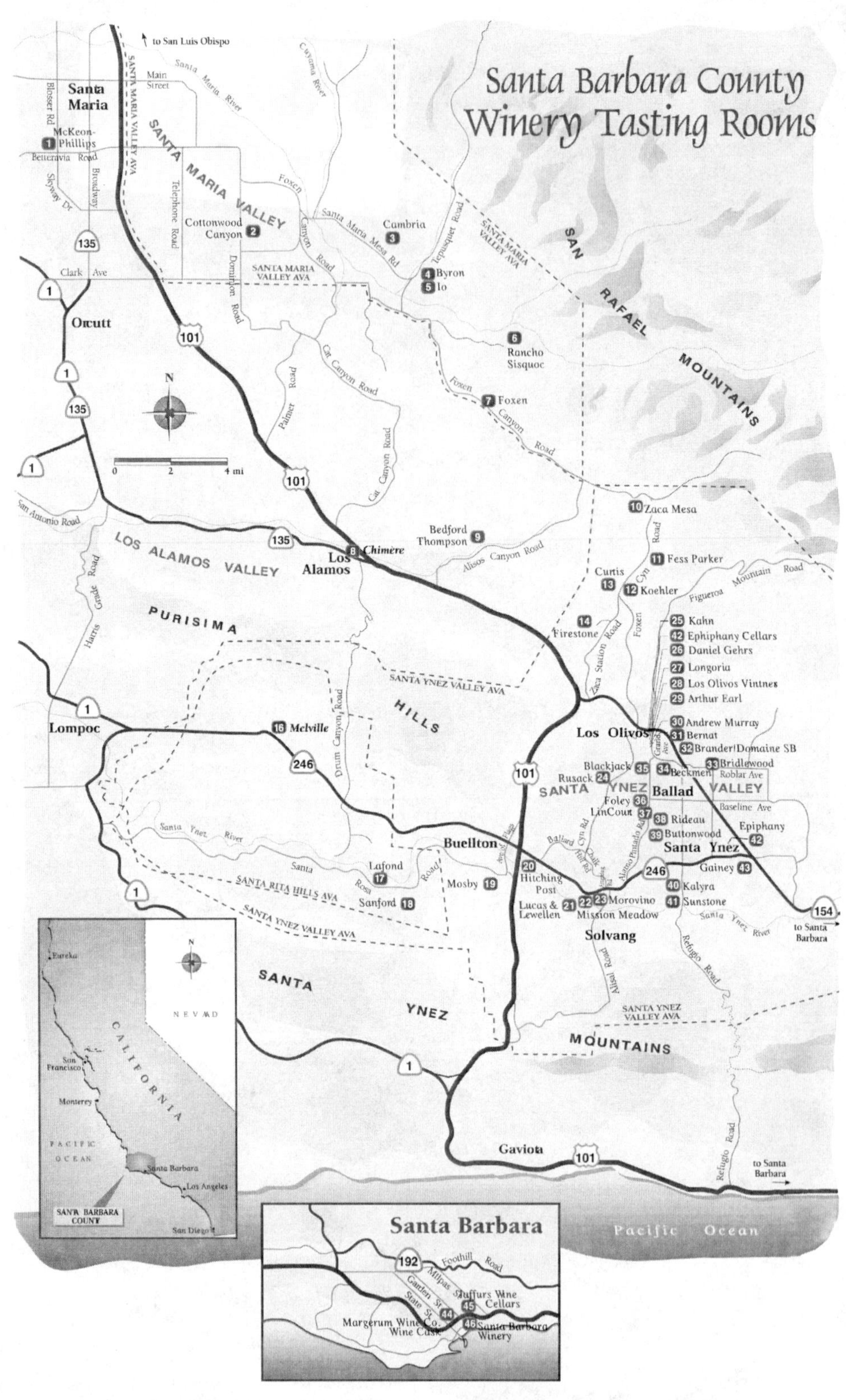

Santa Barbara County Winery Tasting Rooms
Santa Maria
1 McKeon-Phillips
2 Cottonwood Canyon
3 Cambria
4 Byron
5 Io
6 Rancho Sisquoc
7 Foxen
8 Chimère
9 Bedford Thompson
10 Zaca Mesa
11 Fess Parker
12 Koehler
13 Curtis
14 Firestone
16 Melville
17 Lafond
18 Sanford
19 Mosby
20 Hitching Post
21 Lucas & Lewellen
22 23 Morovino
Mission Meadow
24 Rusack
25 Kahn
42 Ephiphany Cellars
26 Daniel Gehrs
27 Longoria
28 Los Olivos Vintner
29 Arthur Earl
30 Andrew Murray
31 Bernat
32 Brander/Domaine SB
33 Bridlewood
34 Beckmen
35 Blackjack
36 Foley
37 LinCourt
38 Rideau
39 Buttonwood
42 Epiphany
43 Gainey
40 Kalyra
41 Sunstone
Orcutt
Los Alamos
Lompoc
Los Olivos
Ballard
Buellton
Santa Ynez
Solvang
Gaviota
SANTA MARIA VALLEY
LOS ALAMOS VALLEY
PURISIMA HILLS
SANTA YNEZ VALLEY
SAN RAFAEL MOUNTAINS
SANTA YNEZ MOUNTAINS
SANTA MARIA VALLEY AVA
SANTA YNEZ VALLEY AVA
SANTA RITA HILLS AVA
to San Luis Obispo
to Santa Barbara
Pacific Ocean
Santa Barbara
44 Margerum Wine Co. Wine Cask
45 Jaffurs Wine Cellars
46 Santa Barbara Winery
CALIFORNIA
NEVADA
PACIFIC OCEAN
Eureka
San Francisco
Monterey
Santa Barbara
Los Angeles
San Diego
SANTA BARBARA COUNTY

Salud!

The Rise of Santa Barbara's Wine Industry

Victor W. Geraci

University of Nevada Press
RENO & LAS VEGAS

University of Nevada Press, Reno, Nevada 89557 USA
www.unpress.nevada.edu

Manufactured in the United States of America
Design by Omega Clay

Library of Congress Cataloging-in-Publication Data
Geraci, Victor W. (Victor William), 1948–
Salud! : the rise of Santa Barbara's wine industry / Victor W. Geraci.
p. cm.
Includes bibliographical references and index.
ISBN 978-0-87417-543-1 (hardcover : alk. paper) | ISBN 978-1-943859-90-0 (paperback : alk. paper) | ISBN 978-0-87417-641-4 (e-book)
1. Wine and wine making—California—Santa Barbara County—History.
2. Wine industry—California—Santa Barbara County—History. I. Title.
TP557.G47 2004
663'.2'0979491—dc22 2003022026

The paper used in this book meets the requirements of American National Standard for Information Sciences—Permanence of Paper for Printed Library Materials, ANSI Z39.48-1984. Binding materials were selected for strength and durability.

Frontispiece: Santa Barbara County Winery Tasting Rooms

This book has been reproduced as a digital reprint.

For Jordan, Victor, and Karime

May this book help you understand
Grandpa's passion for wine and history

Salud!

There is no other liquid that flows more intimately and incessantly through the labyrinth of symbols we have conceived to mark our status as human beings from the rudest peasant festival to the mystery of the Eucharist. To take wine into our mouths is to savor a droplet of the river of human history. —Clifton Fadiman

Contents

Illustrations

Preface

This inquiry into the regional Santa Barbara wine industry unfolds as an eight-part story illuminating the evolution from grape growers to family wine farms, and the resulting vintibusiness structure of the California wine industry. Chapter 1 gives the historical context for American wine by quickly summarizing wine's seven-thousand-year migration from northern Iran, Egypt, ancient Greece, Rome, and Europe. European colonists brought their wine traditions to North America and faced numerous failures in the thirteen colonies. Success came in the second phase (chapter 2), from 1769 to the 1840s, beginning with Spanish and Mexican wine traditions and culminating with the birth of the first commercial California wine industry. After California statehood the industry's third phase exploded with profits and promise as wine businesses copied Gilded Age business techniques and Santa Barbara wineries established themselves as part of the state's new industry. Initial successes crumbled in the fourth phase as moral crusaders dragged the nation into Prohibition and what appeared to be the end of the wine and spirit industry in California, Santa Barbara, and the nation. Phase five (chapter 3) describes the rebirth after the forced hiatus of Prohibition, the Great Depression, and World War II. In this era wine entrepreneurs utilized the concept of family wine farms and capitalized on the entrepreneurial energy of wealthy professionals seeking a back-to-nature experience. It was during phase six (chapter 4) that the market shortage for premium winegrapes drove the industry to reestablish abandoned viticultural areas and develop new regions. During phase seven (chapters 5 and 6) grape growers and winemakers realized that success in the wine industry is a corporate quest. The final phase (chapters 7, 8, and 9) marks the era of vintibusiness, agritourism, and worldwide wine recognition for Santa Barbara, California, and American wines.

Acknowledgments

Although central to my life, wine and grapes have not always been my passion. As a young boy I worked at my father's side in San Diego County vineyards. In our family the tradition of father and son in the vineyard and winemaking spanned multiple generations from Sicily to America. I reluctantly paid my dues during winter, spring, and summer breaks from school and grumbled as I performed the routine vineyard tasks of pruning, hoeing, and picking grapes. Harvest-time visits to the produce markets in San Diego, now part of the Gas Lamp Historic District, and weekends working the family roadside grape-stand tended to bore me, a citified teenage boy. Realizing that I was not cut out for sharecropping vineyards I attended San Diego State University, where I earned a bachelor's degree and two California teaching certificates.

It was during my twenty-year career as a middle-school social studies teacher that I replanted and cultivated my viticultural roots. During this time I refocused my agricultural leanings by moonlighting as a gardener, ornamental horticulture student, and daylily hybridizer. My wine education came from my good friend and teaching colleague Patrick Shaw, who taught me the glories of non-homemade wine. For years we enticed our spouses and children to spend their spring breaks camping at the Napa Bothe campground so that their oenophile fathers could dance with Bacchus in Napa, Sonoma, and Mendocino Counties. Campfire discussions included dreams of someday owning our own family-run winery. Each year we returned with cases of our favorite wines and immediately planned for the next year's pilgrimage. As a history educator I pacified my new passion for grapes by pursuing a master's degree in history and writing a thesis on the raisin industry of El Cajon, California, where my grandfather Michelangelo Geraci had immigrated in the early 1900s. By now I was hooked on both viticulture and history and jumped at the opportunity to complete my doctoral program at the University of California, Santa Barbara, where my research focused on the wine industry of the central coast of California.

This circuitous walk through the vineyards—both literal and figurative—led to this book and my need to express my heartfelt thanks to those who helped me reach this intellectual harvest. The first major acknowledgments emanate from the many people involved in my doctoral process. In 1994 the Santa Barbara County Vintners Association (SBCVA) contracted the University of California, Santa Barbara, Public History program to write a short, tabletop history of the county's wine region. Graduate students Sarah Harper Case, Susan Goldstein, Richard P. Ryba, Beverly J. Schwartzberg, and I undertook the project as a client-sponsored, one-year seminar course. Under the guidance of Professor Otis L. Graham Jr. the team researched, conducted oral interviews, wrote, and published *Still Pioneering: The Story of the Santa Barbara County Wine Industry.* My involvement in the project proved to be an invaluable beginning for research in areas unexplored by the public history project. This monograph utilizes the seminar's oral interviews and investigation and provides a larger, more complete study of the Santa Barbara County wine industry.

Many within the local wine industry supported my research. The past executive director of the SBCVA, Pam Maines Ostendorf, opened doors and always asked what more she could do. Within the industry I thank Rick Longoria, Jeff Newton, and Barry Johnson for their patience in answering my continual barrage of winemaking and grape growing questions. During my graduate studies at the University of California, Santa Barbara, Dan Gainey provided me with a job at the Gainey Vineyards that gave me firsthand access to many of the principals in the story and helped support my work.

Turning one's dissertation into a book expanded the list of those helping to complete this project. A special thanks to R. Douglas Hurt, editor of

Agricultural History, for encouraging me that I had an agricultural story worth telling. A Central Connecticut State University faculty research grant funded finishing touches on the manuscript and completion of a paper for the Society of Agricultural History. The person most responsible for completion of the project is friend and colleague Gordon Bakken, professor of history at California State University, Fullerton. He believed in my story and helped guide its publication.

Most important to this process are those I love the most. My parents provided the multigenerational viticultural heritage that underscores this work. My hope is that through my story my children, Matthew, Gregory, Damien, and Nicole, and my grandchildren, Jordan, Victor, and Karime, will someday come to understand why they had to share me with grapes and wine. To my best friend, confidant, and valued colleague Danelle Moon, who lived this project with me, I owe you more than can be repaid in this lifetime. To all my friends who have listened to this story over and over, I toast you and offer my story one more time. Salud!

Salud!

Introduction

America's post–World War II middle-class, freed by its car culture and disposable income, sought new and exciting ways to relax and enjoy an acquired appreciation of self-indulgent recreation. Throughout the 1960s and 1970s "back-to-nature" enthusiasts planned vacations and short escapes to family wine farms to imbibe wine and enjoy the good life at its source. Visitors marveled at the wine artistry of individual and family wine growers, and secretly (sometimes openly) dreamed of owning their own wine business. In the 1980s and 1990s this oenophile dance between consumer and winemaker continued as tourists faithfully flocked to what looked like a family wine business. In reality, the image of a family wine farm, with its vineyard, tasting room, and tour, had become an advertising strategy for large corporate wine enterprises. Regional wine escapes had become part of a planned complex combination of agriculture, industry, and tourism orchestrated by vintibusiness corporations.[1] An examination of wine destinations like Santa Barbara, California, can help tell this story of the loss of many family wine farms to corporate wine giants.

By the 1980s the United States—more specifically, California—had assumed a leadership position in the wine business. Winery corporations crafted an industry compatible with the nation's economic *pax Americana* and capable of profiting from what historian Olivier Zunz has characterized as a business relationship among national wealth, personal freedom, and well-being. This new international viticultural leadership exemplified Henry Luce's concept of the "American Century," and the everyday business of wine came to portray Zunz's description of middle-class consumerism enhanced by corporate managers, engineers, social scientists, and scientists.[2] A blend of consumerism, agribusiness, government, science, and higher education would convert wine-farms into vintibusinesses.

In the second half of the twentieth century wine agribusinesses and family corporations mastered the basic tenets of capitalist efficiency (vertical integration of grape growing, wine production, and distribution). The cost of doing business at this level proved to be beyond the financial capability of common family farms, and vintners quickly learned to mimic nineteenth- and twentieth-century merger techniques.[3]

A Vintibusiness Case in Point: Santa Barbara, California

The business evolution from grape grower to family wine farm to wine business can be illuminated through the story of the Santa Barbara, California, wine industry. This region, with its Mediterranean climate and history of viticulture, provided the nurturing environment for an industry responding to increased consumer demand. In the end, it became a story of small family vineyards and wine farms being swallowed up by the voracious appetite of Napa mega-wineries and regional artisan vintibusinesses that utilized vertical integration, high levels of capitalization, and large doses of the mystique of wine.

Our story begins in the 1960s, when shortages of winegrapes created "induced innovation." This phenomenon sent viticulturists on a statewide search for regions capable of supporting premium winegrapes.[4] Some growers turned to the state's viticulture tradition. Many others relied on trial and error to discover locations that supported agricultural economic growth, offered tax advantages, contained ample inexpensive land, and provided a good overall economic climate for winegrapes.

A few early pioneers found that Santa Barbara County provided a promising climate and economic infrastructure. Two regions within Santa Barbara County—Santa Maria Valley and Santa Ynez Valley—surfaced as prime locations for the expansion of California's winegrape vineyards. The case for expansion into Santa Barbara County in the 1960s was bolstered by the fact that it ranked twentieth (out of California's fifty-eight counties) in agricultural production; in 1965, agriculture had generated a record $71.2 million for the county's economy. A well-developed infrastructure to support a new major agricultural industry existed by 1965, and rapid post–World War II population growth (40 percent) provided a local consumer base.[5]

Wine Farms, Santa Barbara Style

High start-up costs for wineries and land-use policies meant local operations would remain smaller than those of northern competitors and resulted initially in two distinguishable forms of premium wineries in Santa Barbara County: small commercial (producing 50,000 to 100,000 cases annually) and artisan (fewer than 50,000 cases). The Santa Maria region, with its large commercial vineyards and cheaper land, drew high-case-production wineries while maintaining a brisk business selling winegrapes to out-of-county wineries. These well-capitalized grape growers stabilized contract sales and planted more vineyards, then established winery facilities and began the mass marketing of Santa Barbara County wines.[6]

Smaller artisan or niche market wineries developed in the more expensive Santa Ynez Valley, where winemakers came to depend on the excess premium grapes from the larger Santa Maria vineyards. Most were small, shoestring operations with lower levels of capitalization, smaller acreage, modest production, and ownership by those from other professions (doctors, dentists, lawyers, and entrepreneurs) escaping or retiring from the stress of urban fast lanes to the rural and tranquil images of winery ownership and winemaking.[7]

New, undercapitalized wineries in Santa Barbara County faced the reality that large commercial wineries tied to vineyard operations were more cost efficient. Between 1978 and 1988 land owned by wineries doubled in Napa and the percentage of California winegrapes grown by grape farmers decreased from 70 percent to 35 percent.[8] Economic studies confirmed the common-sense fact that the cost to produce a case of wine decreased as the size of the winery increased. For small wineries initial start-up costs, labor, and low production required higher per-bottle retail prices in order to repay investors. With large wineries, investors achieved greater profits when prices paid for grapes were reduced. Thus, during the 1980s there was a general tendency for the larger wineries to increase their vineyard holdings.

RETAILING THE FAMILY WINE FARM. In Santa Barbara County many local wine growers moved to the vertically integrated scale of operations by borrowing from the 1930s idea of a farm winery or artisan winery that could retail wine to tourists.[9] Success for these artisan wineries depended on building regional product quality, establishing a consumer following, cultivating the image of a winemaker as an artist, increasing tourism for direct retail sales, and having a constant supply of premium varietal winegrapes. By the end of the 1980s Santa Barbara County had a well-defined wine industry with just under ten thousand acres of vineyards and more than twenty-five artisan wineries. In one decade Santa Barbara County had moved from grape farming to winemaking.[10]

NapaBarbara

California wineries could not keep pace with domestic and international consumer demands. For a second time bay-area wineries attempted to meet consumer needs by increasing vineyard acreage. By the mid-1980s more than 70 percent of all California wineries planned to enlarge their vineyards and facilities.[11]

Pressures to expand production outside Napa and Sonoma to the central coast intensified in 1988 when premium-wine sales jumped 20 percent and dominated 45 percent of the total domestic wine market. Eileen Fredrikson, wine consultant and vice-president for San Francisco–based Gomberg, Fredrikson and Associates, noted that cheaper land, recognized grape quality, and high profits drove wineries to the central coast. “This is the market you want to be in,” she observed.[12]

As a result, northern vintibusinesses looked south to the less-expensive Santa Barbara (Santa Maria Appellation) and San Luis Obispo County vineyard lands.[13] Many northern wineries quickly capitalized on Santa Barbara County’s reputation for high-quality winegrapes, and the county’s wineries and vineyards became the target for large wine corporations seeking stable supplies of premium winegrapes. Local grape prices jumped from $1,000 to $1,500 per ton, reflecting an overall minimum 20 percent increase. Between 1988 and 1996 California’s fifteen largest winegrape growers created a "vineyard royalty" that increased their vineyard ownership by 75 percent. Wine World, Robert Mondavi Winery, and Kendall-Jackson vintibusinesses spent over $36 million to assume ownership of more than 6,300 acres of the Santa Barbara County's nearly 10,000 acres of premium winegrapes.[14]

The Local Business of Wine

Many independent Santa Barbara County wineries, mainly situated in Santa Ynez, secured alternative fruit supplies after their loss of Santa Maria grapes to northern wineries. Fears of the demise of the region's independent wineries subsided as local artisan wine businesses either sold their vineyards or wineries, expanded their vineyard holdings and winery production, or adapted new marketing strategies. Funding for the expansion emanated from a recovering California economy that permitted a new generation of professionals to retire to the primal lure and glamor of the wine lifestyle. For some, survival came by selling the winery to an investor willing to merge or modernize and expand the business. Most wineries profited from the high levels of middle-class disposable income and consumer willingness to purchase luxury goods.

Agritourism and Vintibusiness

The threat of a winery oligopoly continued throughout the 1990s. Although large northern corporate vintibuisnesses held two-thirds of the vineyard land, they did not totally control grape production or keep new entrants from the field. By 1996 local vintners, large and small, crushed 45 percent of locally grown grapes for Santa Barbara labels. Most local industry leaders projected continued growth as long as consumer demand for quality wines stayed strong and government policy did not restrict growth.[15] In just thirty years Santa Barbara wine entrepreneurs had reestablished the county's wine industry by adapting Napa-like agricultural and business techniques. Between 1992 and 1996 the production of winegrapes and wine sales increased 85 percent and 78 percent respectively, making local vintibusiness Santa Barbara's largest agricultural sector.[16] By the new millennium the Santa Barbara County wine industry supported more than fifty wineries and twenty thousand acres of premium winegrapes. The small wine-farm was transformed, and fears of a Napa-like urban encroachment of the rural landscape loomed on the horizon; but the "Napazation" of Santa Barbara County had created a successful vinti-business industry that was well positioned for the new century. Tourists and wine enthusiasts would continue to visit the small, family-owned wine farm.

Chapter 1

Northern European Roots and the First American Wine Culture

Wine Traditions

Warmed by an evening of cheap wine Zorba lectured his capitalist friend on "how simple and frugal a thing is happiness." He continued his scolding with a firm reminder that "a glass of wine, a roast chestnut, a wretched little brazier," and "the sound of the sea" are at the soul of the human experience.[1] Nikos Kazantzakis's *Zorba the Greek* captures the depth of wine's mythical role in Western cultural tradition. His chief character provides readers with a living paradigm of the beverage's ability to temporarily release humans from the bondage of everyday life. Moreover, the simple Greek philosopher Zorba reminds his friend, and many readers, that wine imparts a glimpse of the good life.

Inherent in the story is the symbiotic relationship between the grind of daily existence and the need for moments of distraction from its constant burdens. Much like the relationship between Zorba and his business-minded friend, the history of wine has become a tale of capitalist production and consumer experience. Although not entirely analogous, the story exemplifies the need of humans, ancient and modern, to escape to the simple life in an increasingly complex world. One way to achieve this diversion is through wine and its back-to-nature associations. Just as wine's legendary spirit flowed through Zorba's veins, it has streamed for more than seven thousand years through the history of Western civilization. Over time wine culture became the story of a journey, beginning in northern Iran and continuing west to embrace Egyptian, Greek, Roman, European, and American wine enthusiasts.[2] Integral to the story has been the business of viticulture, the science of grape growing, and viniculture, the study of winemaking.

Throughout this journey scholars and oenophiles studied and praised wine for its dual role as a preserved food and as a beverage for feasting and celebrating. Early fascination with grapes and wine provided humans with one of their first domesticated crops as well as with a cultural food heritage. This concern for grapes and wine intensified over the last two millennia, as Europeans and then Americans utilized the food and beverage as a medicinal substance, a major trade item, and a symbol of their God. Thus, wine's role has played itself out in the political and economic dramas of the empires built by the Greeks, Romans, early Christians, European nations, the New World colonies, and modern nation states.

The libation became deeply rooted in Western civilization's economic and political story as early entrepreneurs profited from the lucrative international wine trade. Historical geographer Tim Unwin describes this cultural landscape of viticulture as "an expression of transformations and interactions in the economic, social, political and ideological structures of a particular people at a specific place."[3] Wine and viticulture became historically intertwined with politics, legal systems, cultures, and prevailing economic systems throughout the world. Thus by the fourteenth century viticulture served as one of many symbols of power for Northern and Western European ruling classes. More important, by the seventeenth and eighteenth centuries wine merchants experimented with the mercantile (and later capitalist) ideas of capital, credit, banking, new technology, and marketing.[4]

In America, this history of wine manifested itself as a translocated struggle of a wealthy class in need of an artistic hobby, a wine industry seeking profits, a consumer-focused middle class seeking symbols of the good life, the Jeffersonian agrarian myth, the quest of temperance and religious groups to legislate alcohol morality, and a nation in search of a national public health policy. Wine served as the lubricant for the machines of human movement across continents and oceans and found success and a friendly audience on California's central coast. Zorba could now rest assured that many Americans had finally embraced, on a limited basis, the world's wine culture.

Western Civilization's Wine Roots

Jews and Christians integrated wine into their ceremonies and entrenched its symbolic power in the psyche of future generations. The Old Testament tells how Noah, a tenth-generation descendent of Adam, survived forty days and forty nights on an ark, and then cultivated a vineyard as soon as the floodwater receded. Jewish and Christian scriptures remember how "Noah began to be an husbandman, and he planted a vineyard; and he drank of the wine, and was drunken" (Gen. 9:20–21 KJV). Medical historical researcher Isadore Kaplan believes that this was the first recorded case of alcoholism and that Noah's drunkenness followed by delirium tremens pushed him to banish and curse his son Ham. To this day Jews celebrate their Passover seder feast with enough wine for a minimum of four glasses per guest—not including the glass set for the prophet Elijah. Jewish sacred ceremonies like the bris (circumcision ceremony) and wedding feast also include a symbolic role for wine.[5]

Christians have carried their own wine tradition through the centuries. Their biblical narrative utilizes wine symbolism in liturgical and allegorical instruction for believers and in lessons for candidates seeking conversion. Genesis 27:28 says "God give thee of the dew of heaven, and the fatness of the earth, and plenty of corn and wine." Ceremonial wine symbolism is further established in the book of Numbers 28:7: "In the holy place shalt thou cause the strong wine to be poured unto the Lord for a drink offering." Old Testament scripture continues in Isaiah 24:11 with warnings: "There is a crying for wine in the streets; all joy is darkened, the mirth of the land is gone."

New Testament scripture continues the biblical wine theme. Throughout time, wedding feasts have served as a major celebratory and generational symbol. John 2:3–11 recounts the story of Jesus Christ turning water into wine at the Cana wedding feast so the celebration could continue. Wine becomes the most recognized Christian symbol in the story of the Last Supper, during which Christ symbolically shares his soon-to be-sacrificed blood in a communion of wine (Mark 14:23–24). Mentions of wine in the Bible also provide more practical lessons, as shown in Mark 2:22, which includes a description of proper wine bottling.

After the fall of the Roman empire, religious leaders and wine producers, concerned about maintaining adequate supplies of suitable ceremonial wine and guaranteeing business profits, attempted to manipulate government and religious policies to counteract the continuous economic, social, and political cycles that interrupted wine production. Catholic monastic orders kept the art of winemaking alive by seeking human solutions to pain and suffering. This created a conflict with conservative religious leaders who believed that suffering glorified God and helped pave the path to heaven and a better life. Eventually, wine's image as a healthful beverage and its reinstitution into the European pharmacopoeia in the latter Middle Ages deeply internalized Westerners' beliefs in the value of wine.[6] Today, ironically, reports of health benefits attributed to wine have met opposition in the United States at a time when scientific evidence has corroborated ancient health claims.

A weakening of the wine industry between 1300 and 1600 resulted in a restructured business configuration for European viticulture and viniculture. Population declines, from war and the plague, reduced the demand for wine and discouraged expansion of the industry. Large wineries with vast acreage and multiregional distribution responded by reducing in size and marketing locally. This industry constriction also led to the development of a clear distinction between the quality of wines produced for nobility and those pressed for the masses. Attempts to recentralize in the seventeenth century, based on the needs of new, burgeoning urban centers, sparked a limited resurgence in low-end bulk wine production. As a result, cheap or watered-down bulk wines for the masses proliferated as urban populations increased. Notwithstanding, many wineries maintained production of quality mid-level and higher-end wines for the nobility. They accomplished this while retaining their small regional structure that utilized the best grapes and the best technological practices and promoted the aging of wine for better taste. This small-scale independent regional wine trend, in a modified form, stayed with the industry into much of the twentieth century as small provincial upscale wineries produced limited amounts of high-priced wines for an elite clientele. From these roots can be traced the development of today's premium-wine industry in locations such as Burgundy, Napa, Sonoma, and Santa Barbara, California.

Many of the basic tenets of the modern wine industry developed during this period as people involved in wine production laid the economic foundation for the eventual business practices used in the modern California and Santa Barbara wine industry. Growers specialized in raising specific grape varieties for climatic regions and increased wine quality through the development of bottling and corking of finished wines. Wine entrepreneurs, on the other hand, quickly realized that vertical integration of vineyards and wineries could help control the cyclic boom or bust markets caused by grape shortages or gluts. These same growers also realized that if they were to ensure premium prices for their wines they needed to enforce quality standards. Since growers and the nobility developed close personal, familial, and economic bonds, most looked to political leaders to establish and enforce policies aimed at improving the industry while benefiting governmental coffers through the collection of taxes. Successful wine entrepreneurs learned to streamline business and marketing practices to increase efficiency and ensure higher profits. At the same time, through trial and error, they ascertained ways to adapt to shifting consumer tastes, built regional product distinctions, and increased profits through capital expansion in new vineyards, modern scientific equipment and production techniques, and better marketing.

From all of this was born a modern capitalist industry that left a legacy for future wine merchants, wineries, and growers into the twenty-first century and led to an industry that responded to the new global markets. As politics, governments, war, trade policies, and consumer tastes shifted the industry adjusted to meet consumer demands through mergers and alliances to vertically integrate business structures. This ushered in a cyclic trend of centralization and decentralization that would follow the worldwide industry to Santa Barbara in the last quarter of the twentieth century.

Premium Wines: The Bigger the Wine, the Smaller the Barrel

For centuries class-conscious European consumers and oenophiles have used premium wine to distinguish their social status. Wars in the sixteenth, seventeenth, and eighteenth centuries disrupted premium and table wine trade and production and left wealthy consumers with inconsistent supplies of French, Italian, and Spanish wines. More important, the shortages left the masses without a daily alcoholic beverage. Faced with this shortage these thirsty European wine drinkers found an alternative in cheap distilled whiskey and vodka. Dutch traders, plagued by these wine shortages, switched to brandy (*brandewijn*) until newly financed colonial vineyards in South Africa could export wine to European markets. English and Spanish colonies in the New World provided similar hopes. In the meantime, only rich Europeans could afford wine, further establishing its reputation as a symbol of wealth and power in Western civilization.

The premium-wine industry became fully entrenched in the politics and culture of Western Europe as new technology made the fine wine trade more profitable. In England the business of the wine merchant (*negotiant* in French) prospered when it was discovered that wines could be matured, transported, and stored in glass bottles with shaped corks. As consumer tastes shifted to the new and exotic tastes provided by aged premium wines, as well as to the recently discovered champagnes and port wine from newly developed regional industries, wine merchants shopped worldwide to secure wines. Local and national governments not wishing to miss an opportunity capitalized on the new trade and established wine import taxes to provide additional royal revenues.

In order to expand production these new wine capitalists successfully produced different and better wines with smaller price tags for a larger group of consumers. Worldwide wine shortages occurred as expanding markets, differential customs and duties, and shifting political boundaries led to a rise in wine quality and a reorganization of the international wine trade. By the eighteenth century most wineries required high levels of capital investment, making it impossible for small or poor producers to compete outside their local regions. Only landlords, merchants, and entrepreneurs could afford the long-term investments required by the wine industry. European mercantile systems, in search of cheaper quality wines for the expanding urban centers, turned to their colonies to supply wine to quench consumer thirst.[7]

Wine Emigrates to English Colonial America

Viticulture arrived in the Americas during the Age of Discovery (1500–1750) as European immigrants brought their wine drinking traditions to the New World. Early explorers found that none of the native American peoples had any knowledge of wine or, for that matter, of any fermented spirits.[8] This was not an accident, for the native grape varieties made a very poor quality wine. Over the next three centuries colonial explorers introduced European vines (*Vitis vinifera*) and wines in countless attempts to develop a successful American wine industry. Thus, viticulture took root in South Africa, Australia, New Zealand, Chile, Peru, and North America, including Mexican Alta California, where Santa Barbara would be established.

Sixteenth-century European explorers and settlers quickly found native American vines and had high hopes for an American wine industry. In 1524, while off the coast of what would become North Carolina, Giovanni da Verrazzano found "many vines growing naturally, which growing up, took hold of the trees as they do in Lombardy, which if by husbandmen they were dressed in good order, without all doubt they would yield excellent wines." A decade later Jacques Cartier explored the St. Lawrence River and came across an island he described as having "many good vines, a thing not before of us seen in those countries, and therefore we named it Bacchus Land." The first winemaking in the United States occurred in 1564 when a colony of Huguenots, on the mouth of the St. John's River in Florida, failed to grow enough food for survival but used local Scuppernong grapes to produce twenty hogsheads of wine.[9]

Viticulture arrived in English North America with the Jamestown settlers in 1607, only to suffer numerous setbacks and, ultimately, failure. By 1609 samples of Virginia wine reached Europe. Reports from seamen described the wine as similar to Spanish Alicante.[10] King James I, who hated tobacco, was entranced by wine's possibilities and urged the cultivation of grapes and the production of wine. This led the Virginia Company in 1619 to enact a law that required each householder to plant and maintain ten vines yearly until a vineyard was established. That same year the company provided French *vignerons* to instruct and oversee the viticultural practices. By 1621 more than ten thousand vines were set out; but because of the poor quality of the grapes, little wine was fermented from native vineyards, despite valiant efforts. Two more attempts in the 1630s and 1650s failed. Growers soon realized that European winegrape varietals were unable to survive the climatic conditions found in the Virginia colony. Colonial merchants' dreams of wine profits and freedom from French, Spanish, and Italian wines dimmed. By mid-century hopes for a get-rich-quick wine industry gave way to profitable tobacco production, and wealthy English colonists were forced to continue importing wine from Europe.[11]

Many colonial entrepreneurs were not about to give up on the development of a wine industry, and they placed their hopes in a series of wine trials in the agricultural southern colonies. These experiments proved unsuccessful in the long run. By the eighteenth century the home government no longer believed that the development of the colonial wine industry should be an official policy. With the loss of support from England, wine enthusiasts in 1744 turned to the South Carolina House of Commons for support. In response the Commons offered a £100 prize to "the first person who shall make the first pipe of good, strong-bodied merchantable wine of the growth and culture of his own plantation."[12] It would not be until 1758 that Robert Thorpe would lay claim to the prize and set off a new flurry of interest and experimentation in grape growing and wine production. In 1763 a Huguenot group in New Bordeaux, South Carolina, planted vineyards. They were joined by other French Protestants under the leadership of Louis de Mesnil de St. Pierre. Startup support for the new project came from the colonial assembly and private subscriptions. The American Revolution, however, put an end to the effort.

Southern setbacks in viticulture during the colonial period sprang from the selection of inappropriate varieties for climatic conditions and from political unrest. In 1766, for example, Dr. Andrew Turnbull, a former British consul to Smyrna, imported Greek and Mediterranean cuttings and immigrant viticulturalists to his 101,000-acre Florida landholding, but his effort failed when his Mediterranean agriculture succumbed to tropical diseases. In North Carolina native grapes continued to abound, yet colonists' hopes for a European viticulture industry failed. In Louisiana, a Colonel Ball produced enough wine in 1775 to send a sample of his claret to King George III. His enterprise came to an abrupt end when local indigenous people massacred the colonel and his family during an uprising. Virginia also offered a prize, similar to North Carolina's, and had no takers. Thomas Jefferson made one final pre-revolutionary attempt at viticulture in the southern colonies when he contracted Philip Mazzei, Florentine physician and merchant, to plant vineyards of European varietals near Jefferson's home, Monticello, in Charlottesville, Virginia. The Mazzei project ended when the American Revolution turned Jefferson's attention away from his agricultural endeavors.[13]

These early unsuccessful commercial vineyards suffered from inappropriate agricultural techniques, unstable political and economic times, and the use of inappropriate microclimates for European winegrape varietals. Yet the early colonial entrepreneurial viticultural attempts in Virginia, Georgia, Louisiana, and the Carolinas did not completely discourage American wine businessmen.

Undaunted, wine entrepreneurs attempted viniculture in the pre-revolutionary middle and northern colonies and again suffered setbacks as growers tried to establish European vines and methods in a North American climate and soil ill-suited to the European winegrape varietals. Colonel Benjamin Tasker Jr. and Charles Carroll planted experimental vineyards in Prince George's County, Maryland, and utilized the newly hybridized American-European Alexander grape.[14] By 1796 both projects had ceased to exist.

North of the Mason-Dixon line in Pennsylvania and New Jersey, wine enthusiasts initiated another series of winemaking attempts. Pennsylvania Germans missed their wine and continually experimented with new wine and grape techniques. Benjamin Franklin encouraged the development of native wines and gave directions for winemaking in his *Poor Richard's Almanac.* Throughout the 1760s and 1770s numerous small attempts failed to produce American wines, and some declared that *V. vinifera* was a lost cause in America. By this time Jefferson, realizing that European vines could not stand the cold winters and vine pests of America, had begun to promote the development and use of American native varieties. By doing so American wine pioneers, through trial and error, would be able to determine the correct combination of American soil and climate needed by *V. vinifera.*[15]

Developing the First American Wine Culture

Failures in early American viticulture led wine drinking settlers to substitute new libations while they continued the search for a means to produce their own wine. Yeoman farmers followed their European traditions and developed a subsistence plus *mentalitie* that left grape growing and wine production to gentleman farmers and helped create a mystique in America of wine as a drink for a gentler class. Jefferson, while representing this American gentile class, hoped to cultivate the French, Italian, Spanish, and English tradition of a wine culture for all Americans. These hopes diminished as viticultural failures grew and post-revolutionary Americans turned to cheaper rum that quickly accounted for one-fifth of the value of all imports from England. Jefferson worried that distilled spirits would diminish the vitality of the nation's health. Thus, the quest for an American wine industry intensified as Americans turned to stronger drink. Wine became a means to encourage moderation, and wine entrepreneurs sought new ways to provide adequate supplies of regular wines while increasing profits.

European Americans of the early eighteenth century continued their beverage traditions: They consumed alcohol with every meal and celebrated wet holidays, and many received God with a communion of bread and wine. Even the Puritans had viewed alcohol as the "Good Creature of God," a holy substance, when used cautiously. According to the Reverend James Alexander of Princeton, "The Bible speaks well of wine, even as an exhilarant." As early as 1708 religious leaders such as Cotton Mather had preached moderation and affirmed the preaching of his father, the Reverend Increase Mather, on the value of moderation of this "Creature of God." Most feared that drunkenness, from cheap distilled strong drinks, emanated from Satan. Just before the American Revolution, all ages and social groups consumed alcohol, and foreign travelers reported that America was a nation addicted to drinking. The national consumption rate reached an average of three and a half gallons of alcohol per person per year (more than the present rate of consumption). Nine million women and children drank 12 million gallons of distilled spirits, and three million men drank 60 million gallons.[16]

Alcoholic beverages played a central role in the American lifestyle. Southern masters provided watered alcohol as a work incentive for slaves, parents taught moderate drinking habits by giving their children spirits, and women drank at home or in mixed company at society dinners. Indians received whiskey for payments, young men proved their manhood by overindulging, the military issued distilled spirits to soldiers, and college students relaxed in pubs. Americans often turned to whiskey to complement their meals, which relied heavily on fried greasy foods, butter, and eggs. By 1830 Americans over the age of fifteen consumed an average of more than seven gallons of alcohol a year, or almost three times the modern rate of consumption.[17]

Industrialization, modernization, rural isolation, and impersonal factory systems became ways of life and America teetered on becoming an Alcoholic Republic. Despite these trends, alcohol was not considered a social problem, and informal social groups strictly enforced the regulation of antisocial drinking behavior in the tavern and embraced alcohol as a benign and healthful beverage.[18] Like their European ancestors, most Americans viewed alcohol as a food, as medication for colds, fevers, frostbite, depression, as a way to reduce tension, and as a way for all social classes to enjoy frivolous camaraderie. Local governments monitored drinking through the issuance of tavern licenses and enacted laws aimed at controlling public drunkenness and its related crimes of thievery, lechery, and brutality. As early as 1772 physician Benjamin Rush had concluded that distilled liquor destroyed the body's natural balance. To prove his point Rush quoted reports from the American Continental Army's surgeon general that tied soldiers' ill health to the issuance of rum. Rush reaffirmed wine as a natural and healthy food by comparing sickly American soldiers to Roman soldiers known for their vigor and vitality, and thus recommended moderate amounts of light wine as a substitute for rum. If officials had any thoughts of attempting to control alcohol consumption through taxation, they probably faltered when the federal government faced an uprising in 1794 among western Pennsylvania farmers (the Whiskey Rebellion) over the imposition of an excise tax on whiskey. For these grain farmers, economic well-being depended on turning their crop surplus into whiskey, and they considered the tax discriminatory and detrimental to their freedom and their livelihood.[19]

Alcoholic beverages were part of the overall American experience from the start, and between 1790 and 1830 Americans drank more distilled alcoholic beverages per capita than they have before or since, earning the reputation, according to historian W. J. Rorabaugh, as "the Alcoholic Republic."[20]

Cheap whiskey from surplus domestic grain, coupled with British embargoes during the American Revolution and the War of 1812, solidified Americans' drinking habits. By the second decade of the nineteenth century whiskey flourished as a "liquid asset" when grain-glutted markets took advantage of improved crop distribution methods. New large-scale distilleries capitalized on the fact that America suffered from impure water supplies, lack of milk, wine shortages, and expensive tea.[21]

This national binge inspired a temperance movement in the 1820s that promoted reform measures aimed at moderation through wine consumption and teetotalism. These early reformers started a national debate on the health and social values of fermented and distilled alcoholic beverages. Most people still believed that wine and distilled spirits were a food to be imbibed in moderation. Extreme reformers, on the other hand, focused on the evils of alcohol and attempted to force moderation or even teetotalism on the general public.[22]

Anti-alcohol efforts did not stop the consumption of spirits, and drinking habits became associated with personal freedom and a modern lifestyle. Factory owners, however, needed a sober workforce and sought to decrease alcoholic consumption. They joined with middle-class urban Americans, charged with evangelical and social responsibility, religious leaders, women's temperance groups, and political leaders to bring about an era of temperance reform. American reformers then began to blame economic decay, poverty, and social upheavals on hard drink and pushed for moderation.

Many of the elite reformers favored abandoning distilled spirits for fermented wine, but high prices kept wine out of the reach of most Americans. Wine prices skyrocketed to $1.00 per gallon, or four times the price of whiskey. Thus, rank-and-file Americans flocked to the poisons of whiskey. Many elite drinkers felt guilty paying the exorbitant prices for wine and the import duties on it, which worsened the nation's balance of payments. This situation prompted leaders such as Thomas Jefferson, John Calhoun, and Henry Clay to experiment with vineyards on their own land in the expectation of putting an end to the wine shortage. Despite these problems, journalist Hezekiah Niles prophesied that in time the United States would produce all its own wine.[23]

The developing approach of encouraging moderation in an effort to end alcohol abuses brought a new commitment to establish an American wine industry for producing cheaper wine for all Americans. In 1805, with Jefferson's blessing, Swiss vintners founded vineyards in Vevay, Indiana; but the enterprise quickly folded because of under-financing and inferior quality wines. Continued viticulture failures led Congress in the 1830s to lower wine duties in the hope of finding a cheap wine to lure Americans from distilled spirits. As the duty dropped from fifty to thirty cents per gallon American profit takers mixed inexpensive wines with cheap whiskey and defeated the purpose of the legislation. Determined reformers then successfully steered consumers toward beer, cider, and better eating habits. These measures initially worked; and by 1840 the production of wine and fermented liquor rose to one and one-half gallons per person, and the nation experienced a 500 percent increase in their use. Edward Delavan, secretary of the New York Temperance Society, recognized that "Good men . . . attached the idea of good society to the use of wine."[24] America had the roots of a wine culture.

The First American Wine Industry

Wine industry failures in New England and the South worried those seeking to establish an American industry. Pessimism from these early disappointments gradually lessened as the new nation moved west to lands and climates more suited to grape growing and some commercial successes ensued. President Jefferson told wine enthusiasts that Americans could "make as great a variety of wines as are made in Europe"—"not exactly the same kinds, but doubtless as good."[25] This faith in the ability of Americans to produce wine encouraged wealthy entrepreneurs to blend tradition, quality, science, and market efficiency in an effort to plant the roots of the modern American wine industry.[26]

Frenchman Peter Legaux helped reinvigorate the American viticultural quest in 1793 when he planted a grapevine nursery and 206-acre vineyard in Philadelphia. In 1801, while relying on funds from investment capital raised by a public shareholding company and the Pennsylvania legislature, Legaux restructured his Pennsylvania Vine Company to create a modern wine business. Even with presidential support and state funding, however, he could not overcome the forces of nature, and by 1822 frost, disease, drought, and a caterpillar plague ended this newest American viticultural project.

Other pioneers in the young republic attempted to establish a wine industry for the new nation. Before closing up shop Legeaux's nursery shipped native hybrid varieties through much of the East and Midwest. These sales of vines in Maine, New York, New Jersey, Maryland, Virginia, Ohio, and Kentucky promised a new life for the industry. Some of these vines found their way to Englishman Benjamin Vaughan, who tended native vines in Hallowell, Maine. Vaughan left viticulture records that would later be used by Philadelphia physician James Mease when he wrote about American vines in his *Domestic Encyclopedia.* As wine interest increased, prospective vintners turned to new publications on viticulture. One of the better books, *A Short and Practical Treatise on the Culture of the Winegrapes in the United States of America, Adopted to those states situated to the southward of 41 degrees of north latitude* appeared in Georgetown in 1795.[27] Trial and error began to produce an accumulated knowledge that would lead to eventual success in Ohio and Kentucky.

As Americans began their migration into the Northwest Territories they took the dream of an American wine industry with them. The first of these ventures occurred in 1799 when Jean Jacques Dufour, a viticulturist born and trained in Switzerland, started the Kentucky Vine Company. Like those before him this new American wine entrepreneur endured a false start as plant disease, low yields, and general bad luck destroyed his company. Dufour was undaunted, and in 1802 he convinced Congress to grant him land on the Ohio River, where he planted vineyards as part of his New Switzerland colony. In a very short time Kentucky wines began to reach markets all over the United States, and growers read Dufour's book, *The American Vine-Dresser's Guide*. Sadly, by the 1820s all the vines in the Kentucky enterprise had succumbed to disease.[28]

None of these failures undermined the entrepreneurial urge to establish an American wine industry. In fact, from amid all these setbacks emerged Major John Adlum (1759–1836), who became known as the father of American viticulture. Born in Pennsylvania, the veteran of the War of 1812 settled on a Maryland farm, where he watched insects and disease destroy his first vineyard of European vines. Adlum then moved to Georgetown and initiated a correspondence with Thomas Jefferson that resulted in his planting a new vineyard on native root-stock. Jefferson's belief that a "good wine is a daily necessity" and his detailed notes on his own vineyard failures provided Adlum with the encouragement to continue. Armed with valuable scientific data Adlum started anew, and by the 1820s he had shipped samples of his successful Tokay wine to Jefferson and to James Madison. The immediate Catawba wine successes made him the guru and chief wine propagandist of American viticulture and helped revive interest in American winegrowing. New enthusiasts and prospective growers read Adlum's 1826–1827 treatises *The Vigneron* and *Adlum on Wine Making*.[29]

During this time numerous planters in the Carolinas sought viticulture as an alternative to diversify their slave-based tobacco and cotton agricultural system. First attempts to establish vineyards failed after the South Carolina Society for Promoting Agriculture ran out of funds before finding the right combination of vines, soil, labor, and knowledge. Nicholas Herbemont, a grower, urged the South Carolina senate in 1827 to subsidize emigration of *vignerons* from France, Italy, Germany, and Switzerland in an attempt to establish vineyards. Looking at past failures, the legislature thought the scheme to risky and did not fund Herbemont. In 1828 the Georgia legislature considered promoting olive oil and wine but decided to leave the speculation to a few individuals. Like its predecessors, the industry in this region died.[30]

Commercial Wine Successes: Ohio, New York, and Missouri

Despite many failures, a few scattered, but well-publicized, successes using native grapes served as the catalyst for further attempts at developing an American wine industry. In 1850, Nicholas Longworth, lawyer, horticulturist, and wealthy Ohio developer, used much of his wealth to establish a modern commercial Ohio wine industry. Longworth had moved west after his New Jersey estate was laid to ruins by the British in the Revolutionary War. He invested heavily in Ohio lands and used his real-estate profits to "democratize wine appreciation—to bring it within the ken of ordinary citizens by treating it as something refined and gracious and as part and parcel of America's agrarian ideal."[31]

Longworth decided that American native grapes would be the best commercial answer for the temperance movement's "rallying cry" for a dry white table wine. By utilizing advanced marketing tactics he attacked American snobbery for European varietal wines by creating labels that downplayed the use of native winegrapes, and he advertised his 35,000 gallon annual production as premium wines. He developed a national and international marketing scheme that promoted his Ohio wines in horticultural expositions, fairs, and wine tastings. Within a few years Longworth's vineyard and wine business became a cutting-edge enterprise: He employed experienced German vineyard laborers, used whole berry cool fermentation and racking from the lees, aged the wine in cool cellars, discontinued sugar additives, and used malolactic fermentation. As a result his quality Ohio wines gained national and international recognition. Longworth's successful enterprise was ended when the Civil War interrupted the industry and he failed to secure a stable supply of better grapes.[32]

Another successful commercial winegrape-growing venture emerged in the 1850s with the Hammondsport and Pleasant Valley Wine Company in the newly planted Finger Lakes district of New York. Over the next decade numerous other small vineyards and an agricultural experiment station appeared in the Finger Lakes "grape belt" (New York City, the Hudson Valley, and the Chautauqua region along Lake Erie), where the landscape permitted the air drainage essential to retarding fungus diseases and preventing spring frost.

Regretfully, most of the commercial endeavors faltered. Along the Hudson River, Robert Underhill grew American Catawba and Isabella grapes and helped sponsor the "Grape Cure" regimen of eating five or six pounds of grapes daily to help purify overfed Victorian Americans. The winery failed, but the family left a legacy of hybrid varieties for the region. Other growers such as Frenchman Alphonse Loubat planted vines on forty acres of Brooklyn waterfront, which he pulled out in 1835 when the property became too valuable for agriculture. William Robert Prince, Long Island nurseryman, developed a viticultural nursery and in 1830 published his *Treatise on the Vine.* Prince was convinced that European grapes could grow in America, but he compromised by planting hybrid vines. His dreams and work never developed into an industry.

Hopes for an American wine culture continued out west, in Missouri. In 1859 St. Louis winegrowers formed the American Wine Company. This enterprise was quickly followed by Michael Poeschel's 1861 winery, which became one of the largest wineries outside California, operating until Prohibition and reopening in 1965. Successes such as these prompted leaders in the United States to continue to promote an American wine culture. In 1851 Senator Stephen A. Douglas stated enthusiastically that the "United States will, in a very short time, produce good wine, so cheap, and in such abundance, as to render it a common and daily beverage."[33] Georgetown's John Adlum declared that by 1900 Virginia and the Southwest would have as many acres of vineyards as France and would produce wines equal to France's.

America finally developed a wine industry, born through trial and error, but it still had not found the proper grape varietals and the perfect climatic region that would reduce vineyard problems. As W. J. Flagg pointed out in an 1870 *Harper's Monthly* article, "The question of wine-drinking in America revolves itself into the question of grape growing in America."[34] New hopes rose as vintners began moving beyond trial and error and learned to disseminate information, fund research, form organizations, vigorously market their product, lure investors, and seek governmental support. Universities jumped in and set up experimental stations and departments devoted to viticulture and viniculture. Fairs and exhibitions demonstrated the newest in technology and plant material. The federal government encouraged grape growing, and by 1857 the U.S. Patent Office was making a systematic effort to collect and study native vines capable of supporting a wine industry. In 1862 the newly established U.S. Department of Agriculture brought the federal government assistance to the development of an American wine industry.

The process of building an American wine industry slowed down as the Civil War consumed the nation and funneled resources away from grapes and wine. Wine enthusiasts never lost hope, for they realized that wars have always interrupted the business of daily life. French vineyard peasants, who had endured centuries of war, would have advised American wine drinkers to take solace in their belief that the "good Lord sends a poor wine crop when war starts and a fine, festive one to mark its end."[35] The Civil War and Reconstruction slowed the development of the wine industry in the eastern and southern states; yet there could be no doubt that the country had developed its first wine culture and the beginnings of an industry. By the end of the Civil War American viticultural entrepreneurs sought to redevelop and find new regions capable of supporting large-scale commercial wine production. The nation may not have had a fine, festive crop to mark the war's end, but it celebrated a rebirth of entrepreneurial energy as Manifest Destiny moved grape growing and winemaking farther west.

Chapter 2

Boom and Bust

Birth and Death of the First California Wine Industry

Anyone who knows history . . . must surely know his wines.

—Arnold Toynbee, English historian (1889–1975)

Spanish Viticultural Southwest Beginnings

Winemaking was off to a slow start in the new republic, but determined wine proponents refused to give up on the possibilities of producing quality American wines. Many looked westward to the Spanish colonial empire in today's American Southwest, where commercial winemaking peaked as Spanish soldiers, Franciscan priests, and Spanish entrepreneurs planted vineyards in Alta and Baja California.[1] Spanish commercial winemaking flourished in Alta California when colonizers planted their own vineyards from European rootstock and fermented wine for the Catholic Mass and for table use and provided a commercial trade commodity for presidio, pueblo, and mission settlements.

These viticultural successes increased throughout the eighteenth century as European vines flourished in the hot and dry southwest, free from the East's severe winters, humid summers, disease, and insects.[2] By 1744 a Franciscan priest in the region of modern-day Texas recorded that this land prospered with an abundant fruit yield and "a rich wine in no way inferior to that of our Spain."[3] Traders in the Southwest started buying and selling El Paso and Rio Grande Valley wines. Farther west, Fray Junipero Serra began to build the mission San Diego in 1769, and his followers quickly established a wine trade among the presidios, the pueblos, and the twenty-one missions of Alta California. During this period the Spanish settlers established vineyards in San Juan Capistrano and San Diego, and within a few years the mission San Gabriel (today Los Angeles County) became the *Vina Madre* (mother vineyard), setting standards for grape growing and production of quality wines. As a result, commercial wine trade became common during Mexican rule of the 1820s and lasted until 1833, when Mexican secularization laws stripped priests of the use of their vineyards.[4]

After 1833 mission wine production ceased, and California's wine energy shifted to secular operations. Over the next fifty years wine production centered on the pueblo of Los Angeles, where Americans such as Joseph Chapman, William Chard, and Lemuel Carpenter had established a cottage wine industry with production of around thirty thousand gallons per year. It was not long until a commercial winemaking venture prospered under the guidance of Frenchman Jean Louis Vignes.[5]

Santa Barbara's Spanish Wine Tradition

Early European settlers in Alta California brought this new wine and grape-growing tradition to Santa Barbara Country. In 1769 Spanish explorer Gaspar de Portolá investigated the Santa Ynez Valley in the mountains east of the Santa Barbara pueblo and presidio. Portolá's diarist for the expedition, Father Juan Crespi, praised the triangular valley's fine soil, rolling grassy hills, and abundance of water. Five years later Spanish explorer Juan Bautista Anza also recognized the valley's agricultural possibilities. These observations led Spanish Catholic priests to begin importing cuttings in 1782 from the mission San Gabriel in an attempt to guarantee supplies of sacramental wines for the county's three missions—La Purísima Conception, Santa Ynez, and Santa Barbara.[6]

Over the next fifty years numerous small church and private commercial wineries developed in the area. The vineyards of José Antonio de la Guerra y Noriega (commandante of the presdio of Santa Barbara from 1815 to 1846), for example, yielded an estimated six thousand gallons of wine per year. Presidio soldier José M. Ortega also planted vineyards and, along with de la Guerra, gained a statewide reputation for winemaking.[7] During this same time priests at the mission Santa Barbara planted three vineyards—Vina Arroyo in Mission Canyon, La Cieneguita vineyard near present-day Cieneguitas Road, and the San Jose vineyard near the San Jose Creek in nearby Goleta. The San Jose vineyard contained 2,262 vines on seven and one-half acres; the other two totaled around 3,695 vines.

Land settlement policies of the Spanish government encouraged viticulture. As early as 1794 the Spanish governor Diego Borica granted six leagues of land in the Santa Ynez Valley to the Ortega family with the stipulation that a vineyard be planted. After the Mexican colonization law of 1824 and the Reglamento of 1828, hundreds of secularized land grants appeared throughout California. Most grantees utilized the land to raise cattle for the hide-and-tallow trade and maintained subsistence agriculture for everyday food and wine needs. The resulting wealthy landowning class (the *dons*) of these great coastal *ranchos* secured most of their wine supply from production at local vineyards, making wine a major part of the California and Santa Barbara agricultural scene from the beginnings of European settlement.[8]

When California became a state in 1850 more than eight hundred land-grant cases appeared before the U.S. land commission courts. About six hundred of these cases were resolved; the rest of the land reverted to the public domain. Historical records reveal that Santa Barbara County's forty-four land grants supported numerous successful vineyard plantings in or bordering the Santa Ynez and Santa Maria Valleys.[9] Included in these land-grant vineyards were Alamo Pintado, Los Alamos, Casmalia, Corral de Quati, Cuyama, La Laguna, Nuestra Señora del Refugio, Punto de Laguna, Santa Maria, Sisquoc, Suey, Tepusquet, Tinaquaic, Todos Santos, and La Zaca Rancho.[10] These vineyards were supplemented by production from the missions Santa Barbara, Purísima, and Santa Ynez. The eventual transfer of the ranchos to the Yankee (American) entrepreneurs resulted in the plowing of thousands of acres of rich soil for additional planting of wheat and grapes.[11] Even though California agriculture diversified with new products for a national market, local wine production continued in its economic importance throughout the post–Civil War period.[12]

The Mission Santa Barbara's vineyards, circa 1900, originally provided wine for both religious use and commercial sales. Photograph courtesy Santa Barbara Historical Society

Creating an American Wine Industry: Grafting American and Spanish Viticultural Traditions

California statehood promoted the marriage of the American winemaking experience, east and west, and catapulted American, more specifically California, wines into the international marketplace. This westward flow of wine started in the 1860s as Germans from the Philadelphia Settlement Society established a flourishing wine industry in Missouri, which offered a climate more suitable to grape growing. A by-product of the Missouri wine success was the education of a new generation of wine pioneers who would help bring American technology, research, trial and error, capital, and business ingenuity to what the Spanish had proven to be the perfect climatic conditions for growing European winegrapes in North America.

At first, the fledgling California wine industry, based on Spanish traditions, faced competition for American wine supremacy with wine producers in Missouri, Texas, Florida, Alabama, South Carolina, Virginia, Oregon, Washington, Ohio, and New York. Initially, the older, established regions felt secure: California and smaller regional wines made minimal inroads into their markets during the Civil War. After the war, however, producers in smaller regions like California began to prosper, and eastern growers and producers began to feel threatened.

Acting on their fears, these eastern growers expanded viniculture and viticultural production by utilizing grapes from other markets and increasing vineyard acreage. In 1868 Thomas Welch, dentist and Wesleyan preacher, started a nonalcoholic beverage business in Vineland, New Jersey. An ardent prohibitionist, Welch used the newly discovered pasteurization process to produce a nonalcoholic wine for sacramental use in churches and as a healthful beverage for everyday consumption. This swing from winegrapes to table grapes for pasteurized ("unfermented wine") grape juice shifted eastern viticulture away from quality winegrape production. Simultaneously, the Missouri and Kansas wine industries expanded to fill a gap left by decreased imports of French wine, a reduction caused by vineyard destruction from the phylloxera louse, accidentally imported to France on American vines.[13] In order to compete with the European wine market many American producers, like the Mississippi Valley Grape Growers' Association, employed German, Italian, and Swiss immigrants to plant grapes and establish their industry.

Farther south, vintners in Texas, Florida, Alabama, South Carolina, and Virginia continued to pursue a wine industry. In San Antonio, Texas, groups of German and French immigrants expanded the local wine industry and maintained the region's dependence on hybridized native varieties developed by Thomas Volney Munson, nurseryman and grape hybridizer who became known as the father of the Texas wine industry. Some southern efforts encountered many obstacles to success. In 1894, for example, an Italian enclave in Mobile Bay, Alabama, formed the Alabama Fruit Growing and Winery Association, but prohibition, disease, and a lack of funding soon killed the endeavor. No better luck was found in South Carolina, where the enterprise of French viticulturist M. Carpin failed when disease struck his vineyards. The bad news continued into North Carolina, where antebellum vintners closed after most counties in the state adopted prohibition laws. Partial success could be found in Thomas Jefferson's Virginia, where the dream of a wine industry continued as German settlers established vineyards in Charlottesville and growers founded the Albemarle County Grape Growers' Association. By 1873 the Virginia Monticello Wine Company had won many awards in Paris and Vienna.

Viticulture also appeared in places not normally recognized as wine-producing regions. In the 1880s the Minnesota Grape Growers' Association was formed, and in Utah, at the command of Brigham Young, farmers established a wine industry for communion wines. This off-the-beaten-track quest continued in the Southwest, where growers revitalized the industry in Phoenix, Arizona. Hopes for strong, new, small, western regional successes gathered momentum as wines from the newly established Willamette Valley (Oregon Territory) wine region won awards at the 1857 California State Fair. Washington State also joined this list as winegrowers established their first vineyards with native varietals.

Despite all these new startups, it would be new plantings in California's Los Angeles basin, central valley, and Napa that would eventually control the American wine industry. Vigorous competition for wine superiority resulted in the "big three" of American wine production: California, Ohio, and New York.[14] By the end of the nineteenth century California led America in wine production by wedding eastern and midwestern winegrowing knowledge with western climate and Spanish traditions.

California's First Commercial Wine Successes

After 1850, California exploded into the national wine scene as southern California, specifically the Los Angeles region, led the nation in winemaking. The region, gaining its reputation from the Mission grapes left behind by Spanish colonials, produced sparkling wines, Angelica (sweet wine), and Aguardiente (brandy). Just prior to the Civil War production of these local wines exceeded 500,000 gallons per year, a figure that topped Guernsey County, Ohio, the former United States leader.[15] Jean Louis Vignes, California's first commercial winemaker from Bordeaux, France, had emerged in the 1830s as a local industry leader in Los Angeles, where he capitalized on the Mediterranean climate and made wine for brandy.

In 1855 Vignes sold his thriving enterprise to his nephews Jean Louis and Pierre Sainsevain, who quickly expanded the operation by purchasing grapes and increasing production to more than 125,000 gallons of brandy. Most of their product was sold in San Francisco through the wine marketing firm of Kohler and Frohling.

Vignes's operation was not alone in the new Los Angeles region. Tennessee native Benjamin Wilson had established his San Gabriel Valley Lake Vineyard in 1841, and by the 1850s he was producing 50,000 gallons of wine from 160 acres of vineyard. Wilson's sweet wines and port could be found in markets from San Francisco to the East Coast. A bad year in 1866 discouraged Wilson, however, and he leased the vineyards to his son-in-law J. De Barth Shorb. Matthew Keller, another entrant to the California industry, came to the Los Angeles region in 1851 and quickly planted vineyards on his 13,000-acre Rancho Malibu near Vignes's El Aliso vineyard. In a short time Keller's winery produced 100,000 gallons per year and established a reputation for quality by planting European wine varietals (Pinot Noir and Cabernet Sauvignon) and advocating the new wine science techniques of Louis Pasteur and Eugene Hilgard. The depression of the 1870s forced Keller to lower his standards, and his business slowly dwindled until his death and the sale of the land by his estate.

Winegrape growing expanded statewide and soon included San Diego, Santa Barbara, Monterey, Napa, Sacramento, and Sonoma Counties. Between 1856 and 1862 California agricultural reports boasted that the number of grapevines statewide had increased eightfold with the help of favorable governmental policies and the infusion of capital by investors. In a move symbolic of the new wine enthusiasm, the 1859 California legislature bolstered the new industry by excluding vineyards from taxation and started a long tradition of assistance to the state's wine and grape-growing industry. Further government support came in 1861 when the state legislature, in conjunction with the state agricultural society, pledged to find the "ways and means best adopted to promote the improvement and growth of the grape vine in California."[16] As we will see, favorable tax status did not necessarily give the new industry clear sailing.

Agoston Haraszthy, a Hungarian immigrant who came to be known as the father of the California wine industry, quickly moved to take advantage of the state's supportive mood. He traveled throughout Europe, collecting more than 100,000 cuttings from 1,440 varietals to use as experimental rootstock for California microclimates. He dedicated himself to improving American wine through a process of replanting with better grapes and following the European model of premium wine production. At his Buena Vista Rancho in Sonoma County, Haraszthy propagated hundreds of thousands of rooted cuttings from more than 165 varieties in his nursery and supplied California growers with more than 14 million vines between 1855 and 1859. This new growth failed to keep up with consumer demands, however, and average imports of wine exceeded 500,000 gallons annually between 1858 and 1861.[17]

Antebellum wine entrepreneurs experienced a vicious wine competition between regional industries in Missouri, Ohio, New York, and California. Eastern vintners accused California wineries of selling their wines under counterfeit French and German labels, a charge that was often true.[18] In a counterattack eastern vintners placed California labels on inferior wines. The competition intensified as low-priced European wines poured into the American market. Quality deteriorated further as market shortages lured unscrupulous wine men to stretch production by adding sugar to low-quality grapes and by using free-run juice for white wine and bitter, low-quality, second-press juice with skin and seed residue for red wines. To make matters worse, greedy California growers and winemakers also maximized their profits by picking grapes before they were ripe, ignored sanitary concerns by failing to clean green and rotten berries out of bunches, disregarded basic cleanliness standards in the fermentation process, used barrels previously employed for other purposes, and sent wine to market before it was ready. Amazingly, many of these inferior wines sold for prices above their French counterparts.

The wine industry's development during the Gilded Age followed that of other food processing industries.[19] New consumer demands resulted in expansion, and technological advances drove up the productivity of agriculture through modernization of cultivation, transportation, and marketing. State and federal governments provided university research and development, and farmers shared their knowledge (gained by trial and error) through conversations, journals and treatises, and the formation of trade associations. Most important, agricultural government planners and legislators produced landmark legislation that supported the nation's movement toward an industrial and agribusiness economy through the passage of the Morrill Act, the Homestead Act, and the Hatch Act, and the creation of the U.S. Department of Agriculture. Governmental support also came at the state level when the 1862 California legislature passed the Wine Adulteration Act to enforce truth in labeling. The spirit of innovation, long characteristic of winemaking, was intense in California.

A new generation of reputable California winemakers and industry leaders promoted a series of acts, educational programs, and associations aimed at improving grape and wine quality in the cooler regions of northern California. Leaders like George Husmann, Missouri viticulturist, nurseryman, writer, and professor of horticulture, promoted increased home consumption of wine to combat intemperance. Husmann gained viticultural prominence and expert status on grape growing in the new western regions with his 1863 book, *An Essay on the Culture of the Grape in the Great West,* and his 1866 publication, *The Cultivation of the Native Grape, and Manufacture of American Wines.* He believed so strongly in the possibilities of California that in 1883 he took his growing expertise to the Napa Valley, where he planted his own vineyard.

Another industry leader, Theodore Hilgard (lawyer, judge, and man of letters from the German community of Belleville, Illinois) came to California with his son Eugene and became the champion of increasing quality through science, or, as he believed, through "rational winery practice."[20] The junior Hilgard later became a professor of agriculture and viticulture at the University of California, Berkeley, and the director of the College of Agriculture Experiment Stations. These men, and others, recognized the advantages of the region, with its moderate climate, its proximity to urban populations, and its trade opportunities through San Francisco Bay, and helped move the wine industry north to every county of the bay region.[21]

Further commitment to improve the industry with science and technology continued throughout the 1880s and inspired wine historian Paul Lukacs to refer to grapevines as "machines in the garden."[22] With the help of the University of California staff, grape growers authorized the establishment of a Board of State Viticultural Commissions in 1880. The board of commissions immediately placed its complete faith in scientific grape growing and wine production practices to enable the production of consistent quality wine that consumers would embrace. This philosophy became the centerpiece for the state's leap to national and international prominence. To further enhance the new industry, the board promoted the marketing of California wine at state, national, and world expositions and fairs. Many of these innovations sprang from the research and development programs established by Dr. Frederic Bioletti at the recently established University of California at Berkeley Experiment Station.

Yet, in a strange twist of events, it was Mother Nature in the form of plant pests and disease that helped rectify many of the state's quality issues. Phylloxera (root louse), which favored California winemakers briefly in the 1870s by destroying virtually all French vines, turned upon and destroyed California's vineyards in the 1880s at the same time Pierce's disease (bacteria spread by sharpshooters) was devastating the Los Angeles industry. In the long run, pests and disease benefited the industry by purging the state of its inferior Mission grape and allowing forward-thinking wine entrepreneurs to replant with more favorable European winegrape varietals. The pestilence also acted as a mechanism to rid the state of many marginal and disreputable growers and producers. Get-rich-quick winegrowers either could not afford or refused to spend money to restart their businesses. Los Angeles's troubles shifted the industry's entrepreneurial energy to the northern part of the state, where cool-climate, "premium wine" grapes could flourish. The few remaining vineyards of the southern region switched to table grapes, raisins, and sweet after-dinner wines.[23]

California winemaking, like its European counterpart, faced the cyclic convulsions of glut and bust. The state's winegrowers, like other nineteenth-century American farmers, encountered economic spikes and peaks accentuated by three depressions that flattened the national economy near the middle of each of the post–Civil War decades. The historical wine industry cycle of boom and bust would continue to plague the California industry and eventually lead producers to pioneer cooperatives and vertically integrate business structures as a means of softening the destructive power of these cycles.

Birth of California Vintibusiness

By the 1880s grape growing and winemaking, and U.S. agriculture as a whole, entered the modern agribusiness era, characterized by mechanization, marketing, new scientific techniques and processes, mergers, corporations, and dependence on urban markets. Two forms of wine enterprises grew to prominence, challenging the myth of the small family wine-farm and bringing America into the international wine industry. The first of these forms was that undertaken by wealthy entrepreneurs who gravitated to the industry and approached their new endeavor, like any other business enterprise in the Gilded Age, with vertical and horizontal integration and with corporate mergers that created vintibusinesses. The second was that of successful businesspeople who entered the field as a retirement or hobby enterprise, running what insiders today refer to boutique or artisan wineries.

In 1894 seven well-financed San Francisco wine merchants founded the California Wine Association (CWA) in an attempt to vertically integrate from vine to store and produce consistent quality wines in enough quantity to supply national and international markets. The impetus for the organization came from English accountant and financier Percy Morgan, who created the monopoly as an entity capable of controlling supplies and stabilizing fluctuating prices. As the director of CWA Morgan cared less who drank or why they drank wine as long as members profited. Under his leadership the California industry quickly moved from local to national and international markets with high volume urban sales. One could truly say Morgan became a Gilded Age captain of the wine industry. CWA achieved control of the American wine market by 1900, when it purchased the Andrea Sbarboro and Pietro Rossi Italian Swiss Colony enterprise (north of Sonoma, California) after a "wine war" in eastern markets that nearly bankrupt Sbarboro and Rossi. The organization included more than fifty wineries by 1902 and controlled two-thirds of the state's wine production, which grew from 18 million gallons in 1895, to 23 million in 1900, 31 million in 1905, and 45 million in 1910. Wine historian Paul Lukacs credits Morgan with "the introduction of wine as a manufactured commercial product, one with a consistent character and brand identity in the marketplace."[24]

The only real California competitor to CWA was the San Bernardino County (Cucamonga Valley) industry, which comprised twenty thousand acres of grapes, twice the size of Napa, and was lead by Secondo Guasti and his Italian Vineyard Company. The company developed winegrowing expertise by hiring Italian families to run the operation and controlled four thousand acres of vineyards by 1915. Organizations like these helped stabilize the industry between 1890 and 1910 and allowed California wine production to more than double during this period.[25]

California's wine industry, like its peers in specialized crop agriculture, grew rapidly as wineries aligned themselves with the growth of urban markets and their rising consumer income. Enthusiasm for the future of the California wine industry seemed bright as the twentieth century began, and by 1913 the Golden State's emerging wine industry accounted for 88 percent of the nation's annual production of 50 million gallons of wine.[26] While Southern California winemaking efforts focused on the sweet wine industry in the Cucamonga Valley, the majority of the wine industry's entrepreneurial energy continued to flow to the San Francisco Bay region, which became home to at least one hundred commercial wineries.

Napa soon led the state in premium wine output, with Sonoma second, and Los Angeles third by the end of the century. Premium bay-area wines could now be purchased in the eastern United States, Asia, South America, and Europe. Embedded in this industry success story is the basis for the almost complete collapse of the industry in the 1920s. The wine industry fell under the control of investors and financiers interested only in profit. Lukacs believes that "large scale commercial winemaking obscured wine's essential identity, making it appear to many Americans to be but another form of alcohol."[27] Thus, the wine industry became a prime target for the Prohibition Era. One bright hope for the future was found in producers such as California fur trader and wine producer Gustave Niebaum, of Inglenook Winery. Although he successfully created a niche premium winery, he did not have to depend on wine as his primary source of income.[28]

Commercial interest in grape growing in Santa Barbara County dates back to 1892 when local boosters advertised with lithographs promoting the agricultural possibilities of the region's climate and coastal location. Photograph courtesy Santa Barbara Historical Society

The First Santa Barbara Commercial Wine Industry

As the mission and Spanish-Mexican eras ended and California celebrated statehood, many local wineries, established by mission priests and military commanders of the Santa Barbara presidio, passed into private commercial hands. In June 1871 James McCaffrey, graduate of the California Mechanics' Institute, purchased the San Jose vineyard in the Goleta district of Santa Barbara County. He quickly added 3,300 vines and built a 25-by-45-foot adobe winery complete with wine presses and open-top fermentors. When McCaffrey died in 1900 his widow sold the winery to Michele Cavaletto, an immigrant from the Italian Piedmont region, who ran the winery until the beginning of Prohibition.[29]

By the late 1860s Santa Barbara County ranked third in California wine production: The region's small wine entrepreneurs produced 5 percent of the state's wine. Most famous was Albert Packard, a Rhode Island lawyer, who purchased 250 acres and established what was probably the first successful commercial winery in Santa Barbara. Packard planted his vineyard on the west side of the city (west of De la Vina Street between Carrillo and Canon Perdido Streets) where the property's previous owner, Felipe de Goycochea, second commander of the Santa Barbara presidio, had established a vineyard in the late eighteenth century.

Packard understood European winegrape growing and applied the technical and scientific knowledge of the time. He knew that premium wines required a cool growing region and was quoted in a local news-

Albert Packard established the region's first successful commercial winery, La Bodega, in 1865.

Photograph courtesy Santa Barbara Historical Society

paper, saying that "the wine making season is several weeks later here than elsewhere in California, owing to our proximity to the sea coast."[30] Packard believed he could make a fortune with viticulture and planted his estate with vines imported from Spain. As the vines came into production in 1865 he constructed the two-story adobe La Bodega winery with a capacity of 80,000 to 90,000 gallons. With the help of Boston winemaker Ed Breck and a Mr. Goux, a winemaker from Bordeaux, Packard produced his wines under the El Recedo (The Corner) label and shipped most of his wine to Los Angeles, to San Luis Obispo, and as far away as Texas. The winery produced a quality Claret that commanded prices double that of its Los Angeles competitors. By the turn of the century local speculation suggested (though it was not documented) that Anaheim disease had destroyed the vineyard, much as it had devastated the vineyards of Los Angeles.[31]

Local records do not reveal outbreaks of Anaheim disease in other Santa Barbara County vineyards. In fact, despite the Packard setback, Santa Barbara County moved forward in its quest for a modern wine industry, and by the 1890s an estimated forty-five vineyards, on about five thousand acres, had been planted in the area. While many were located behind the coastal range in the sparsely settled Santa Ynez Valley, optimistic winemakers had not given up on the south-facing coastal shelf in and around the small town of Santa Barbara. Small vineyards still dotted the city itself, and there was plenty of evidence that the grapevines could thrive there. The huge Montecito vine, planted (legend has it) in 1812, produced six tons of grapes per harvest and was cut down in 1876 to serve as a display at the Philadelphia Centennial Exhibition to lure investment money for the development of the area's agricultural enterprises. A larger Carpinteria vine planted in 1842 developed a trunk with a circumference of nine feet and by the 1890s was said to produce ten tons of grapes a year. Yet, the south-facing coast of Carpinteria proved to be inhospitable to ambitious grape farmers. Colonel Russell Heath's ten thousand vines and two-story winery, for example, were brought to ruin as coastal moisture nourished destructive mildew in the vines and grapes.[32]

Perhaps the most successful commercial vineyard in the area was planted twenty-two miles off the coast of Santa Barbara on Santa Cruz Island. In the 1880s French immigrant Justinian Caire planted a vineyard

Maria Louisa Dominguez seated under the La Parra Grande grape arbor in Montecito near the community of Santa Barbara. The 86-year-old diseased vine was cut down in 1876 so it could be exhibited at the Philadelphia Exposition. Photograph courtesy Santa Barbara Historical Society

with premium European varietals such as Zinfandel, Cabernet Sauvignon, Pinot Noir, Petite Syrah, Muscat, and Riesling on his island property. Caire managed his six hundred acres of grapes with Italian workers, and by 1910 his winery averaged 83,000 gallons of wine per year. Santa Cruz Island wine pleased loyal wine-drinking customers between Los Angeles and San Francisco.[33] Prohibition ended the profitable enterprise.

Out of this mixed record in Santa Barbara County local observers inferred a hopeful message. A local 1883 promotional history of Santa Barbara and Ventura Counties ran this advertisement:

> There are in the two counties not less than 400,000 acres of land which are capable of producing grapes of good quality. . . . The warm and protected valleys of the Santa Maria, Santa Inez and Santa Clara, with their lesser tributary valleys, with the sloping lands which surround them, form the natural home of the vine, and could, if occasion demanded, produce sufficient wine of a high quality to supply the utmost demands of commerce. In these sheltered and fruitful regions there is found, in the highest degree, the conditions for successful viniculture.[34]

Historian Hubert Howe Bancroft wrote in 1888 that the mission Santa Barbara had been "famous for its choice wines and profuse hospitality."[35] Howe went on to note that Santa Barbara County produced greater crop

The Carpinteria grapevine, La Vina Grande, lived from 1842 to the mid-1920s and was listed in the Guinness Book of Records as the largest grapevine on record. Photograph courtesy Santa Barbara Historical Society

yields than Napa and Sonoma Counties and that the only disease to strike the area had been mildew. Bancroft also stated:

> It will probably not be long, before some of the large ranchos of this district [Santa Ynez] will be subdivided and offered for sale. Rumor mentions La Zaca, Corral de Cuati, and Jonata Ranchos. . . . Experts in wine-making rank the Jonata and College Ranchos as first vine land. The soil and climate seem well adapted to grapes.[36]

But these Santa Barbara–area hopes were not so much over-optimistic as premature. Wine entrepreneurs with investment capital were to settle on lands and wineries near the fast-growing region of San Francisco, where ocean and rail transport connected it to the eastern United States and the world. By contrast, Santa Barbara County was still inaccessible and thinly settled. In 1870 the city had only 2,898 citizens and was con-

Santa Cruz Island Chapel at its 1891 dedication, surrounded by vineyards planted in 1884.

Photograph courtesy Santa Barbara Historical Society

nected to the north-county Santa Ynez and Santa Maria Valleys by the treacherous San Marcos stage road. Stearns Wharf steamer service provided the only trade outlet until 1887, when the Southern Pacific railroad connected the area to both Los Angeles and San Francisco. California's wine entrepreneurs would for many decades concentrate their larger commercial efforts in an arc around the city of San Francisco.[37]

Prohibition and the American Wine Industry

California winemakers started the twentieth century with high hopes. The state's population soared to more than 1,485,000, and national wine consumption grew to .3 gallons per capita per year. By 1910 this demand, although low by European standards, was enough to consume the 50 million gallons that the industry produced. The state's share of the national wine market had grown from 50 percent to 88 percent, and the only serious rivals were European wines.[38]

Enthusiasm for the future of the California wine industry seemed bright as the twentieth century began; but a dark cloud on the horizon—the temperance movement—was clearly visible in California and Santa Barbara. State lawmakers had given communities the option to decide if they wanted to be "wet" or "dry." In 1874 the founding of Lompoc as a "dry" town within Santa Barbara County symbolized a national battle that was to be fought on many fronts from the early 1800s through the twenty-first century.[39] Anti–alcoholic beverage forces gained momentum at both the state and national levels during the Progressive Era, as seven states joined the "dry" list between 1907 and 1912. Even though hard (distilled) liquor was the main target for extinction, moral reformers also took aim at wine.[40]

Most American wine drinkers and producers were stunned when the century-long prohibition movement achieved national success with the 1919 passage of the Eighteenth Amendment, which prohibited "the manufacture, sale, or transportation of intoxicating liquors within the United States." A 1913 temperance victory in Congress had allowed dry states to design and enforce their own alcohol commerce laws, and by 1919 thirty-three states were already dry. The War Prohibition Act of 1918, designed by agricultural officials to save foodstuffs for the Great War in Europe (World

War I), foreshadowed the 1919 passage of the Eighteenth Amendment—over the veto of President Woodrow Wilson. Minnesota congressman Andrew J. Volstead, with anti-saloon league aid, quickly pushed the Volstead Act through Congress and provided enforcement provisions that ensured the United States would become a dry nation. In the end, Prohibition slowed down American alcoholic consumption, brought to a close an era of working-class saloons, and served as one of the more successful alliances of upper and middle classes to legislate morals and habits.[41]

Ironically, Prohibition also served to increase home winemaking in the United States, and most of the wine came from California grapes. Government agencies issued permits for commercial manufacture of vinegar, sacramental wine, medicinal wines, industrial alcohol, and flavorings, and for home winemaking. From these records and others it can be gleaned that home manufacturing of wine skyrocketed: Wine production jumped from an estimated 50 million gallons per year before Prohibition to 76.5 million gallons per year during Prohibition as home winemakers were permitted to produce 200 gallons of wine per year for family use. Herbert Hoover's Wickersham Commission counted more than 45,000 legal winemaking permits in California alone and in 1931 concluded that "it appears to be the policy of the government not to interfere with it."[42] Per capita wine consumption climbed from .47 gallons per year in the fifty years before Prohibition to .64 gallons of wine per capita per year during Prohibition and showed some persistence in that increase at .53 gallons per year after repeal.

Although wine consumption increased, the commercial wine industry collapsed as bonded American wineries fell to fewer than 140 in 1932, from a high of more than 700 in 1919. Grape growers, on the other hand, prospered as red grape prices in 1921 jumped from $25 to over $82 per ton. Still, realizing that Prohibition killed the formal wine industry, vineyardists sought stability for their remaining grape market. Anxious California grape growers formed the California Vineyardists Association in 1926 and quickly signed up more than 750 of the state's growers. The association aimed to stabilize grape prices, secure markets, and enhance distribution systems throughout the nation and the world.

The 1932 presidential election left no doubt that the nation was tired of

Prohibition. A wet California legislature, a wet U.S. Congress, and a wet President Franklin D. Roosevelt approved 3.2 beer and a 12 to 14 percent watered-down sweet carbonated sacramental wine and gave doctors the right to prescribe wine. As a result wine production tripled between 1932 and 1933. Good news for the wine industry came on December 5, 1933, as the nation repealed Prohibition.[43]

The legacy of Prohibition haunted the wine industry for decades. California winegrape growers lost much of their premium winegrapes when they converted vineyards to thick-skinned varieties that could be shipped to eastern home winemakers. People who continued to drink wine learned to accept cheaper sweet and low-quality dry table wines. Most confusing was the fact that repeal permitted each state to establish its own liquor laws. Originally nineteen states remained dry—Mississippi being the last to repeal Prohibition, in 1966. The regulatory dilemma became more complicated as some states allowed the sale of wine in grocery stores, while seventeen others created state or municipal monopolies (package stores) for the sale of alcoholic beverages. Thus, the wine industry eventually faced forty-eight (later fifty) different sets of regulations for transport, sale, taxation, license fees, and distribution of wine.

Further complicating the problem was the federal government's unofficial nonsupport policy for wine production. Under Roosevelt's New Deal, Assistant Secretary of Agriculture Rexford Tugwell adapted the age-old position that wine could promote moderation in alcohol consumption and proposed that wine be exempted from federal taxation. This moderation proposal met the wrath of Missouri congressman Clarence Cannon, a member of the House Appropriations Committee and lifelong prohibitionist, who used his congressional power to block any help for the wine industry. Cannon's stubborn tenacity on these issues lasted for thirty years, until his death in 1964. His political clout allowed him to force the Department of Agriculture to strike the word *wine* from all of its publications for fear of losing funding for its programs, in essence creating a government policy in which wine was no longer considered an agricultural product.[44]

In the struggle to rebuild after the hiatus of war, depression, and Prohibition the wine industry became its own worst enemy. Forward thinkers in the industry, such as Andrea Sbarboro, had anticipated the efforts of prohibition forces and had formed the California Grape Protective Society in 1917 to counter prohibition's anti-wine sentiments that were closely tied to immigrant nativism and anti-city rhetoric. Sbarboro failed to garner the support of his industry peers, however, and wine became closely tied to corporate hard-liquor distillers. The situation worsened as members of the industry openly battled over issues of bulk wine versus premium wines, sweet versus dry wines, high alcohol versus low alcohol, and, most important, over the question of whether wine is a food or liquor. Wine writer Leon Adams commented in the 1930s that most of the major players in the industry thought of wine "as a skid-row beverage" and were only interested in profit margins.[45] Others continued the battle against wine's growing image as just another distilled alcohol and attempted to unify the industry against Prohibition. Wine pioneers like Adams and A. P. Giannini, founder of Bank of America, unsuccessfully made an attempt to unify industry members into what was later named the Wine Institute.

Worse yet, many Americans grew to believe that all alcohol consumption was immoral. Anti-liquor forces remained strong and sought new ways to restrict consumption and save Americans from moral deprivation. Historian John C. Burnham credits repeal of Prohibition, and the transition back to the "bad habit" of drinking, for a new or neoprohibitionist movement in the latter half of the twentieth century.[46] The quasi-legal status of wine was reinforced when the wine industry remained under the jurisdiction of the Bureau of Alcohol, Tobacco, and Firearms and not the "friendlier" Food and Drug Administration. In less than one century America and California had created and lost a wine tradition. Throughout the twentieth century the liquor industry as a whole continued to struggle with anti-alcohol forces, and winemakers attempted to rebuild and recreate the California premium international wine industry.

Chapter 3

The California Wine Revolution

California's Post-Prohibition Rebirth

With the repeal of Prohibition California's grape growers scaled up production and began rebuilding their industry with the advantage of new scientific viticultural knowledge and techniques. It would be in the second half of the twentieth century that the wine industry would have, in the words of Henry Luce, editor-in-chief of *Time* publications, its "American Century." The industry had weathered two world wars, Prohibition, and the Great Depression, though it had not been devastated by war as had its European counterparts. The American wine industry was poised for its rebirth. After more than three hundred years of false starts American wines were finally flourishing, and the industry faced no major global competitors, a booming Cold War economy, newfound scientific and technological advances, and a national lust for consumption. The American—more specifically, the California—industry rose to world prominence in less than a quarter of a century. Wine writer Paul Lukacs described this miracle growth as a three-phase process: Wineries first patterned themselves after European models, then shifted to a California style of scientifically mass-produced low- and high-end wines, and finally matured as winemakers sought to graft the old traditions to the new California style.[1]

As a by-product of Prohibition, most consumers had switched to sweet wines with high alcoholic content. U.S. wine consumers had preferred dry wines by 2 to 1 in 1900, but sweet wines were favored 4 to 1 by the end of Prohibition. Members of the international wine community feared what

American Prohibition might do to the world dry wine market. In 1932 Italian premier Benito Mussolini, as well as others, warned that after Prohibition Americans would have to reeducate themselves in order to be able to "enjoy the noble and delicate pleasure afforded by light, tasty and refined wines."[2] The resulting wine trend brought an expansion of sweet wine production in the Central Valley, where the number of bonded wineries doubled in 1933. At the end of World War II this preference for sweet wines peaked as three out of every four bottles of wine produced were fortified.[3] American wine had become identified as just another form of cheap booze or distilled alcohol. The quality of the wine was low, and much of the potential market was retained by noncommercial family wineries.

California's now-legal wine trade became one of the few industries to expand during the Great Depression. Early concerns over the altered American wine palate subsided as early as 1939, when wine writer Frank Musselman Schoonmaker added California wines to his import line (giving them varietal names rather than generic European regional titles) and American war veterans returned from Europe with an appetite for dry table wines. Despite consumer shifts, industry leaders worried how more than 380 U.S. wineries set to reopen would cope with cooperage shortages, consumers short on cash, different wine regulations for each state, outdated equipment, and poor-quality vineyards.

In order to navigate these industry problems California wineries formed the Wine Institute in San Francisco, which by 1935 boasted a membership of 188, or 80 percent, of the state's wineries. Further cooperative rebuilding of the industry came in 1938 when the California Department of Agriculture helped establish the Wine Advisory Board, which mandated membership for the state's wineries and assessed a per-gallon tax to pay for a national wine campaign. Also at this time the University of California's viticulture and enology programs at Berkeley, under the leadership of viticulturist A. J. Winkler and enologist Maynard A. Amerine, moved to the Davis campus. California had reestablished the marketing and scientific roots for its new wine industry.

With Prohibition ended, winery and grape-grower cooperative associations flourished and quickly learned to lobby for favorable federal policies. Just after the repeal of Prohibition, cash-strapped wineries collaborated to reduce heavy taxes from the Federal Alcohol Control Administration (FACA). Relief came in 1938 when the Wine Institute convinced state and federal legislators to allow the industry to pro-rate grapes (guarantee farmer crop prices, as was done for other agricultural commodities) and included the industry under the California Marketing Act with its forced participation and payment of gallonage assessments. FACA memb-ers then addressed the ongoing fear of a grape glut by convincing governmental and agricultural leaders to authorize funding by Bank of America of a diversion program to stockpile grape-brandy for later sales. These methods, like many New Deal programs, fell short, and in the long run it would be the beginning of World War II in Europe that boosted the demand for California wine.

The post-depression industry relied heavily on bulk wine sales (80 percent of all wine produced), which favored large growers and winemakers. Most Napa wineries, with their smaller facilities, heeded the advice of University of California, Davis, professor Dr. Frederic Bioletti and fought to establish their market share by emphasizing the sale of smaller quantities of premium wines at higher prices. In time, this decision required industry members in Napa to find new winemaking techniques and more efficient business practices that could lower costs and raise profits. Thus, over the next few decades innovators such as Andre Tchelistcheff, Carl Bundschu, the Beringer brothers, Roy Raymond, Louis Martini, and Robert Mondavi established better vineyard practices, planted superior grape varietals, and utilized new technology.

National and international marketing for small (retail) and large (bulk) wineries faltered under the remnants of Prohibition. During the years immediately following the repeal of Prohibition the federal government and the forty-eight state legislatures grappled with the concept of "farm wineries."[4] These post-Prohibition discussions focused on whether wine was a food or an alcoholic beverage and whether wines, grown and produced on family wine farms, could be sold at their source, as could other agricultural products. California state policymakers moved to allow small family-operated wine farms to promote themselves through tasting rooms and direct sales. In the end, repeal policies allowed each state to develop its own wine policy.

World War II and, inadvertently, federal policies brought Napa premium wine to the forefront as European wines failed to reach the American market. This new international role began as early as 1936 when the Federal Alcohol Administration Requirement #4 mandated certified labels for varietal bottled wines (51 percent of the wine had to be crushed from one varietal), thus forcing the premium-wine industry to begin moving from bulk to bottled wines. The shift continued into 1943, when the War Production Board crippled bulk wine distribution by using the last of seven hundred wine-tank railroad cars for the war effort. Further support for the premium-wine industry came with the government's wartime purchases of raisin grapes (54 percent of all grapes crushed for wine at the time), forcing wineries to depend on premium winegrapes for bottled wines. Optimistic premium producers like Edmund Rossi, president of Italian Swiss Colony, correctly predicted in 1944 that dry wine would eventually surpass the dessert wine industry. World War II served as the vehicle to help the industry develop national brands, increase acreage of premium grapes, and establish the practice of at-winery bottling, as well as bringing about a massive influx of capital for modernization.

The infusion of entrepreneurial money gradually altered the image of the California wine industy. At first a small group of California winemakers attempted to improve the public's attitude toward its product by making better quality wines. Leaders in the movement were Edmund and Robert Rossi of Italian Swiss Colony (third-largest post-Prohibition U.S. winery), who with the Grape Growers League (later, the Wine Institute) lobbied for advertising campaigns to help consumers accept table wine as a food beverage.

California had developed a premium-wine industry, but a new trend on the horizon threatened this new movement. In 1942 National Distillers bought Italian Swiss Colony for $3.7 million and started what later observers called "the Whiskey Invasion."

After World War II the California wine industry experienced a transformation that lead to the centralization of the industry in Napa. This concentration patterned itself after the general agricultural trends of the 1950s toward larger farms, fewer farmers, new technology, mechanization, and increased efficiency and production. In 1955, John H. Davis, director of the Moffett Program in Agriculture and Business at the Harvard School of Business, delivered a speech in Boston, entitled "Business Responsibility and the Market for Farm Products," in which he coined the term *agribusiness* to describe this centralizing process. In his speech, Davis predicted that agribusiness, which embodied the spirit of a second agricultural revolution and which offered vertical integration of production and marketing, would run business-farms of the future.[5]

Following World War II, California commerical wineries, bolstered by favorable governmental policies, reentered the national and international wine marketplace, consolidated, and began the process of reeducating an ignorant American wine consumer. In a move that appeared to consolidate the industry overnight, large liquor companies in the eastern United States (Seagram's, Schenley, and National Distillers) made major investments in California wineries. By 1945 large distillers controlled half the nation's commercial wine production. This influx of much-needed capital for expansion and rebuilding saved the industry, but the postwar "bigger is better" philosophy, which led to the centralization of the wine industry in Napa, resulted in a drastic reduction of bonded wineries: 271 in 1960, down from 1,300 in 1936.[6] The liquor companies, however, lacked both the knowledge of winemaking and the patience to rebuild the industry, and within a few years ownership of the state's wineries reverted to resident entrepreneurs whose main interest was winemaking.

As wineries fell back into the hands of wine businesses they began the process of reeducating U.S. consumers. During the postwar decades American consumption of flavored sweet wines increased from 100 million gallons in the mid-1940s to 145 million gallons in the mid-1950s. Premium winegrowers, Robert Mondavi in particular, began a public relations drive that led to the formation of the Premium Wine Producers Board (adjunct to the Wine Advisory Board), which initiated comparative tastings and defined premium wine by quality and price. Further changes occurred in 1958 when government regulations legalized "pop" wines, so called because they had enough carbon dioxide to cause a small "pop" when the bottle was opened. This led the way to the popular light fruit wines of the late 1960s, and in 1971 retailers sold more than 41 million gallons of "pop" wines. That same year Americans used $346 per million dollars of income to purchase wine, up from $301 in 1969. Not to be forgotten in this new market were many women who now viewed themselves as equal to men in all aspects, including consumption of alcoholic beverages.[7]

As grocers filled store shelves with brand names like Boone's Farm, Annie Green Springs, Sangria, Ripple, Bali Hai, Key Largo, Spanada, Tyrolia, and Thunderbird, rising postwar disposable incomes encouraged many vintners to begin bottling their own up-scale wines for lucrative retail sales.[8] As a result America experienced a wine revolution marked by increased consumption and a consumer shift from cheaper, sweet, high-alcohol wines to premium dry table wines. Curious consumers wandered through store aisles without the knowledge of how to match quality and price value. Since Prohibition had destroyed American wine connoisseurship and created a nation without wine authorities, consumers were forced to rely on trial and error to find what tasted good to them. Within a short time wine writers in newspapers and magazines would come to the rescue.

During the 1970s America developed a new educated class of oenologists, and California wine increased in quality and prestige while rising to prominence in the world wine market. New wine professionals organized the American Society of Enologists and the Napa Valley Wine Technical Society to initiate experimentation and disseminate information. Between 1964 and 1974 California bonded wineries grew from 231 to 311 facilities and winegrape acreage more than doubled from 136,758 acres in 1965 to a high of 322,044 acres in 1974. The increase was led not by pioneers but by the eight largest wine companies, which increased their hold over the market from 42 percent in 1947 to 68 percent in 1972.[9]

By the 1960s consumer preference for dry wines propelled the California premium-wine industry once again onto the world market. Rising disposable income levels made wine more accessible as one of life's finer luxuries, and this in turn enticed vintners to begin bottling their own wines for retail sales rather than shipping them as bulk products to be bottled by national wholesalers. These new marketing goals targeted an unsophisticated wine audience and depended heavily upon retraining and reeducating the general public through advertisements in magazines and on the new medium of television, and by training hotel and restaurant staffs.[10]

Post-Prohibition Wines in Santa Barbara

After the repeal of Prohibition in 1932 it would take decades for the state's wine industry to replant vineyards, modernize production facilities, and reeducate wine drinkers accustomed to cheap, sweet, bulk wines. Santa Barbara County's wine industry struggled out of the devastation of Prohibition with a false start by two local commercial winemakers, Umberto Dardi and Benjamin Alfonso. On 9 October 1933, Dardi, an Italian farmer, obtained bond number 3577 to produce 1,100 gallons of wine on his property near Kellogg and Patterson Streets in Goleta, a neighboring community to Santa Barbara. The enterprise ended in tragedy in August 1937 when Dardi declared bankruptcy and, not long afterward, both he and his daughter died in bizarre home winemaking accident.[11]

The second wine enterprise, while not a human tragedy, still ended in failure. In April 1935 Benjamin Alfonso received bond number 4228 to operate the Old Santa Ynez Winery on land that was once part of the College Rancho in Santa Ynez Valley. He quickly constructed a wooden structure with cement floors and tin roof to enclose his press, crusher, storage tanks, and fermentation tanks with a capacity exceeding 3,000 gallons. Bureau of Alcohol, Tobacco, and Firearms (BATF) records for 1936 and 1937 show that the winery had problems from the start: large amounts of spoiled wines, ongoing failure to file required bond forms, and numerous leaking tanks, which Alfonso was forced to destroy. The winery closed in 1940 when Alfonso faced BATF charges of illegal winemaking. That same year Alfonso sold the land, thus ending Santa Barbara County's first attempts at post-Prohibition wineries.[12]

Bacchus Arrives on Santa Barbara's Mountain Drive

The wine tradition was far from dead in Santa Barbara, for in the foothills behind the city, along the winding road appropriately named Mountain Drive, could be found a flourishing outpost of the 1950s Bohemian lifestyle that kept the local wine dream alive for the next two decades. In the 1940s Bobby Hyde, the developer of the Mountain Drive community, bought a fifty-acre parcel along the winding road. He began to sell sections to young men and families that he found compatible with his free and artistic lifestyle. Wine lover Bill Neely, a potter and summer park ranger, and architect Frank Robinson joined Hyde and helped rebuild the community's wine tradition.

Mountain Drive residents celebrated with frequent festivals and parties based on the spirit of Bacchus. The year's main event was an October grape stomp that began with a motorcade to San Luis Obispo County to pick winegrapes. Upon return with the grapes the community leaders would select a wine queen, who would inaugurate the stomp dressed only in a crown of gilded grape leaves. "The way the [Mountain Drive] wines were being made," confessed Stanley Hill, a participant, "was too haphazard." He admitted, however, that "it was a hell of a lot of fun, stomping around in the vat with a bunch of naked cuties."[13] Neely experimented with plantings of Folle Blanch, Semillon, Corbeau, and other cuttings from UC Davis's Department of Enology, but he was defeated by fire, gophers, and rocky soils. Hill, on the other hand, had limited success with Cabernet Sauvignon and Pinot Noir grapes. The Santa Barbara region still awaited the rearrival of a commercial wine industry.

California's Wine Revolution

As Mountain Drive residents experimented with winemaking, post–World War II California commercial wineries reentered the national and international wine marketplace after a twenty-five-year hiatus imposed by Prohibition, depression, and war. As noted above, within one generation American wine improved in both quality and prestige and quickly rose to prominence in the world wine market.[14]

The crucial moment of self-realization for the California industry came in 1976 with the famous Bicentennial blind tasting of French and California wines in Paris, France. In what *Time* called "The Judgment of Paris," French wine experts named Stag's Leap Wine Cellars 1973 Cabernet Sauvignon and Chateau Montelena's 1973 Chardonnay superior to Bordeaux and Burgundy competitors.[15] Most important, the tasting inspired American winemakers to raise their standards and, in the words of wine writer Paul Lukacs, to "begin thinking of 'world class' as a goal."[16] The event proved to be such a milestone that the Smithsonian Museum of American History commemorated its twentieth anniversary with a two-day recreation of the tasting and celebrated the role of wine in American history.[17]

The blind tasting in Paris heightened the intensity of a series of planned and incidental industry growth factors that had began as early as the mid-1950s. The wine renaissance of the 1960s and 1970s brought a shift in consumer tastes, and wine sales increased in conjunction with an expanding population, strengthened consumer incomes, and dreams of rising social status. In the long run the changes resulted in a new California style of winemaking that dominated the industry worldwide.[18]

Along with increases in consumer consumption came the switch to premium table wines. The ancient mystique of wine began to catch on as Americans switched to premium table (dry) wines as a symbol of social status.[19] At the same time, wine's historic social and religious symbolism helped provide legitimacy for a variety of social movements in the 1960s that sought to address the chaos and injustice of the post-war world. Business-savvy wineries tied wine's social status and the period's romantic back-to-nature spirit with their rural settings that elicited mysticism and romance capable of bringing a natural peace to people's minds.[20] The national shift toward dry table wines proliferated further as health-conscious Americans read Dr. Salvatore P. Luca's *Wine as Food and Medicine.* Luca, University of California professor of preventive medicine, described in his book how wine could be used as a natural tranquilizer, cholesterol reducer, vitamin, and digestive aid.[21]

These trends led to a dramatic jump in U.S. per-capita wine consumption, from 1.51 gallons per adult in 1963 to a 1971 high of 2.37 gallons per adult.[22] California winemakers quickly moved to make more affordable premium wines available to the new market. Wine marketers realized that Prohibition had destroyed the American fine-wine tradition and that this was their opportunity to rebuild the industry by redefining "the best" to be the new California style that utilized science to produce fruit-flavored wines based on quality grapes. Over the next two decades California moved the world industry from generic blended wines to varietal-designated and vintage-dated wines based on the philosophy that quality grapes make quality wines. Trail-blazing winemakers and entrepreneurs moved to produce a California tradition capable of producing world-class wines.[23]

In order to pull off this wine coup the industry needed a cadre of professionals. It was not long before these trained leaders in oenology and viticulture graduated from the University of California at Berkeley and Davis and in short order provided the means to mass-produce premium table wines.[24] California's use of cool fermentation, hygienic processing and bottling, cultured yeast, and scientific vineyard management became a world standard for winery efficiency. More important, efforts to reeducate consumers succeeded and the American public began to expect reasonably priced premium wines.

Consumer taste shifts were only the beginning of the process. America's postwar economic growth fueled major economic changes for the industry. Favorable tax climates for investors helped wineries expand as federal, state, and local tax concessions made it advantageous for individuals and companies to invest in vineyards and wineries. The industry did not offer high profit margins but did offer considerable growth potential in an inflationary period, thereby drawing professionals (doctors, dentists, lawyers, retired corporate officers, investors, entrepreneurs) and their capital to rebuild the industry.

These revolutionary changes lead to an unprecedented growth of the industry in the 1960s and 1970s requiring a high level of investment in land and technology. Capital for this expansion came from wine entrepreneurs who adapted the business techniques of large businesses to a fragmented industry. For the wine industry this meant a gradual trend toward centralization, or merging of wine-, alcohol-, and food-processing corporations.[25] These new large wineries instituted marketing techniques that utilized the popular press, television, radio, and tourism (tasting rooms and vineyard events) to develop an expanding market.[26]

This growth led to an ever-increasing need for new land to fill the demand for additional winegrapes. Wineries in an expansion mode, seeking premium winegrapes, looked beyond the counties of Napa, Sonoma, and Mendicino to new vineyard lands in the central and south coast regions of California.[27]

Napa Seeks Premium Winegrapes

The first response of San Francisco Bay–area wineries and vineyards to grape shortages was to plant new local vineyards; but rapid postwar urban expansion had encouraged many farmers to sell their land as its value rose, and the result was escalating land prices in the regions best suited for winegrapes. After a half-decade (1960–1965) of unprecedented urban sprawl agricultural activists moved to counter the loss of prime agricultural lands that threatened the vineyards of the San Francisco Bay region.[28] Bay-area counties patched together local laws that exclusively zoned land for agricultural use, based on farmers' arguments that these parcels provided a sense of community, helped secure economic diversity, preserved historic and aesthetic values, and secured open space for recreational and health benefits.[29]

Soon the threats of urban sprawl reached statewide audiences, and farmers and environmental activists temporarily joined forces to lobby state legislators to curb the loss of agricultural and open-space lands. In response, legislators passed the California Land Conservation Act of 1965 (called the Williamson Act) and the Property Tax Assessment Reform Act of 1966.[30] These laws established a statewide voluntary county-participation program based on property tax incentives that were designed to save valuable farmland.

These policy measures slowed the conversion of California farmland to urban uses, but sales of land for viticulture increased. Small and medium winegrape growers increasingly found it more profitable to sell to a new generation of gentleman farmers from the cadre of doctors, dentists, lawyers, business executives, and agricultural entrepreneurs seeking the 1960s' version of the good life—the wine industry. These high-income investors purchased land, planted grapes, and under the existing tax laws, avoided paying taxes by writing off all invested income and capital improvements as losses. If investors sold the land several years later it was taxed at the lower capital gains tax rate. This system created a tax dodge whereby no permanent economic loss was suffered by investors and vineyards functioned as a laundering mechanism for entrepreneurs with excess wealth. The window of opportunity for these advantages only lasted until the 1976 Tax Reform Law amended the Internal Revenue Service Codes to exclude vineyard investments as a form of tax write-off.

Without the generous tax advantages farmers, grape growers, ranchers, and investors then sought other means to create an efficient, high-profit industry. Farmers seeking diversity and chasing agricultural "hot" crops converted row cropland, dairies, and fruit and nut lands to vineyards. California table- and raisin-grape growers capitalized on the grape shortage and investor interest by selling their grapes for bulk wine juice. Ranchers, on the other hand, utilized vineyards as a way to achieve an agricultural diversity capable of stabilizing earnings while avoiding profit-eating property taxes. Investors, seeing an opportunity for short-term profits, got caught in the mystique of the wine lifestyle and also avoided high property taxes and inflation through vintibusiness capitalization.

By the late 1960s the demand for vineyard land reached a fever pitch. The need for more premium winegrape vineyards became even more apparent as wine industry reports showed a doubling of U.S. wine consumption between 1963 and 1974.[31] The upward trend in total U.S. wines consumed slowed to 10.4 percent per year in 1972, when dry table wines topped 50 percent of all wines consumed. To meet the nation's thirst, marketers nearly quadrupled foreign wine imports, from 14,369,000 gallons in 1964 to 51,394,000 gallons in 1974. Further strain on the California grape crop came as world markets also paid top dollar for California grapes. An Italian immigrant colony in Caxias Do Sul, Brazil, imported California grapes to meet the needs of its own industry.[32]

Economic reports from the early 1970s fostered the idea that the U.S. wine industry was woefully short of premium winegrape acreage. In 1973 Maynard Amerine predicted that "150,000 acres of new vineyards are to be planted throughout the state in the next several years and the variety of grapes to be grown on each acre will be matched to the climate and soil conditions of that acre to yield the best quality grapes."[33] Amerine's prediction proved correct.

The search for new winegrape lands heightened throughout California, the United States, and the world.[34] Economic projections from the Bank of America and the Wine Institute provided market-growth data and the encouragement for developers, grape growers, bankers, insurance companies, and gentleman farmers to move into action.[35] Prompted by these business possibilities, investors reached out to researchers from UC Davis and California State College, Fresno, for the research and development technologies to guide the establishment of the new expanding California wine industry.

Most in the industry knew that regional microclimates matched with appropriate varietals held the secret for the selection on new vineyard lands. Vintner Robert Mondavi utilized science, but added the caveat that science mostly helps oenologists and viticulturists avoid absolute failures. The California wine industry needed more premium winegrape acreage in regions where real estate prices and other economic opportunities offered reasonable profit margins. Thus began a decade-long search for the state's best winegrape growing areas.

Rediscovery of Santa Barbara Viticulture

Economic historian Alan L. Olmstead chronicled how regional American agricultural industries become location specific as a result of "induced innovations" brought about by marketplace factors.[36] In the case of the California wine industry, winegrape shortages sent viticulturists on a statewide journey to find the regions capable of supporting premium varietal winegrapes. Some growers of the 1950s and 1960s quickly turned to the state's past records and combed new and old economic and research reports looking for indicators left by fellow farmers, business investors, and universities. Many used trial and error to discover locations that supported agricultural economic growth, provided tax advantages (federal, state, and county), contained ample inexpensive land, and offered a good overall economic climate for winegrapes.

A few early pioneers found that Santa Barbara County provided a promising cool climate and economic infrastructure needed for success. Two regions within Santa Barbara County—Santa Maria Valley and Santa Ynez Valley—surfaced as prime locations for the expansion of California's winegrape vineyards. Santa Barbara County in the 1960s was buoyed by its healthy agricultural economy, ranked twentieth among California's fifty-eight counties, and 1965 brought an all-time high of $71.2 million to the county's general economy.[37] Because the local community had the infrastructure necessary to support another major agricultural industry—banks, farm service businesses, housing, water, roads, and schools—it could draw much needed venture capital. As a result many West Coast corporations in San Diego, Los Angeles, and San Francisco moved to diversify their portfolios with investments in food processing and agriculture, and wineries and vineyards became first-rate investment opportunities.[38] But like most state agricultural communities, the county faced urban expansion pressure on agricultural land.

Rapid population growth (40 percent) between 1960 and 1965 placed Santa Barbara County in the third position as the fastest-growing county in Southern California (behind Orange and Ventura Counties).[39] Projections for the future pointed to new growth as the University of California built its Santa Barbara campus and the Air Force developed missile facilities at Vandenberg Air Force Base in Lompoc. The 1966 Security First National Bank report projected that Santa Barbara County would grow at a rate substantially higher than of the state and that Goleta, Carpenteria, and Santa Ynez would become the county's high-growth areas. Although the report made no mention of viticulture it was apparent that Santa Barbara County was economically ripe for all types of agricultural expansion.[40]

In January 1965 the Santa Barbara County Agricultural Extension Service, in conjunction with Marston H. Kimball, UC Davis bioclimatologist, issued an extensive report on the climate of Santa Barbara County.[41] The study pointed to climatic conditions capable of supporting winegrape growing. Data for the report were gathered at stations in what is today the heart of the Santa Ynez and Santa Maria viticultural area—La Zaca, Lompoc, Solvang, Santa Ynez, Los Alamos, and Sisquoc Ranch. The report noted that mild temperatures were the rule in Santa Barbara County and that precipitation came in a concentrated period between November and April. It also boasted that sunshine was abundant throughout the county, although low cloudiness during summer nights brought cooling effects to the coastal points and western valleys of Santa Ynez and Santa Maria.[42]

The report described the geography of the Santa Ynez and Santa Maria River Valleys and their maritime climates. The Santa Ynez Mountains, with elevations to 4,000 feet, parallel the coastline from Point Arguello to the eastern edge of the county and outline the westward flow of the Santa Ynez River, which empties between the San Rafael Mountains and Purisima Hills (elevation 1,200 to 1,700 feet) to the north. The southern Santa Ynez Mountains (elevations from 800 to 2,600 feet) encircle present-day Lake Cachuma and the Los Padres National Forest to the east, and form a series of low hills to the west as the river empties into the Pacific Ocean near Surf. This allowed the maritime moderating climate to work its way up the long narrow Santa Ynez River Valley that widens at Lompoc, the report noted. The Santa Maria Valley, on the other hand, was described as a triangular area about 20 miles long and 15 miles wide with its apex near the town of Sisquoc and its base along the San Luis Obispo Bay. The Cuyama River flows westward and empties into the Santa Maria River, which is also joined by the Sisquoc River. More important, the report gives precise climatic data including frost, fog, precipitation, temperature, growing season, heat summation, and elevation.[43]

An intricate climate map pinpointed areas where grapes could be grown and even compared growing information to data from UC Davis.[44] The report identified a coastal zone that ran between 8 and 30 miles inland up the two river valleys. Direct ocean influences included summer fogs with a temperature-modifying effect that was present 75 to 85 percent of the time in the upper Santa Maria Valley (Garey to Sisquoc Ranch) and the western valley floors of Santa Ynez (Lompoc to Solvang). By 1965 county farmers had available data that could support decisions to plant region I and II premium winegrape varietals based on the University of California Amerine/Winkler index.[45] A few winegrape pioneers in the northern part of the state quickly realized that the economic infrastructure and climatic data all supported winegrape expansion into Santa Barbara County.[46]

Chapter 4

Santa Barbara Pioneers Plant Winegrapes

You get the best vintage from well-cared-for grapes.

—Ovid, *The Art of Love*

California premium winegrape shortages during the 1960s and 1970s forced bay-area wineries to look elsewhere for fruit and encouraged independent agricultural entrepreneurs to plant vineyards in the central and south coast counties of Monterey, San Luis Obispo, and Santa Barbara. The arrangement proved profitable for both factions as northern wineries negotiated contracts for the premium fruit as soon as the vines were brought into production.

Between 1964 and 1978 viticultural pioneers planted winegrape varietals in Santa Barbara County's Santa Maria and Santa Ynez Valleys. Men like Uriel Nielson, James Flood, Harold Pfeiffer, Bob Woods, Louis Lucas, Dale Hampton, and Bob and Steve Miller established large commercial winegrape vineyards in what would become the Santa Maria appellation. Close behind were the smaller individual, corporate, and family vineyards of Boyd Bettencourt, Giff Davidge, Pierre Lafond, A. Brooks Firestone, Marshall Ream, Jack McGowan, Richard Sanford and Michael Benedict, Fred Brander, and Bill Mosby in the Santa Ynez Valley.

The county's two wine areas developed around the entrepreneurial energy of local viticultural pioneers. After accumulating investment capital in other professions, these men gambled that their personal resources and skills as architects, retired business executives, ranchers, real estate developers, doctors, and dentists could develop a viticultural region. In a relatively short time they successfully planted 5,836 acres of winegrapes—half of the total that the local industry reached in the early 1990s. Favorable market conditions allowed for a temporary cooperative spirit, whereby vintibusiness operations in the north (Beringer, Wente Brothers, Geyser Peak, Christian Brothers, Monterey Vineyard, Paul Masson, Sebastiani, Wine Sonoma, and United Vintners) utilized Santa Barbara County grapes to expand their wine production capacities.

Commercial Viticulture for the Santa Maria Valley

In the early 1960s the area's first two pioneers, Uriel Nielson and Bill De Mattei, both from Central Valley grape-growing families, planted more than 100 acres of vineyards in the Santa Maria Valley. The two had first noticed the region in the late 1930s when as students at UC Davis they had worked on a research project that had sought out and mapped California coastal climates best suited for premium winegrape growing.[1] After World War II both men studied the climates of French winegrape regions and compared their results with the weather microclimate records they had collected at numerous California airports. Their conclusions directed them to the cooler region I and II Santa Maria and Santa Ynez Valleys of Santa Barbara County.[2] By 1964 they acted on their research data and purchased land in Santa Maria for the purpose of experimenting with premium winegrape varietals like Cabernet Sauvignon, Pinot Noir, Chardonnay, Johannisberg Riesling, Sauvignon Blanc, and Sylvaner.[3]

Nielson and De Mattei selected Bill Collins, an experienced grape grower from Delano, California, as the vineyard manager for the project. Collins, like his employers, believed that the region was "one of the rare places in the world where high quality wine grapes" could be grown. More important, he believed that the region could produce "better quality wine than those produced in Napa Valley." Collins's faith in the region was given a boost when Christian Brothers Winery quickly contracted for the vineyard's grapes. In Collins's words, "If a rancher said he was going to start a vineyard, he would find a winery representative at his door the next day offering to contract for his future production."[4]

The project's initial yields exceeded four tons per acre, and northern wineries paid $400 per ton for the grapes. With production costs averaging about $1,000 per acre, Collins felt that a "family with 40 acres of high quality grapes" could "make a hell of a good living."[5] Thus, he predicted that numerous local growers would follow suit after this initial project. Later, in a Pacific Gas and Electric Customer monthly bill insert, Collins was quoted as predicting that the region would someday have more than 5,000 acres of vineyards producing premium winegrapes.

Not far away a third pioneer decided to enter the Santa Barbara vineyard business. In 1952 James Flood III purchased the 37,000-acre Rancho Sisquoc with capital acquired from the sale of his 200,000-acre Rancho Santa Margarita to the federal government for establishment of Camp Pendleton Marine base, just north of San Diego, California.[6] From the outset Flood looked for ways to diversify the cattle ranch operation and increase the land's overall productivity. In 1963 Flood hired Harold Pfeiffer as ranch manager, and the two immediately considered growing winegrapes.[7] A promising series of negotiations with Almaden Winery in the early 1960s inspired Flood to ready his Sisquoc Mesa lands for vineyards by installing an irrigation system. The deal fell through when Almaden changed hands, and Pfeiffer converted more than 1,000 irrigated acres to sugar beet production.

When neighbors De Mattei and Nielson began planting their vineyards just to the north, Flood began to think again of viticulture. Flood and Pfeiffer both felt they had the perfect microclimate for winegrape growing, and in 1968 they planted grape test plots with cuttings from the Nielson-De Mattei vineyard. They utilized the mesa area of the property, just above the Sisquoc riverbed, because of its almost frost-free microclimate and low riverbed elevation (300 feet) that allowed fog and air movement preferred by many winegrape varietals. Expansion continued in 1968 and 1969 when Pfeiffer purchased more grape clippings from De Mattei and Nielson and established a nursery that was used to plant 29 acres in 1970, 48 acres in 1971, 28 acres in 1972, and a final plot of 87 acres in 1974.[8] Practical advice for vineyard planting came from Paul Masson's vineyard manager Joe Carrari.

By 1972 Santa Barbara County vines planted in the 1960s began to bear fruit, and local growers searched for secure markets for their expanded future production. At first the crops went chiefly to the Oakville Winery in the north, and from 1974 to 1979 Sisquoc benefited from a six-year contract with Bob Meyer of Geyser Peak. Continued statewide grape shortages convinced Santa Barbara–area growers to expand even further. In 1977 Ed Holt was brought on as the new vineyard foreman, and he helped plant the 200-acre Rowan vineyard on the upper mesa. But the largest of the Santa Maria pioneering efforts was yet to come.

In the late 1960s another agribusiness family from Delano, California, George A. Lucas and Sons (established in 1943), decided to expand its 1,500-acre grape farming operation into Santa Barbara County. After graduating from college Louis Lucas ran the family's table- and raisin-grape business in Bakersfield, California. He began to toy with the idea of raising European varietal winegrapes and in 1968 joined the American Society of Enologists. Lucas and his brother George then decided to find inexpensive quality land with appropriate climate for winegrape growing and began a series of trips through the south and central coast regions looking for premium winegrape vineyard land. They decided that the Santa Maria Valley had the characteristics they sought.[9]

The brothers, along with business partner Dale Hampton, eight-year family employee and high school friend from Delano, spent 1969 researching the area's soil and climate, studying existing grape test results, evaluating water resources, and reading about California's two-century tradition of winemaking.[10] Because they "didn't want to follow the same train of thought everybody else did," they decided to find a location where grapes could be profitably grown by utilizing the newest in technology and winegrape science.[11]

The brothers' research led them to the Santa Barbara County's Tepusquet rancho lands of the Santa Maria Valley, at the confluence of the Cuyama and Sisquoc Rivers. Irrigation proved to be no problem as local water-well test-holes identified the area's ability to provide plentiful water. Local real estate agents confirmed the availability of cheap land ready for planting and directed the brothers to the favorable Pacific Gas & Electric Report. Additional support for the overall project came in the form of the 1970 Bank of America Wine Industry Report that projected a decade of wine-industry growth.[12] The brothers spoke with De Mattei (Luis's Delano Little League coach) and Nielson, long-time neighbor ranchers from Delano. A positive response from these trusted fellow ranchers further raised their hopes. The final convincing data came when Brother Timothy of Christian Brothers winery, who had been purchasing grapes from the Nielson Vineyard, told the Lucas brothers that he “would consider paying Napa Valley prices” for local grapes.[13]

The family corporation moved into action and put some properties together to form a limited partnership stock company, the first such venture in the history of California grape production, and established the Dalmatian Vineyards Associates. The venture attempted to form lease options, purchase land, rent parcels, form termed leases, or whatever was possible to create an economically feasible project that would attract investors and “looked like farmers had done it.”[14] Attempts to get Dean Witter, E.F. Hutton, and other major investors to underwrite the project faltered, and in the end, the small firm of Beckman and Company from San Jose, California, undertook the project’s funding on a best-effort basis.

The Lucas brothers planned a model vineyard and used only heat-treated rootstock for the deep gravel soil that was free of phylloxera and oak tree fungus. Plans included the use of grape varietals considered best for the region I to region II climate: Cabernet Sauvignon, Pinot Noir, Pinot Chardonnay, and Johannisberg Riesling. Automated irrigation systems, virus-resistant grape stock varieties, machine harvesting to reduce labor problems, frost protection systems, metal trellises, five 20-acre-feet reservoirs, and numerous 1,000-foot-deep wells rounded out the prospective growth plan. The ten-year prospectus promised limited investors a 10 to 60 percent annual profit on their investment along with 12 percent tax deduction for the first three years.[15] The deal failed to attract enough investors, however, and rather than continue, the brothers returned every investor’s money. Later they reflected that they were “about five years ahead of their time.”[16]

The brothers decided to find another way to plant their vineyards and sought the expertise and resources of family and private financiers. One would-be backer, Alfred Gagnon, senior partner in a major consulting firm, upon receiving the refund of his $50,000 investment, decided that it “must have been a good deal for somebody if they felt they could do it for themselves.”[17] Upon further investigation of the region Gagnon decided in

1969 to come on board as a 50 percent partner. Thus, with Gagnon's money and expertise and some farm equipment supplied by the Lucas brothers, a limited partnership emerged, creating the Tepusquet Vineyards. The enterprise received a gigantic boost in 1970 when Beringer Winery signed a five-year renewable contract for the grapes. Banks now jumped at the opportunity to provide the rest of the credit needed for the project. Eventually the plan raised $3.5 million and developed approximately 1,200 acres of vineyards. Dale Hampton planted the Tepusquet vineyard and acted as the vineyard manager. Over the next few years Hampton also helped establish the 350-acre Paragon Vineyards for Jack Niven and the 190-acre Delon White vineyard, both close to the Tepusquet Ranch. Santa Barbara now had the start of a commercial winegrape industry.[18]

Much of the expertise necessary to plant the rest of the newly expanding Santa Barbara industry would come from the ranks of the Tepusquet venture. Three of the Tepusquet planners formed the Coastal Farming Company in Santa Maria. General partners for the firm included Dale Hampton, in charge of field operations, Joe Tucker, irrigation expert, and Garth Conlan, who acted as the business officer.[19] Over the next few years Coastal Farming either created or consulted on 2,000 additional acres of vineyards.[20]

Another small planting of vines took place on the Suey Ranch, owned and operated by the Newhall Land and Farming Company in Santa Maria. The Newhall family purchased the Suey Ranch in 1921 after William Randolph Hearst acquired their central coastlands for his mini-empire. Bob Woods, hired as general ranch manager in 1966, sought ways to further diversify the 3,500-acre ranch and pursued dry farming, cattle ranching, and the growing of lemons, avocados, and sugar beets. In the late 1960s Ed Mirassou, northern winery owner, and his son Peter visited the Suey Ranch with statistics in hand from the oenology program at UC Davis and convinced Woods to plant a vineyard with sixteen winegrape varieties from the UC Davis winegrape nursery. Woods later admitted that he "didn't know anything about grapes" and "had never drank wine."[21] Yet by 1969 they had planted 25 to 30 acres of Pinot Noir and a few acres of Cabernet Sauvignon in what would be named the Rancho Vinedo Vineyard. The experiment seemed successful and grew to more than 1,000 acres by the end of 1973. In 1971 the vineyard movement continued with the establishment of the 90-acre Camelot Vineyard and the 533-acre Katherine's Vineyard, both located eleven miles east of Santa Maria on Santa Maria Mesa Road.[22]

More was yet to come as financial institutions like Prudential Insurance sought profitable agricultural investments. Entrepreneur Harley D. Martin used successful planting reports and the favorable 1970 Bank of America report in his prospectus that convinced Prudential to lend him $2.9 million to form a limited partnership for the creation of the Sierra Madre Vineyard Inc. Martin purchased 1,000 acres of the Suey Ranch in Santa Maria and contracted with Dale Hampton's Coastal Farming Company to plant 850 acres of winegrapes.[23] Mismanagement of the vineyard resulted in its failure by 1975, and Prudential Corporation convinced Superior Court Judge Arden T. Jensen to place the property in receivership with Dale Hampton's Coastal Farming Company to protect the company's assets. Hampton quickly brought 630 acres of the premium winegrapes back into production and shipped all the grapes northward for inclusion in less-expensive wines.[24]

Cold War military base expansions on the Pacific Coast led to the condemnation of the central coast agricultural holdings of the Broome family (now Point Magu, site of an air base and a state park). Bob and Steve Miller, fourth generation members of the Broome family, spent a good part of the late 1960s investigating 300 to 400 ranch sites statewide to replace the family's holdings. In 1968 they purchased the 35,000-acre Rancho Tepusquet from the Allan Hancock family (La Brea Interstate bank).[25] Between 1968 and 1972 the Millers planted row crops on the land and closely watched the development of neighboring vineyards at Rancho Sisquoc, Uriel Nielson's 110 acres, and the Lucas's Tepusquet Vineyards. Successes on those vineyards motivated the Millers to plant 640 acres of winegrapes in 1972.[26]

The Millers wanted the best vineyard possible and hired Dale Hampton to plan and plant their vineyard. Bob Miller later reflected that "one of the things he pioneered [first at Tepusquet, then at Bien Nacido Vineyards and other vineyards] was the concept of using metal stakes in the vineyard." When people began to call it a "Cadillac vineyard," the Millers decided to name the vineyard Bien Nacido—a Mexican expression for being born with a silver spoon in your mouth.[27]

Hampton's Coastal Farming partner Garth Conlan convinced the Millers to plant UC Davis–registered grapevines and enrolled them as "certified increase nursery stock."[28] Not only would this meet the need for future cuttings but the registry made the vineyard eligible for free advice from the university's viniculture department.[29] Additional consultation for the new vineyards came from Vince Patrucci of the Enology Department at California State University, Fresno. By the mid-1970s grapes from those first years went north to Wente, Martini, Sonoma Vineyards, ZD, and Fetzer. In the nearby Los Alamos Valley, Mary Vigoroso followed the movement, planting 350 acres of Pinot Noir, Cabernet Sauvignon, Zinfandel, and Chardonnay grapes intended for sales to large wineries.

Santa Ynez Viticultural Enterprises

Just south of Santa Maria, in the adjacent Santa Ynez Valley, agricultural speculators planted smaller vineyards to help alleviate premium winegrape shortages. These corporate, individual, and family operations helped meet the demand for premium winegrapes but were more susceptible to the cyclic characteristics of the viticultural marketplace.

The region joined the move to growing winegrapes in 1967 after a false start when Daniel J. Gainey, Josten Jewelry partner and Santa Ynez Arabian horse breeder, launched a vineyard project on his 1,800-acre Santa Ynez ranch. Gainey directed his ranch manager Don Bryant and assistant manager Barry Johnson to study the possibilities of winegrape growing in the region. Their favorable report convinced Gainey to plant a 10,000 cutting grapevine nursery for the projected vineyard. In 1968, as planting time approached, Gainey decided that he was not sure about grape growing and sold the cuttings to another nearby vineyard venture.[30]

Not far from the Gainey Ranch, Boyd and Claire Bettencourt faced rising taxes and the threat of losing the family farm, a common plight in the 1950s and 1960s. Determined not to lose their second-generation dairy farm, they searched for various means to diversify production and keep the ranch ledger in the black.[31] Their neighbor Giff Davidge, who later became their partner, referred them to the Pacific Gas & Electric brochure in which Collins had projected that vineyards could do well in Santa Barbara County.[32] Inspired by the report, the Bettencourts visited the Salinas, California, area and investigated newly established vineyards in that region.

The Bettencourts then visited Boyd's classmates from UC Davis, Nielson and De Mattei, to study the initial results from their Santa Maria vineyard. Bettencourt remembered they had searched the entire state evaluating the proper climate and soil combinations for vineyards. In 1966, following his friends' advice, he cautiously proceeded into the winegrape industry. The initial planting, in 1966, included fifteen acres of vines with the addition of five acres per year for the next two years. Nielson and Di-Mattei's vineyard manager Bill Collins served as the vineyard consultant for the Bettencourts and used many of the nursery vines from the aborted Gainey project. By 1969 the twenty-five acre vineyard began production and negotiated contracts that channeled grapes to the Paul Masson Vineyards and Winery.

In 1971 Richard Sanford and Michael Benedict planted their Sanford and Benedict Vineyard at the western end of the Santa Ynez Valley near Santa Rosa Road. Sanford, born on Palos Verdes Peninsula, graduated from UC Berkeley in 1965 with concentrations in geography and geology. He then spent three years in Vietnam as a Navy destroyer navigator. After his tour of duty he traveled through the Burgundian region of France and began to dream of a life in agriculture. He also toyed with the ideas "of vertical integration of the wine business" and "growing a crop, manufacturing a product, and then marketing it."[33] He had no agricultural experience and thus went through the agonizing decision of whether to go to UC Davis for a master's degree in enology or to plant a vineyard and learn through trial and error. Prompted by the Bank of America's 11 percent growth prediction in 1970, tax advantages at the time, and being "a little bit crazy," Sanford decided in that year to go directly into business.[34]

Sanford searched for a location to grow Chardonnay and Pinot Noir grapes that offered a climate to match that of France's Bordeaux and Burgundian regions. The geographer/geologist found that the Santa Ynez Valley in Santa Barbara County offered the long, cool growing seasons and maritime influence similar to that of Burgundy and Napa. With his partner, Benedict, who was trained as a botanist, and backed by financial investors, Sanford planted 110 acres of grapes nine miles west of Buellton along the Santa Ynez River on the 738-acre ranch that was once part of the original Santa Rosa land grant. The vineyard expansion continued.

In the 1950s Dean Brown, third generation Betteravia (Santa Maria) cattle rancher, purchased the 2,200-acre Rancho Corral de Quati. Successes on the cattle ranch created tax problems for Brown, forcing him in the late 1960s and early 1970s to look for ways to diversify the ranch and take advantage of the current tax laws.[35] Conversations with his friend Giff Davidge got Brown interested in using grape growing as a tax write-off. He hired Dale Hampton to plant and manage the vineyard and figured ways to write off soil ripping, soil fumigation, purchase of plants, stakes for vines, installation of an irrigation system, and labor. By 1972 the

Richard Sanford in the doorway of his adobe winery at Rancho La Rinconada. Photograph courtesy Sanford Winery and Vineyard

100-acre vineyard included Cabernet Sauvignon, Chardonnay, Riesling, and Pinot Noir cuttings from UC Davis, and grapes from the vineyard were sold to Martini and to Geyser Peak. Brown's neighbors soon followed his planting lead.

Seeking an investment opportunity, automobile tire industrialist Leonard Firestone, who was also U.S. ambassador to Belgium (1974–1977), purchased 550 acres of Rancho Corral de Quati in 1971. Firestone immediately looked for ways to develop his new investment. The previous owner, Dart Industries, had commissioned Vince Patrucci to do a feasibility study on growing winegrapes on the ranch. The report predicted that the area could produce Cabernet Sauvignon grapes capable of commanding prices from $1,000 to $1,200 per ton.[36] Additional good news came when Coldwell-Banker Real Estate agents T. Hayer and Richard Dick commissioned the California Farm Management (San Joaquin Valley) group to conduct an agricultural feasibility study of the rancho Corral Di Quati.[37] This study, along with evidence from the Sisquoc's 32-acre test plot, the Bettencourt-Davidge vineyard success, and Dean Brown's 100-acre La Zaca Vineyard, pointed to the possibility of successful grape growing in the region.

Firestone then directed his son, A. Brooks (who retired, at age 35, after twelve years with the family-owned Firestone Tire and Rubber Company), to investigate and report on the ranch's agricultural possibilities. The younger Firestone studied data from the UC Davis survey and neighbor Dean Brown's ten-year weather study. Overall, Firestone's study found that subterranean springs provided ample water and that a western maritime influence, between the San Raphael and Santa Ynez Mountains, afforded the ranch a UC Davis region I and II grape-growing classification. The study also reported that the area averaged 16 inches of rain per year, with little or no rain during harvest times, and that its sand to gravely loam soils made the perfect growing medium for winegrapes. The most convincing evidence for both Firestones came from the trial-and-error success that had prompted local farmers to rate the area "brilliant" for winegrapes. Both Firestones believed that these farmers looked "like they know what they're doing."[38] Convinced by these feasibility studies, Leonard Firestone began planting 260 acres of classic winegrape varietals—

Chardonnay, Sauvignon Blanc, Gewürztraminer, Riesling, Merlot, and Cabernet Sauvignon—and placed Brooks in charge of the project.

Brooks used this opportunity as a way out of what he considered the rat race of the large corporate life. Firestone Tire and Rubber Company had gone public in the 1970s, and the role of the family in the business was unsure; in the words of Brooks, "We just didn't fit."[39] Fortunately, he was able to utilize his father's investment in Santa Ynez as an opportunity to create an active farming career.[40]

Further Santa Ynez planting continued throughout 1972. Marshall Ream, vice-chairman of Atlantic Richfield Corporation, while on a vacation with his wife at the Alisal Guest Ranch in Santa Ynez Valley, discovered where he wanted to retire. He purchased a 1,800-acre ranch and took note of the real estate agent's observation that the area was perfect for winegrapes.[41] Statewide market indicators like the success in Monterey County and the Bank of America report enabled Ream to bring together an investment group that included himself, Los Angeles real estate agent John C. Cushman III, Stanford economics professor John T. McDonald, former Standard Oil president Joseph Harnett, agricultural developer and consultant Thomas J. Simpson, Montana cattleman and real estate investor Charles E. Westwood, and Carl L. Kempner, managing partner of Hamershlauh/Kempner Company.[42] Using tax-law benefits, the group funded the purchase of 1,500 acres and immediately planted 200 acres with winegrapes.

Not all of the planters started on the large scale of Firestone and Ream. In 1972 Montreal architect Pierre Lafond decided to plant 72 acres of vines on his 105-acre Santa Ynez Valley ranch. Lafond needed winegrapes for his Santa Barbara winery (established 1962), which had been producing non-grape wines with purchased fruit. Lafond recalled, "I couldn't buy enough grapes to make my wine."[43] He entered the expansion frenzy from a different direction: He would grow winegrapes for his established winery. Lafond devised a plan whereby he could "gradually but steadily improve [his] ability to make fine wines."[44] Bill Collins became the vineyard manager for the newly planted Valley View Vineyard in Santa Ynez.

Continued vineyard growth occurred in 1973 when Bob Woods retired from the Newhall corporation's Suey Ranch operations and moved his

An 1982 photograph of Pierre Lafond, founder of Santa Barbara Winery. Photograph courtesy *Santa Barbara News-Press*

family to their Rancho Vinedo property. The retired ranch manager ran a small herd of Angus cattle and in 1973–1974 planted 27 acres of Chardonnay, Pinot Noir, and Gamay grapevines. His "idea was [to] have half of the ranch in white grapes and half in red grapes." According to Bob Woods, "The knowledge was deficient around these areas as to what we should grow, what would sell, and what would be beneficial." Woods's decision to grow Pinot Noir was "based on the fact that everybody else was Cabernet Sauvignon and this was [another] red." He claims that it was a personal decision made when he "flipped a coin."[45] Woods also knew that he could not compete with the huge Lucas and Newhall ranches for Cabernet Sauvignon vineyards. Through trial and error and pure luck Woods picked a perfect microclimate for Pinot Noir and Chardonnay. His Rancho Vinedo vineyard received little if any frost, needed little irrigation, and enjoyed a long, cool growing season. Most of the fruit from those first years was brokered through San Francisco grape broker Joe Ciati for northern wineries.

Another 1973 entry into this planting spree was Jack McGowan. The former McDonald-Douglas executive hired Hampton to plant and maintain vineyards on land adjacent to Alamo Pintado Road just outside the Danish community of Solvang. The initial planting included 12.5 acres of Cabernet Sauvignon on the lower acreage and 3.5 acres of Merlot and 9 acres of Cabernet Sauvignon on the upper, or La Questa, vineyard.

Dr. Bill Mosby moved to the Santa Ynez Valley in 1958 and opened a dental practice in the nearby town of Lompoc. Throughout the 1960s and 1970s both he and his wife, Jeri, planned on an agricultural retirement on their ranch and carefully watched as vineyards popped up throughout the county. In 1969 their initial retirement planting of 60 acres of row crops ended in a disastrous flood. Undaunted by their first agricultural disaster, they decided to try viticulture. Bill approached his college fraternity brother Bob Gallo, from the Gallo Wines family, who sent them experimental cuttings. In 1971 the Mosbys planted test plots of Merlot, Cabernet Sauvignon, Gewürztraminer, Chardonnay, Sangiovese, and Nebbiolo grapevines from Gallo. The experimental plots prospered, and the Mosbys searched for additional land that could support premium winegrapes.[46]

In 1976 the Mosbys found a favorable vineyard location and purchased 206 acres of the Rancho La Vega ("the meadow" in Spanish) south of Buellton and planted 18 acres of Gewürztraminer and Chardonnay grapes. The ranch carried with it the mystique of past rancho days: Dr. Roman de la Cuesta and his wife, Micaela, had received the ranch as a wedding present in 1853 from her father, Francisco Cota. The property still contained the original adobe homestead and its attached carriage house. Thus was born Vega Vineyards, a family venture to sell winegrapes to wineries.

Long Beach dentist Walter Babcock and his wife, Mona, purchased 100 acres near Lompoc in 1978 as an agricultural escape from city life. The Babcocks, like the Mosbys, sought the quiet agricultural life of Santa Ynez and planted lima beans the first year. Conversations with neighbors like the Bettencourts, Firestones, and Branders convinced them that grapes would be a profitable and glamorous agricultural enterprise. So in 1979 the Babcocks planted 30 acres of vineyards and embarked on a new venture. Within a few years they expanded the vineyard to 50 acres.[47]

In 1979 Robert and Donna Marks purchased 110 acres in the Buellton area as a family retreat and hobby farm. Their Rancho Dos Mondos provided lumberyard owner Robert a runway for his private airplane and an opportunity for the family to experiment as "sundown farmers."[48] Early agricultural endeavors with wheat, garbanzos, and flower seeds (African daisies) proved to be far too labor intensive and unprofitable. In an attempt to diversify the ranch the family planted 3 acres of Chardonnay in 1980, and family and friends spent their spare time maintaining the vineyard. The vineyard grew to include 18 acres and one part-time agricultural worker.

The surge of small vineyard planting continued into the early 1980s. In 1981 Long Beach investor Paul Albrecht planted his four-acre 11 Oaks Ranch vineyard at the intersection of Alamo Pintado and Baseline Avenue, two miles north of Solvang and adjacent to Carey and the La Questa Vineyard. Two years later Betty Williams planted her 39-acre Buttonwood Farm across from the 11 Oaks Ranch and Carey vineyards. By the end of the 1970s Santa Barbara's Santa Ynez and Santa Maria Valleys contained a number of premium winegrape vineyards, most of which shipped fruit to northern wineries.

The Wine Revolution Continues

Throughout the 1970s and into the mid-1980s increases in premium-wine consumption continued to encourage many winegrape growers to court the dream of producing fine wines with their fruit. This transition from grower to producer (or to grower and producer) was motivated by the favorable market signs reflected in Bank of America's 1973 report, fair trade laws, a 1977 Morton Research Corporation evaluation of the wine market, and the 1977 move by the Santa Barbara County Board of Supervisors to allow wineries on preserved farmland.[49]

By 1973 reports documented that between 1967 and 1972, American premium wine consumption increased by 65 percent.[50] This spectacular five-year surge was due in part to a shift in the public attitude toward wine as a fashionable and pleasurable beverage, but the increase also reflected population growth and rising incomes that allowed for purchases of luxury items.[51] The 1970 report had projected consumption of 400 million gallons by 1980; the 1973 report upgraded this figure to 650 million gallons.[52] Californians drank more wine than the rest of the nation, and wine national consumption increased at a faster pace than beer and distilled spirits.[53]

Clearly American tastes for dry table style wines exceeded what had been forecast.[54] The Bank of America report credited this shift in part to a change in demographics, as more people reached legal drinking age (18 to 21, depending on individual state laws), and in part to more wine being sold in restaurants and grocery stores.[55] Increased consumption could also be attributed to the fact that people were being educated in the art of drinking wine.[56]

All indicators pointed to continued growth in wine consumption, and the supply of grapes and wine increased during this period. By 1972 reports placed Californians third, behind the District of Columbia and Nevada, in per capita wine consumption, and the Golden State's wine share of the U.S. wine market grew to just under 71 percent of the nation's total. More important, the Bank of America report projected continued increases in foreign imports despite devaluation of the dollar that made French, German, and Spanish wines more expensive but did little to affect the supply of cheaper Italian wines.[57] Observers noticed that plenty of room existed for expansion of wine sales for all California wine regions.[58]

"Grape Farmers Never Get Rich"[59]

By the mid-1970s many Santa Barbara County growers began to lament that their premium winegrapes were blended into bulk northern wines and it became apparent that wineries—not grape growers—were profiting most from the expanding industry. Operating profit margins for wineries jumped more than 40 percent while grape costs declined, and the cost of materials as a percent of sales decreased from 62 percent to less than 50 percent in 1974.[60] These same growers feared a settling out of the marketplace as Napa acreage and winegrape tonnage nearly tripled.[61] The pressing question for the fledgling Santa Barbara grape growers was how to get the highest possible price for their grapes. Most realized that a local wine industry would help establish the region's reputation and secure the best prices for local fruit.

Santa Barbara vineyard owners feared that a decade of statewide planting of winegrape vineyards could lead to a bust in the market and diminish their grape profits. The 1973 Bank of America report had conceded that grape growing was a risky proposition. The history of the winegrape industry had always been one of boom and bust, underplanting and overplanting. The report also warned that sometime between 1978 and 1980 the supply of grapes for crushing would far exceed the amount required.[62] Despite these warnings, Santa Barbara County vineyard planting continued with Cottonwood Canyon Vineyard in 1973, Ballard in 1974, Brander in 1975, and Sweeney Canyon in 1979. Many of the original pioneers—Lucas, Miller, Bettencourt, Ream, Firestone—feared market gluts and dreamed of permanent winegrape contracts or, better yet, their own wineries to ensure usage of their estate grapes.

Cost-efficient vertical integration of vineyards and wineries became a reality in the 1970s, and marketing reports confirmed the success of bringing vineyards and wineries together. The 1977 Morton Research Corporation's wine market report showed a general trend toward vertical integration within the industry and promoted these vertically integrated wineries as a more competitive means to maximize profits through the utilization of winery-owned and -produced grapes.[63] In 1978, Bank of America's third wine report blamed the recession in the early 1970s for the wine industry downturn in 1973 and 1974 and confirmed that wine consumption and grape prices continued to rise within their predictions from the 1970 and 1973 reports. The study further projected that the $3 billion retail wine industry would continue to grow at a 6 percent rate well into the 1980s and blamed the short downturn on nothing more than a "settling out" of inefficient wineries and grape growers. Those who failed to read the market signs correctly had made the "big mistake" of not realizing that they had to process, market, and sell their new products in an efficient manner.[64] The report was a call for vertical integration in the wine industry.

By the late 1970s vertical integration of vineyard and winery became the industry trend. From large corporate vintibusinesses like Coca-Cola and Gallo to family enterprises like Mondavi, wineries and vineyards statewide began to integrate.[65] Within Santa Barbara County many grape growers attempted to create stable winegrape sales through production of their own wines and contract sales to other wineries.

The bottom line for Santa Barbara growers and winemakers was that the United States had undergone a strong growth in wine demand and that projected average growth rates of 8.6 percent per year far exceeded the state's estimated production capacity. Experts based these figures on the presumptions that the economy would remain stable, wine prices would not outstrip disposable personal income, and the projected consumer increase in wine usage would continue. Faced with this data the Santa Barbara County wine industry quickly moved into an era of establishing wineries and gaining recognition for its vineyards and wines.

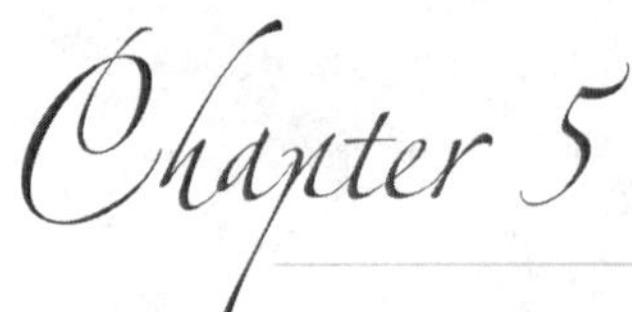

Santa Barbara Develops Wineries

1970s–1980s

Wine expresses the historical moment of a country.[1]

—A. Brooks Firestone, Santa Barbara County winemaker

The Winery Boom Spreads to Santa Barbara

By the 1970s California premium-wine production could not satisfy increased domestic and international consumer demand. As we have seen, Santa Barbara agricultural entrepreneurs responded by planting vineyards and exporting their fruit to northern wineries. Many of these grape-planting pioneers quickly learned a major business lesson of viticultural history: Vertically integrated vintibusinesses stand the best chance of surviving the continuous boom and bust cycles. In the long run, the victors are those capable of controlling their supply of premium winegrapes.

By the late 1970s and early 1980s Santa Barbara's numerous pioneer growers faced a market glut when their rapidly planted vineyards matured and produced many grape varietals unsuitable for local microclimates. Dale Hampton recalled that there was a "romance" about wine that motivated investment in viticulture by many professional people with little experience. They "got into the romance of wine and this romance created a lot of acres of grapes." Errors in selecting varietals for cool region I locations left growers with some poor-quality, overproduced winegrapes. Hampton admitted that in the Santa Maria Valley "we planted way too damn much Cabernet" and that it "never ripened properly." Over time, through trial and error, growers discovered that the Santa Maria Valley produced wonderful Pinot Noir and Chardonnay winegrapes. At the same time, they discovered that the Santa Ynez Valley proved best for growing Merlot and Riesling varietals. Winemaker Stephan Bedford recalled, "We were doing a very poor job of grape growing in the 1960s and 1970s."[2]

Despite these problems the planting continued through the 1970s and culminated in the devastating Santa Barbara County grape gluts of 1980, 1981, and 1982.[3] Grape prices dropped drastically, and many growers plowed their fruit under in an attempt to stabilize prices. State agricultural leaders had warned growers not to overplant, advice that was ignored statewide. As vast vineyard plantings in Monterey, Paso Robles, and Santa Barbara matured within a few years of each other, growers came to understand that the Santa Maria Valley would profit most by keeping its superior Chardonnay and Pinot Noir grapes out of the bay-area blending process.

In 1988 Stephan Bedford served as the winemaker at Rancho Sisquoc Winery and later became partner in his own Bedford Thompson Winery and Vineyard. Photograph courtesy *Santa Barbara News-Press*

As a consequence, many growers responded by investigating the possibility of merging their vineyards with local wineries. This would create a market for excess fruit, and, it was hoped, local wine would in turn win recognition and make county grapes more valuable. Looking back, Kate Firestone, Brooks Firestone's wife and business partner, recalled that people "started dreaming in the early seventies" about starting a small winery.[4] By 1975 Santa Barbara County's thirty-two commercial winegrape growers tended 3,864 acres in the county. Yet the county had only four vintners, and the largest of these—Firestone—had yet to market its product. In less than a decade the county's wine industry had developed an overwhelmingly agricultural tilt, and many local growers realized that increased American wine consumption profited wineries more than farmers.

The American wine boom of the 1960s and 1970s peaked in the early 1980s when per capita wine consumption of generic wine actually declined. This was bad news for bulk table-wine sales and great news for the Santa Barbara premium winegrape growers. John Fredrikson, in *Wines and Vines,* referred to one aspect of this decline in consumption as "the silver lining in the gloomy wine picture," for premium wines.[5] During the 1980s consumption of premium wines increased dramatically. Industry leaders watched as the premium-wine market surged from 4 percent of the market in 1980 to 22 percent in 1989.[6] Affluent consumers with increasing amounts of disposable income gravitated to more expensive, higher quality Chardonnay and Pinot Noir wines. Further support for the development of local wineries came with a weakening dollar, which led to reductions of foreign premium-wine imports and increases in exports of California wines.

Exceptional market conditions for premium wines in the 1980s motivated Santa Barbara winegrape pioneers to vertically integrate their vineyards with wineries as a means to utilize their high-quality winegrapes and take advantage of the premium-wine market. This merging of vineyards and wineries had taken place in reverse in the 1960s and 1970s in the bay area as wineries sought to control vineyard lands. The logic was the same for both Santa Barbara and northern wine businesses: In the premium-wine market a successful winery must secure a reliable supply of

Kate Firestone with Igor Brudniy, Ukrainian hotelier, at Firestone Vineyards in Santa Ynez.
Photograph courtesy *Santa Barbara News-Press*

reasonably priced quality fruit. Noted University of California wine expert A. J. Winkler warned as early as 1960, "If you don't control the grapes, you can't consistently make a quality wine, because sooner or later somebody's going to buy those grapes out from under you. So if you're going to make quality wine, you've got to control the grapes."[7] Santa Barbara growers began merging their vineyards with small wineries to keep control of some of their local fruit and reap the benefits of rising wine prices.

High startup costs for wineries and local land-use policies meant that Santa Barbara County operations would remain smaller than those of northern competitors. These factors also resulted in two distinguishable forms of premium wineries in the county, small commercial (50,000 to 100,000 cases) and artisan (under 50,000 cases).[8] The Santa Maria region with its large commercial vineyards and cheaper land drew larger (high-case production) wineries while maintaining a brisk business selling winegrapes to out-of-county wineries. Smaller artisan or niche market wineries developed in the more expensive Santa Ynez Valley, where winemakers came to depend on excess premium grapes from the larger Santa Maria vineyards. By the end of the 1980s Santa Barbara County could boast more than twenty-five wineries that utilized winegrapes grown locally on 10,000 acres. Even then, larger growers continued to ship the majority of their grapes to northern vintibusinesses.

Vertical Integration, Santa Barbara Style

As the first Santa Barbara vineyards of the 1960s and 1970s began to produce grapes, many growers realized that vineyards were only one means by which to enter the industry. They also realized that the year-to-year instability of grape prices threatened their future. It was no great leap of logic when many decided to vertically integrate grape growing and winemaking as a means to protect their operations.

Undercapitalized growers starting up wineries in Santa Barbara County faced the reality that large commercial wineries tied to vineyard operations were more cost efficient. Economic studies confirmed the commonsense fact that the cost to produce a case of wine decreased as the size of the winery increased. For small wineries, initial startup costs, labor, and low production required higher per-bottle retail prices in order to repay investors. With large wineries, investors achieved greater profits when prices paid for grapes were reduced.[9] Thus, during the 1980s there was a general tendency for the larger wineries to increase their vineyard holdings. Between 1978 and 1988 land owned by wineries doubled in Napa and the percentage of winegrapes grown by grape farmers decreased from 70 percent to 35 percent.[10]

This also happened in Santa Barbara County. Many local winegrape growers were forced to move to the vertically integrated scale of operations on the model of the small regional premium-wine vintibusiness. Borrowing an idea from the 1930s of a farm winery that could retail wine to tourists, many growers developed artisan wineries.[11] Success for these artisan wineries depended on building regional product quality, establishing a consumer following, providing the imagery of a winemaker as an artist, increasing tourism for direct retail sales, and having a constant supply of premium varietal winegrapes. In order for this to occur, growers and newcomers to the business convinced themselves and other investors that efficient production and new technology would produce adequate profits on their returns—in the long term.

Vertical integration followed different directions in Napa and Santa Barbara. After the 1960s, Napa vertically integrated backward: Established wineries purchased vineyards. In Santa Barbara County the integration moved forward, as growers responded to rollercoaster winegrape prices by crushing and bottling their own fruit. Despite their different path, Santa Barbara County wine developers succeeded, by the 1980s, in creating one of the wealthiest agricultural communities in America.[12]

These external economic pressures forced Santa Barbara growers to consider winemaking, and most searched for a means to finance these very expensive modern wine facilities where risks were high and profits accumulated over the long term. Complicating the issue was the established and highly competitive regional wine industry in Napa, Sonoma, and Mendocino Counties, which eventually sought to stabilize its premium grape needs by buying up prime Santa Barbara County vineyards.[13]

Financing was not the only problem that faced Santa Barbara County winery startups. Wineries, of any kind, were new to the county's pro-agriculture Board of Supervisors, which had protected local vineyards, along with other agricultural enterprises, under the Williamson Act. Requests for issuance of conditional-use permits for Firestone and Santa Ynez wineries in the mid-1970s started a discussion of whether wineries were agricultural endeavors or just processing plants. One commissioner worried that "unless restrictions were laid down, a number of them might be strung along principal highways as roadside wine stands."[14] Glenn Janssen, Santa Barbara County agricultural agent, reported to the supervisors that the region's grape prices had only averaged $397 per ton while expenses exceeded $450 to $550 per ton in the county.[15] Many local growers argued that they could no longer rely on Beringer, Wente Brothers, Geyser Peak, Christian Brothers, Paul Masson, Sebastiani, and United Vineyards to contract area grapes. In 1977 County Farm Adviser George Goodall told the board that wineries were a "unique crop," agriculture all the way to the bottle.[16]

The issue resolved itself as the Santa Barbara County Board of Supervisors slow-growth advocates compromised with growers. In a 1977 board of supervisors meeting Louis Lucas optimistically projected that by 1980 San Luis Obispo and Santa Barbara Counties would come into full production and that 10 to 15 percent of California's premium winegrapes would be produced on the Central Coast.[17] Local industry leaders wanted to ensure that they had markets for these grapes. Although cautious, the board ruled to allow the slow growth of vineyards to continue and opened the door for managed establishment of small wineries on preserved agricultural land. These wineries were intended as a future market for the county's premium winegrapes.

Even though supervisors accepted wineries as agriculture they balked at the development of wine factories that were physically disconnected from agriculture. In 1982 the County Planning Commission proposed that all county winemakers secure half of their grapes from local vineyards so that wine production would be tied to local agricultural output. Luis Lucas of Tepusquet Vineyards spoke for local growers, who feared that under these rules exports to northern wineries would be restricted. Dale Hampton worried what would happen to new local wineries in years of short supply if they could not import more than half of their grapes.[18]

Growers and supervisors reached a compromise that protected county agriculture, secured grapes for wineries, and maintained a tourist-friendly wine region. Dianne Guzman, director of the county's planning commission, negotiated a deal between planners and vintners that allowed wineries on agricultural lands to purchase no more than 50 percent of their winegrapes over a five-year period from outside Santa Barbara and San Luis Obispo Counties. The restriction did not apply to wineries on industrially zoned land.[19] In 1985 the board relaxed its strict interpretation of the Williamson Act and utilized transfer of development rights to permit some developers to establish commercial wine facilities, if they complemented the rural setting and permitted some public recreation.[20]

Cost considerations and county land-use policies helped local developers form competitive, smaller-scale operations patterned after Napa's artisan wineries of the 1950s and 1960s. The region would see the development of small- to medium-sized wineries, where the owner could be the winemaker and maverick winemakers could experiment and handcraft wines.[21] Under the pressures of the modern wine marketplace Santa Barbara County developed two distinct types of artisan wineries.

First came the larger, well-funded artisan wineries that produced 50,000 to 100,000 cases per year. Their scale of vintibusiness allowed them to market handcrafted wine at premium prices and compete with well-established larger premium commercial wineries to the north.[22] Firestone, Zaca Mesa, Tepusquet, and Central Coast Wine Warehouse utilized this model first and were later joined by Fess Parker, Cambria Winery, Byron, and others. From the earliest days people like Louis Lucas, Marshall Ream, Leonard and A. Brooks Firestone, and Bob and Steve Miller had harbored this dream, and now some wineries were fulfilling it. Well-capitalized grape growers stabilized contract sales, planted more vineyards, established winery facilities, and began mass marketing Santa Barbara County wines.

A smaller, artisan winery also developed out of this era. This was the shoestring operation with lower levels of capitalization, smaller acreage, modest production, and ownership by those from other professions escaping or retiring from the stress of urban living to the rural setting, artistry, and tranquil images of winery ownership and winemaking. These operations functioned on the French model of a small, vertically integrated operation of vineyard, winery, and marketing designed to counteract the evils of fast-paced urban life and allow for the artistic creation of wine. Vintner Andre Tchelistcheff mentored the creation of many of these boutique operations and firmly believed that "the apostolic mission of the future belongs to the small wine grower."[23] Their success would be based on whether they found a market niche or later sold their business to larger wineries.

Growers to Winemakers

Larger commercial artisan wineries became successful in Santa Barbara County as they integrated local vineyards and wineries. By 1973 it became apparent to Brooks Firestone that "too many people in California were putting in grapes" and there would soon be an overabundance of grapes. He began to wonder if it would be better "to make wine out of these grapes." So the younger Firestone acted on his instincts and convinced his father that "the farmer always gets screwed."[24] Within one year of planting the first vineyards Brooks put together a twenty-year winery prospectus based on conversations with wine business men and women—such as Don Chappellet of Chappellet Winery, Bud Van Loben Sels of Van Loben Sels Vineyards, and Russ Green of Simi Winery. Their advice was not all optimistic. At a meeting with Andre Tchelistcheff in his Napa home, the wine guru asked Brooks, "How much money are you prepared to lose?"[25] Despite Tchelistcheff's warning, both Firestones believed that a long-term large capital investment in the fledgling Santa Barbara wine industry would succeed.

In 1975 the Firestones launched the region's first modern-day commercial winery. Their $7.5 million effort began with a three-way partnership that included Leonard Firestone's Santa Ynez land, Brooks's skills as a business manager, and capital from the Japanese wine and spirits producer Suntory Limited of Japan. Leonard's longtime friend Keizo Saji, president of Suntory Limited, contributed the initial cash financing and provided his company's expertise in the area of alcoholic beverage production, marketing, and distribution.[26] In 1976 the newly constructed 40,000-square-foot redwood and fieldstone winery, north of Santa Ynez, housed their first grape crush under the guidance of winemaker Anthony Austin. The enterprise got off to a good start and gathered its first recognition in 1978 when the winery's 1977 Johannisberg Riesling won a double-blind tasting at a San Francisco competition. In 1981 Firestone's 1978 Chardonnay won "Best of Show" in a London tasting.

Not far from the Firestone vineyard Marshall Ream also began to worry about markets for his Zaca Mesa vineyards. He faced the same economic problems as the Firestone group: Winegrapes alone do not seem to produce sufficient profits. In 1976 Ream's investment group, armed with Monterey County success stories and the 1973 Bank of America report, produced its first wines in rented Monterey County winemaking facilities.[27]

John Cushman, later the owner of Zaca Mesa, remembered, "At the time, vertical integration was the key."[28] Years later winery general manager Jeff Maiken reflected, "I'm sure that they felt that by starting a little operation like this with all the expertise and run it like a big business that they could make a big success out of it." The romance of the wine industry influenced business. Maiken recalled they also felt that it would "be nice just to have a little weekend getaway" that provided the mystique of owning "a piece of a winery."[29]

In 1982 the partnership put together a plan to triple their production over a two-year period. The investment group consolidated its winery and several vineyards into a single company with assets in excess of $11 million. These capital assets were then used as equity to finance an additional $3.5 million in loans from Aetna Life and Casualty, Crocker National Bank, and the Farm Production Credit Corporation for improvements and expansions.[30] They hired Ken Brown, graduate of Fresno's School of Enology, as winemaker, and they expanded the facility from 7,500 square feet to 20,000 square feet and upped production from 20,000 cases to 60,000 cases per year.[31]

In the nearby Santa Maria Valley the Lucas brothers' Tepusquet vineyards survived a rough first decade by selling winegrapes to as many as twenty-seven northern wineries. Napa vintners like Mike Grgich of Chateau Montelena (one of the winners of the famous 1976 Paris tasting) used Santa Barbara grapes for one of his award-winning wines. Yet the Tepusquet vineyard only broke even on the best years.

Tepusquet partners Gagnon and Lucas visited France in 1976 and 1978 and researched ways of making a profit in a small regional wine industry. Again the answer seemed to be vertical integration of vineyard and winery. In 1982 Dale Hampton and Lucas told the Santa Barbara County Board of Supervisors that county growers shipped 92 percent of their grapes to northern wineries and earned mediocre profits. They argued that local growers could only make a profit by processing some county winegrapes and establishing a reputation for the region's wine quality. According to Lucas, "They [Napa] were cutting us and buying our grapes on the side at cheap prices."[32] Later that year Tepusquet winery made its debut.

Commercial integration of vineyards and wineries continued throughout the 1980s. In 1987 Fess Parker entered the Santa Barbara wine industry. Parker had become an American icon for his roles as Daniel Boone and Davy Crockett in Walt Disney productions between 1950 and 1970. Parker capitalized on his success as an American popular culture star when he eventually entered the Santa Barbara County wine industry.[33]

Parker and his wife, Marcey, had had no interest in wines or ownership of a winery during their earlier years. In fact, Parker claimed that he "didn't care for wine in the mid-fifties."[34] It was his involvement with real estate development that led to his burgeoning taste for fine wines. In 1964 he moved his family into a Bel-Aire (Los Angeles) home and discovered that the property's adjoining garden hillside contained an old-fashioned wine cave. Parker decided that their new home would also serve as a center for business entertaining and thus proceeded to fill the cellar with fine wines. Over the next twenty years the Parkers got used to drinking fine international wines.[35]

It would not be until the early 1970s that the Parkers would become interested in grape growing and wineries. Fess had grown up on a Texas cattle ranch, and in the 1960s he fulfilled a lifelong dream when he purchased his Santa Ynez escape and retirement ranch. Over the next twenty-five years the Parkers looked for ways to diversify their ranching business, and they studied the development of the early Nielson, Lucas, Firestone, and Zaca Mesa wine enterprises. At one point they began to consider winegrape growing and visited Professor Amand N. Kasimatis, with the viticulture program at California State University, Fresno, but other work and family commitments kept the idea on a back burner.[36]

A conversation with longtime friend Dale Hampton in 1985 prompted Parker to reconsider establishing a vineyard and winery. While serving as the master of ceremonies for the fledgling Santa Barbara County Vintners Association, Parker met many of the local industry's pioneers who tried to convince him to enter the wine business. Their recommendations seemed good, so Parker conferred with local friend and real estate agent T. Hayer and began the search for land on which to grow grapes. Later that year he purchased a 714-acre Los Olivos ranch, which became Fess Parker Winery and Vineyard.

In launching his enterprise, Parker used the recognition and connections he had gained during his years as an actor to compensate for his lack of winemaking experience. He believed that "if you know too much about something you are not likely to do it."[37] With his son Eli and the rest of the family, Parker plunged into the industry and hired Jedd Steele, 1991 International Winemaker of the Year, as their winemaking consultant. After an arduous struggle with the county board of supervisors the Parkers constructed a 11,700-square-foot winery with a separate 4,800-square-foot wine storage building adjacent to a newly planted 60-acre vineyard.

Santa Barbara Niche Wineries of the 1980s

The great majority of new wineries during this era developed as small artisan facilities designed to ferret out a niche in a growing national and international wine marketplace. Most could be found in the Santa Ynez Valley, though they relied on winegrapes from the adjoining Santa Maria Valley. This eclectic group of wineries varied from cooperatives to small artisan wine businesses and independent winemakers.

COOPERATIVES. One way to form a competitive winery, some concluded, was to bring small growers together in one location to produce their own labels while sharing equipment, staff, and facilities. Continued uncertainty in grape markets in 1976 convinced eight Santa Barbara County vineyard owners to form the Los Vineros ("the vineyard owners" in Spanish) Cooperative Winery. The co-op owners comprised Uriel Nielson, Bob Woods, George Ott, Eric Caldwell, Charlotte Young, Boyd Bettencourt, Bill Davidge, and Dean Davidge. California had a history of such wine co-ops going back to the 1950s.[38] Industry watchers at the time touted the ability of these cooperatives to secure large loans, receive tax breaks, and procure grape contracts for their members. In 1976 Los Vineros opened its facility in Santa Maria and formed a partnership whereby each member owned his or her own vineyards and was tied to the winery by right of first refusal. They agreed that all cooperative-produced wines were to be blended from members' fruit so as not to favor one vineyard over another.

The hopeful founders built a substantial facility, bonded the winery, and custom crushed and cellared Los Vineros labeled wines with the help of winemakers such as Bob Lindquist, Mary Vigeroso, and Jim Clendenen. In 1977 the winery took the valley's first gold medal at the Orange County Fair. Despite the optimistic beginning the winery failed in 1985. In the words of Ernest Gallo, "By its nature, a cooperative was primarily a producer, not a marketer." His brother Julio Gallo saw co-ops as an "honest attempt by growers to bring some stability to the grape industry . . . but co-ops were not the answer."[39] Los Vineros Winery confirmed the reflections of the Gallo brothers—it lacked a marketing program. Bettencourt agreed when he confirmed that "farmers are great people about growing things and so forth, but they are not marketers."[40]

In the late 1980s a second and more successful Santa Barbara cooperative enterprise opened when numerous local and state winemakers made reputations for themselves on the 600-acre Bien Nacido Vineyard. The vineyard's owners, Bob and Steve Miller, designed a style of "custom growing" winegrapes for individual winemakers. Local independent winemakers like Jim Clendenen and Bob Lindquist were so successful with the Bien Nacido grapes that the Miller brothers constructed the Central Coast Wine Warehouse facility for their use. Thus, small winemakers secured grapes, grape growers secured contacts, and wine enthusiasts consumed the premium wines made under Au Bon Climat ("the good climate"), Brandborg Cellars, Caparone, Chansa Cellars, Gary Farrel Wines, Hitching Post, Lane Tanner, Page Mill, Qupé, Richard Longoria Wines, Steele Wines, and Whitcraft Winery labels, to name a few.[41]

ARTISAN WINE BUSINESSES. During the 1970s and 1980s a variety of individuals established themselves in wineries. The cultural mystique of wine and its association with the good life have historically made this an attractive avocation. In Santa Ynez Valley professionals such as doctors, dentist, lawyers, and entrepreneurs responded to the primal lure of the land and established artisan wineries (usually producing under 10,000 cases) on small vineyards in the valley.[42]

In 1977 J. Campbell Carey, James Campbell Carey, and Joseph Carey (all practicing physicians) formed a family corporation and purchased the twenty-five-acre McGowan La Questa vineyard. The Careys dreamed of establishing a family winery that could provide retirement opportunities and a business to hand down to future generations. They converted the ranch's old dairy milking barn into a winery and augmented their grapes with Chardonnay and Sauvignon Blanc grapes from the adjoining forty-acre Adobe Canyon Vineyard.[43]

The Careys launched their operation in 1979 and hired winemaker Rick Longoria, whose background spanned Buena Vista Winery in Sonoma, Chappellet Winery in Napa, and Firestone in Santa Ynez. They then created an immediate cash flow by producing and releasing Sauvignon Blanc, Cabernet Blanc, and Blanc de Noir wines. That same year Longoria established their long-term premium wine business by producing 6,000 cases of Merlot, Cabernet Sauvignon, Chardonnay, and Sauvignon Blanc wines. Longoria later recalled that these local wineries were "in competition with all the other winemaking areas in the state: Napa, Sonoma, Santa Clara" and that in these formative years they confidently believed themselves "part of a viable winemaking region."[44]

In 1979 Bill and Jeri Mosby decided to add a winery to their Vega Vineyards. Jeri Mosby reflected that it had become apparent to them that "there's a conflict of interest between winegrowers and winemakers." Growers want maximum tonnage and wineries want low-production, intensely flavored winegrapes.[45] The Mosbys decided to enter the premium-wine market with a slow-growth plan based on the family's expertise and judicious reinvestment of profits. Technical advice would come from their son Gary, who had recently graduated from UC Davis with a degree in viticulture and enology and had experience as a winemaker for the Edna Valley Winery in Paso Robles. The vineyard manager position fell to their second son, Michael, a graduate of California State Polytechnic College in San Luis Obispo. Bill, who had grown up in an Oregon agricultural family, relied on his medical training to help in the technical aspects of the process. Jeri found her niche as the tasting-room manager and events planner, and their third son, Rick, served as Bill's assistant.

Like others, this family operation aimed at more than business success. Jeri, and others in the industry, often mentioned that "the quality of the people involved with the wine industry is pretty high, and . . . most of them don't have to make tonight's dinner out of what they sell in the tasting room today." Jeri said they were attracted by the quality of their competitor colleagues, who maintained the status of "gentleman winegrowers."[46]

David and Margy Houtz escaped to Santa Ynez in 1979. David, a retired Santa Monica real estate executive, and Margy, a systems analyst and homemaker, brought their four children to a 38-acre ranch two miles south of Los Olivos, off Highway 154 at Roblar Road. They constructed a 50-by-50-foot California-style redwood-sided winery with a tasting room, lab, and guest apartment. Their "Peace and Comfort Farm" grew to include a residence, garden, horses, goats, chickens, ducks, geese, quail, and guinea pigs. In 1982 they planted sixteen acres of Chardonnay, Sauvignon Blanc, and Cabernet Sauvignon grapes with the help of Dale Hampton and Jeff Newton. Then with the help of winemaker Rick Longoria the Houtzes established a goal of producing 3,500 cases per year in what they called a "down-home farm winery." This image manifested itself in the Houtz Vineyard label, which portrayed two lambs in an eighteenth-century-style engraving reminiscent of Bach's well-known "Sheep May Safely Graze" cantata.[47] In 1984 the winery was bonded and hired winemaker John Kerr, formerly of Jekel, Chalone, and Ventana wineries.

Within a few years of planting their vineyard, another family quickly discovered that small-scale winegrape growing provided little economic security. Walter and Mona Babcock experimented with vertical integration of vineyard and winemaking in 1982 when they crushed some of their grapes at the Los Vineros Winery. Falling grape prices and initial success with their wines convinced them to vertically integrate their operation and to encourage their son, Byran, to pursue graduate studies in viticulture and enology at US Davis. The day after Bryan graduated in 1984, the Babcocks poured the foundation for their winery. The parents retired to their agricultural dream and their son began a career on the family ranch.[48]

In 1987 Richard Dore, a former banker, and Bill Wathen, former Chalone viticulturist, founded Foxen Vineyard with the aim of producing world-class Cabernet Sauvignon. Both had started making Cabernet as a hobby on the 1838 Spanish land-grant rancho of English sea captain Benjamin Foxen, Dore's great-great-grandfather. The partners broke the usual pattern and decided to make wine first and use profits to help defray the cost of planting their own vineyard. At first they used only purchased grapes from Sanford and Benedict, Daly-Forthman Vineyard, and Rancho Sisquoc. Then the "Foxen boys" used what Wathen referred to as "prescription farming": "If you can't own the vineyard, it's nice to have a say in the farming."[49] They quickly moved production from 500 to 2,400 cases per year and in 1991 planted an eleven-acre vineyard. Much of their sales were dependent on their well-earned reputation as the Santa Barbara County "Dean Martin and Jerry Lewis of winemaking."[50]

The influx of wine investors continued into the late 1980s. In 1987 Norman Beko, retired computer entrepreneur, sold his Graphics Resources Corporation, acquired the Wine Exchange (a wine brokerage firm), and purchased forty-five acres of Chardonnay grapes in San Luis Obispo County from Prudential Financial.[51] Not willing to lose momentum, he purchased the eighty-acre Cottonwood Canyon Vineyard the next year from Prudential.[52] The vineyard, named after a beautiful setting of cottonwood trees, contained twenty-eight acres of vineyards in the canyon and forty-three acres of Chardonnay and Pinot Noir grapes on the surrounding hillside. Beko committed his enterprise to integrating his established vineyard with a winery. His business plan included a long-term growth strategy that started with part-time employees, part-time consultants, and rented facilities and eventually led to a full winery and tasting room on the vineyard site.

During the 1980s the artisan-marketing niche grew to include wineries designed to be more than an avocation. These endeavors marketed 10,000 to 50,000 cases yearly for local tourist sales and for more distant national and international markets. Centered in the Santa Ynez Valley they vertically integrated their local vineyards and purchased additional grapes from larger Santa Maria vineyards.

One of the first in this category was C. Frederick (Fred) Brander. In 1962 Brander's parents escaped political and economic unrest in Argentina and immigrated to Santa Barbara. Once in America they sent their son, Fred, to Harvey Mudd College, where he received a degree in chemistry. The junior Brander then studied enology at UC Davis.[53] In 1971 Brander worked for Mayfair Wines in Santa Barbara, a wine wholesaling business, and eventually opened up a small wine import company that specialized in wines from France and his native Argentina. But Brander was more interested in becoming a winemaker and worked part of the harvest at Dry Creek Vineyards in Sonoma to increase his skills in producing Sauvignon Blanc wines. In 1975 he convinced his parents to establish a forty-acre vineyard in the Santa Ynez Valley and in 1980 received the bond for the Brander Winery. Over the next few years Brander expanded the operation and in 1984 he added a pink Chateau winery and tasting room to the facility.[54]

Another entrant in this 1980s winery boom was the Sanford Winery. Sanford and Benedict had produced their first vintage in 1976 from a jointly owned vineyard, but the dream dissolved quickly. In 1980 the partnership between Richard Sanford and Michael Benedict fell apart, and Benedict purchased Sanford's interest in the vineyard. Sanford was not willing to give up on the lure of the wine industry, and in 1982 purchased the 738-acre Rancho El Jabali, part of the original Santa Rosa land grant. With his wife, Thelka, he developed a long-range plan to plant grapes and produce premium wines in an artistic, scientific, and environmentally balanced winery. For the first few years Sanford leased winery facilities from the Edna Valley Winery in San Luis Obispo, and in 1983 he assembled his own interim winery facilities in Buellton. In a short time they reached

Entrance to the Rancho El Jabali, Sanford Winery and Vineyard. Photograph courtesy Sanford Winery and Vineyard

their 30,000-cases-per-year goal with grapes purchased from Santa Barbara County vineyards.

Continued successes in the Santa Barbara wine industry prompted the Gainey family to reinvestigate the possibility of a winery to diversify their Santa Ynez agricultural enterprise. In the late 1960s Daniel J. Gainey had decided that the timing was wrong for a winery. As the 1980s winery boom hit Santa Ynez he reconsidered grapes and winemaking as a means to diversify the ranch's agribusiness endeavors. He knew that he would be able to start a vineyard cheaply because he already owned the land and the operation could share equipment and labor with the rest of the ranch.[55] Gainey was not willing, however, to invest the personal capital to compete with Firestone or the Zaca Mesa group.

In 1983, with the help of marketing experts, ranch manager expertise, and financial analysis, Gainey launched an artisan vineyard and winery operation centered on a retail premium wine business. Chamber of Commerce tourist studies showed that the nearby community of Solvang was the third most popular visitor attraction in California, just behind Disneyland and Hearst Castle. Confident that this tourism could support a retail winery operation, the family got approval from Santa Barbara County Planning Commission and constructed a 22,000-square-foot winery designed to give visitors an educational experience about how grapes become wine.[56] This was not a new idea. Tasting room sales, bolstered by educational tours, had started in 1934 at the Napa Beringer winery.[57] According to Barry Johnson, general manager, this marketing strategy allowed the winery to "grow our own grapes, make our own wine and sell all we make, right from the winery."[58] In 1982, wine writer Dan Berger commented that the "rambling, ranch-style facility is so carefully designed that it looks as if it were cut from a textbook on how to make wineries."[59]

Canadian Pierre Lafond provides an anomaly in the development of the 1980s winery movement. He followed the Napa backward integration pattern and moved from a winery to integrate a local vineyard. In 1962 Lafond had opened El Paseo Cellars, a wine and cheese shop, in Santa Barbara's Old Paseo section. Under the encouragement of Mountain Drive residents he secured a bonded license and began to make light everyday table wines for sales in his shop. He thus became the first small local com-

The Gainey Vineyard and Winery. Photograph courtesy Gainey Vineyard and Winery

mercial wine enterprise since Prohibition in Santa Barbara and moved from his garage to his present location at 202 Anacapa Street, two blocks from the beach. Statewide grape shortages forced Lafond to switch to production of pomegranate, strawberry, plum, cranberry, and olallieberry (similar to blackberry) wines from frozen juices.

By 1971 Lafond decided that if he wanted to produce grape wines he needed to integrate his operation with a vineyard. Therefore, in 1972 he purchased 105 acres of land along the lower Santa Ynez River and planted 72 acres in winegrapes.[60] Lafond's Santa Barbara Winery entered the premium commercial wine industry in 1981 when he hired Bruce McGuire, from R&J Cook Winery on the Sacramento Delta, as the full-time winemaker. Driven by Lafond's entrepreneurial spirit and McGuire's expertise the winery steered itself into the premium-wine industry. Between 1985 and 1986 Lafond modernized and expanded production to 35,000 cases per year and based his marketing on the fact that his was the state's only beachside winery. The waterfront retail tasting room in the downtown tourist center of Santa Barbara quickly accounted for 90 percent of all the wine sales for Lafond's enterprise.[61]

By the end of the 1980s Santa Barbara County had a well-defined wine industry with just under 10,000 acres of vineyards and more than twenty-five wineries that had moved in one decade from grape farming to winemaking. The next step was the development of consumer recognition that would successfully market the region's premium wines.

Chapter 6

Santa Barbara Gains Recognition

Back of the wine is the vintner,
And back through the years his skill,
And back of it all are the vines in the sun,
And the rain and the Maker's will.

—Anonymous Vintner's Ode

As we have seen, winegrapes and wine came to Santa Barbara County with the missions and flourished until Prohibition devastated the commercial wine trade. Upon repeal the industry slowly reappeared as local pioneers first planted vineyards in the 1960s and 1970s and subsequently developed two forms of wineries. By the 1980s Santa Barbara County had developed premium vineyards and a regional wine industry. But the fledgling local wine industry confronted a disorderly market that was controlled by boom-and-bust cycles, shifts in consumer tastes, and both domestic and foreign trade struggles. Overcoming these problems required continuous efforts stretching from technology, to marketing, to industrial organization, to politics, and consumer education.

Most Santa Barbara vintners realized that name and label recognition required their immediate attention. Jim Fiolek, vice-president of marketing for Zaca Mesa winery, and others reflected that both medals and publications meant a boost in sales for small wineries.[1] Local wine entrepreneurs remembered how the 1976 Paris competition boosted California wine sales, and they sought this type of prestige and profits for the county.

Building this recognition became an arduous and multifaceted campaign.

Bay-area winemakers had achieved world recognition by establishing a "California wine style," blending science and traditional handcrafted techniques to produce reasonably priced, high quality, and consistent wines. In the 1980s Santa Barbara wineries built on these foundations to achieve regional, state, national, and world identification. On a parallel front, wineries sought further perfection of their business structures and additional governmental support to enhance regional recognition. Local industry members influenced the establishment of two new American Viticultural Areas (AVAS), demonstrated the quality of their wines, marketed the region through the Santa Barbara County Vintners Association, and developed high-profile labels that were built on both winery and winemaker reputations. By the 1990s consumers worldwide learned to recognize Santa Barbara premium vintages on shelves in grocery stores and wine shops.

The Wine Industry Responds to a Turbulent Market

The postwar emergence of a globally competitive California wine industry came against a backdrop of a turbulent marketplace plagued with incoherent regulatory rules that sought to ensure wine quality through federal and international trade laws. To overcome this the statewide industry struggled for recognition in the world marketplace by developing a distinctive product designed to reacquaint American consumers with the wine tradition.

Through it all, California wines continued to grow in market share and Santa Barbara County developed its market presence based on premium wines produced from grapes of exceptional quality. Local winegrape growers and wineries concentrated their efforts on developing their niche in the newly established California wine style. Recognition would eventually result from a process of borrowing and adapting techniques from Napa. Santa Barbara County would develop appellations, establish a vintners association, and utilize marketing techniques that eventually reached a wide spectrum of wine consumers.

Santa Barbara Appellations

For Santa Barbara grape growers and newly established wineries a first step in recognition would come with two AVA designations. In the early 1970s most American wine consumers divided national wines into two categories—corked and capped. Through education California vintners created a wine-savvy consumer who, by the 1980s, wanted to know whether a bottle of varietal designated wine was worth the ever-increasing price tag. Industry members feared that premium wines could become "indistinguishable, at face value, from similar products," a commodity that consumers purchased based on price alone.[2] Regions like Santa Barbara, with a burgeoning reputation for artisan wineries and premium wines, feared this commodification of their product. They believed that appellation designations would help upscale oenophiles choose their quality product.

In Europe, independent government agencies determine regional labels to assist consumers in selection of wines. In the United States, however, the body that taxes and regulates the industry—the Bureau of Alcohol, Tobacco, and Firearms (BATF, today's ATF)—also designates appellations. Most BATF officials have little knowledge of what Rick Theis, Sonoma County Grape Growers Association, considered to be the fact that the "quality of the wine is determined in the vineyard, not in the location of the winery. Wineries and brands come and go but the land remains unchanged."[3] Thus, it became a marketing task of local wineries, grape growers, and trade associations to define, sometimes after the fact, the characteristics of AVAs. Santa Barbara County received two early designations and then spent two decades building its reputation.

The BATF designated Santa Barbara's first region in 1981 when the agency recognized the Newhall Land and Farming Company petition to name the Santa Maria Valley as an AVA. The agency defined the area as encompassing the 7,500 acres of vineyards growers had planted on the region's funnel-shaped, flat valley floors and sloping hillsides. Growers and winemakers further defined the locale as a cool region I, based on the UC Davis scale of heat summation, with well-drained sandy loam to clay loam soils capable of nurturing Chardonnay, Pinot Noir, Merlot, Sauvignon Blanc, Cabernet Sauvignon, and Johannisberg Riesling grapes. The BATF defined the AVA as being based on the Santa Maria River Valley with northern boundaries formed by the plummeting slopes of the San Rafael Mountains at a point near where Highway 166 intersected the section line just southwest of Chimney Canyon. Regulators defined the western boundary as Highway 101.[4]

Two years later, in 1983, the BATF recognized the Santa Ynez Valley as Santa Barbara County's second AVA and described its geography as the area that surrounded the Santa Ynez River. They defined the northern boundary as the Purisima Hills that separated the valley from the Los Alamos Valley, and the southern boundary became the Santa Ynez Mountains that separated the valley from the south coast. Lake Cachuma and the Los Padres National Forest formed the eastern boundary; the western boundary was the place where the Santa Ynez Valley narrows and is separated from the Lompoc Valley by the Santa Rita Hills. Based on the Winkler and Amerine viticultural heat summation scale the AVA was identified as a cool region I to II growing area with a beneficial maritime influence.[5] With the establishment of two AVAS Santa Barbara County had achieved the first step toward wine recognition. The geographic names on wine labels now included Santa Barbara, Santa Ynez, and Santa Maria. Consumers could now link quality county wines to their geographic location.

Santa Barbara County Vintners Association

The formation of the region's two AVAS prompted local growers and vintners to establish a trade association designed to promote their grapes and wines. After observing Napa and Sonoma AVA marketing techniques Santa Barbara County vintners moved to promote regional, national, and international recognition by modeling themselves after their northern counterparts.

Local growers and winemakers realized that in order to survive in the wine industry they needed to organize and promote their region. More important, many outside the region felt the same about Santa Barbara. Robert D. Reynolds, executive director of the Wine Growers of California, was optimistic about central coast vineyards and predicted that Santa Barbara County grapes would rank "very near the top."[6] This prompted many to adopt a Napa-like business strategy that could secure a place for them in the larger California, U.S., and global markets. Initially, many of the local wineries participated in the California Central Coast Wine Growers Association that lumped Santa Ynez and Santa Maria with Paso Robles; but many wanted more specific geographic recognition. In 1981 local growers and wineries, seeking an opportunity to sharpen their region's image, formed the Santa Ynez Valley Viticultural Association (SYVVA).

No sooner had SYVVA come together than the members realized that the association excluded most of the region's Santa Maria vineyard land. This prompted a 1983 move by Rick Longoria, Richard Sanford, and fifteen other Santa Barbara County winemakers, wineries, and growers to expand the SYVVA into what would become the Santa Barbara County Vintners Association (SBCVA).[7] Funded with a $25,000 grant from the statewide wine commission, members drew up an organizational mission statement "to support and promote Santa Barbara County as a premium wine producing and winegrape growing region and to enhance the position of Santa Barbara County wines in the world marketplace."[8]

Once established, the association sponsored promotional events to build regional recognition. Members knew that tourism was an important factor in enabling the region's small artisan wineries to sell directly to consumers and that "wine tourism is the ultimate brand differentiator."[9] In 1985 Rick Longoria, first SBCVA president, established the tradition of the yearly Vintner's Festival, which over the years brought thousands of people to the local wine country for food from top restaurants, educational exhibits, enjoyment of popular musical entertainment, and locally grown foods. The organization produced a tourist brochure and sponsored wine-tasting events in San Diego and Washington, D.C. Many individual wineries supplemented the regional exposure by establishing a regular schedule of winery events to draw weekend tourists from the Los Angeles region.

Initial success of the association led members to seek an expanded role for the group. In 1987 the SBCVA board of directors under President Jim Fiolek hired Pam Maines Ostendorf as its first full-time executive director. Ostendorf quickly moved into action and organized promotional and advocacy events aimed at consumers, industry members, community organizations, and governmental agencies. The new director faced financial difficulties as membership dues and festival profits failed to cover association costs. Again the association turned to the California Wine Commission for support, and the board of the SBCVA submitted and won a regional project proposal requesting matching funds to promote Santa Barbara County wines. Between 1986 and 1990 the SBCVA used profits from festivals and matching moneys from the commission to fund media visits, posters, brochures, maps, and seminars.

During the 1990s the SBCVA stepped up marketing and advertising campaigns. They hired a pamphlet-distribution company to circulate their brochures in tri-county (Santa Barbara, San Luis Obispo, and Ventura) restaurants, hotels, gas stations, visitor centers, train stations, airports, and travel and car rental agencies. Ostendorf's office also established a series of press releases and press kits designed to draw California newspapers, filmmakers, and wine writers to the region. Ongoing projects included biannual trade wine-tasting event and a server seminar series that educated hundreds of local restaurant and hotel servers, owners, managers, and chiefs about Santa Barbara wines. A community-governmental relations luncheon kept the industry in the eyes of local leaders and informed them of the contributions of the industry to the local economy. Advocacy roles for the association also included membership in professional wine organizations, government watches, and the building of a professional library to keep members informed about new industry developments. The SBCVA also published a history of the Santa Barbara County wine industry in conjunction with the Public History Program at UC Santa Barbara.[10]

By 1999 the association had grown to nearly one hundred members (wineries, growers, vineyard managers). It encouraged wineries within its ranks to promote themselves by organizing one-day, tourist-friendly wine trips based loosely on the region's two AVAs—Foxen Trail (Santa Maria AVA) and Santa Ynez Triangle (Santa Ynez AVA). The Foxen Trail included a one-day, twenty-mile trip along Foxen Canyon Road to the Andrew Murray Vineyards, Cottonwood Canyon Vineyard, Foxen Vineyard, Bedford Thompson Winery, Fess Parker Winery, Rancho Sisquoc, Byron Winery, Firestone Vineyard, and Zaca Mesa Winery. The Santa Ynez Valley Wine

Trail took visitors on a circuitous triangular route that brought together Gainey, Sunstone, Santa Ynez, Buttonwood, Curtis, Los Olivos, and Brander Wineries. Santa Barbara County now had a trade organization to promote its wines.

Quality Wines Bring Label Recognition

Trade association activities would be of little use without the production of high-quality winegrapes and wine. By the early 1970s pioneers like Dale Hampton feared that as more than 310 northern wineries imported 92 percent of Santa Barbara County's grapes, chances for local recognition would be blended into oblivion.[11] Winemaker associations, government regulations, and advertising provided some relief for the problem but real success would come from the award-winning wines produced and marketed by the county's twenty-two wineries.

Throughout history wine regions have risen and fallen based on their ability to produce quality wines and adapt to the marketplace. Regions fail if economic issues are not addressed, whether one is speaking of the overplanting that occurred in Campania after the eruption of Mount Vesuvius in 79 A.D., Burgundy's fourteenth-century agrarian crisis, or the plowing under of grape crops in Santa Barbara County in the mid-1980s.[12] Santa Barbara winegrape growers and vintners learned to become responsive to methods of production, labor, research and development, and consumer preferences. Like most industrial producers, wineries offered various levels of product quality in order to appeal to a wide range of consumers and their pocketbooks. Santa Barbara's small-scale premium wineries shunned the Gallo-dominated bulk-wine market and aimed for the middle- and high-end product lines that afforded them the greatest profitability. Economic stability for the local industry would, in the long haul, be dependent upon the ability of wineries to consistently produce and market high-quality, competitively priced premium wines.

Santa Barbara County rapidly developed a reputation for high-quality premium wines as local vintners, large and small, garnered awards. Region and winery (label) recognition came as larger commercial producers like Firestone and Zaca Mesa broke into national and international markets and smaller local wineries gained acceptance in regional markets closer to home. As the county's premium wines reached retail outlets, satisfied consumers began to recognize local labels. Many area wineries also attempted to break into the super-premium market, where wine collectors pursued handcrafted wines from their favorite wineries and winemakers. In the end, wine writers recognized the region and oenophiles developed loyalties to their favorite wines.

By the late 1970s there were signs that the area's wineries could make quality wines out of the region's premium winegrapes. The first recognition came in July of 1978 when the *New York Times* featured Firestone Winery in its Sunday magazine. A few months later Anthony Austin, Firestone winemaker, won a double gold medal in London for the winery's Chardonnay. In 1978, 1981, and 1982 Zaca Mesa won state awards for every varietal it produced, and in 1983 its Central Coast Cabernet was named one of the best red wines at the International Wine Center in New York.

Consumers, overwhelmed by shelves burgeoning with choices, look to wine writers for suggestions on new and exciting wines, wine regions, and up-and-coming winemakers. These writers, in their quest for wines to intrigue their readers, spread the word of a region's potential. In 1976 wine writers Hugh Johnson and Bob Thompson wrote about the Santa Maria Valley:

> Most of the awesomely fast development of a 5,000 acre vineyard district has taken place on bench land that looks south, in the European tradition. Climate regions I and II prevail in spit of the southerly latitude because the tail of the great coastal fog bank curls easily and regularly into the Santa Maria's valley. The southerly exposure and the frequent mists have caused some skilled observers to think that this might, just might, be the place in all California for Pinot Noir. It'll take some years before anyone will know.[13]

Two years later *New York Times* wine writer Frank J. Prial visited Santa Ynez and proclaimed that Firestone, Zaca Mesa, and Sanford and Benedict were wineries to watch in the future.[14]

It would be a matter of a few more years until the general wine press discussed and praised Santa Barbara wines and winegrapes. Sunset's 1969 edition of Bob Thompson's *California Wine Country* did not mention Santa Barbara County, but the 1977 edition noted, "Farther south, in Santa

Barbara County, 6,000 acres of vines have been planted since 1971 and the Firestone family operates a pioneering winery." The 1979 edition said that "from the viewpoint of visitors . . . there has been a tremendous revolution in the state's wineries since 1968," and seven Santa Barbara County wineries were mentioned.[15]

By the early 1980s Santa Barbara wines had won recognition worldwide. Firestone, Zaca Mesa, and Santa Ynez Winery had garnered medals for their Pinot Noirs, Chardonnays, and Rieslings.[16] In 1981 Sanford Winery and Zaca Mesa had wines listed as "recommended" in *Wine Spectator*, where Zaca Mesa was a regular advertiser.[17] So extensive was Firestone's international recognition that the winery was honored by a visit of England's masters of wine.[18] In the later half of the 1980s it was not unusual to hear that local vintners took a double gold at the International Wine Competition in Toronto, international medals at the Quantas Cup Wine Competition in Australia, or four gold medals at the San Diego National Wine Competition, where they represented 3 percent of the wines entered and won 48 percent of the medals.[19] By the mid-1980s, however, many in the industry worried that too many competitions and awards confused consumers in what Frank Prial referred to as shelf after shelf of wines "beribboned like so many generals."[20]

Additional viability for the region came when President Ronald Reagan served local wines in the White House and established his Western White House on a ridge overlooking both the Santa Ynez Valley and the south coast. Brooks Firestone said that his business increased tenfold after the president served his wines, and he predicted that the region would break into the lucrative Washington, D.C., market. James Carey, though a critic of Reagan policies, realized the possibility of presidential recognition and put his politics aside when he sent a case of his Carey Vineyards estate bottled Adobe Canyon Chardonnay to the president.[21] Over the next few years guests of and diplomats for Republican and Democratic presidents drank wines from Firestone, Zaca Mesa, Sanford, and Gainey, to name a few.

Wine writers began to mention the region on a regular basis, and *New West* called the region a "piece of paradise." In 1987 Anthony Dias Blue, *Bon Appetite* wine editor, named Santa Barbara County "one of the better wine regions in the country." Wine writer Matt Kramer described Santa

Maria Chardonnay as "lush, rich, intense and succulent," "not easily bullied by breezes, heat or sunshine," "bottled sunbeams." Accolades continued in 1996 when *Wine Spectator* described the ruggedly beautiful south central coast as "an adventure for wine drinkers and tourists alike," and deserving of the title of California's "other coast."[22]

The 1990s proved to be a decade of rave reviews for Santa Barbara County. Most major wine writers and wine trade and consumer publications praised the region. In the *Wine Advocate,* wine writer Robert Parker noticed that one-fifth of the wines honored in the *Wine Advocate*'s December 1998 issue were from Santa Barbara County, a respectable showing for a county with one-sixth of the grapes and one-tenth of the wineries of California. That same year *Food and Wine* honored Santa Barbara's Bien Nacido vineyard as among one of California's greatest. Wine author and Master of Wine Mary Ewing continued the tribute when she stated, "Clearly, the most exciting new viticultural areas in California—if not the entire country—are in Santa Barbara County." In 1999 Jon Fredrikson, renowned San Francisco wine consultant, told two hundred winemakers at Firestone Vineyard that Santa Barbara "is really the Silicon Valley of the California wine industries."[23]

Name Recognition for Independent Winemakers

Those who enjoy the luxury of specialty artisan wines tend to form followings for the artist/winemaker they patronize. An elite few collect expensive wines and speak a special jargon as they drop the name of their favorite wine artists. They relish the opportunity to rub elbows with winemakers who become minor celebrities. Every wine region making upscale wines needs a certain amount of this snobbish recognition to build a regional reputation.

Many winemakers readily took up the wine mantle and carried their artist message to elite oenophiles. These self-proclaimed wine geniuses clearly understood that Americans embrace field-specific superheroes into their hearts and support their endeavors with an open pocketbook. In many ways this is not dissimilar to the cliques and patronage systems that historically have supported all artists. In the 1960s winery owners Robert Mondavi, Joe Heitz, Louis Martini, Karl Wente, and Dolph Heck became the superstars. By the 1970s a more savvy media realized that the industry was more specialized and winemakers became the new superstars.[24]

Regional wine recognition for Santa Barbara County in the 1970s through the 1990s included a group of talented artisans whose names became buzzwords for upscale regional, state, national, and international wine consumers. Customers quickly learned to recognize wines from winemakers like Firestone, Sanford, and Lafond; but elite status also came to a number of independent winemakers who produced wines without physical plants and vineyards—winemakers who conducted business through post office boxes and borrowed, leased, rented, and bartered facilities and equipment. Their trademarks were their high-priced, small-production (usually fewer than five thousand cases), premium-handcrafted wines that were marketed on the reputation of their persona.

These independent winemakers developed techniques to stay competitive with the larger commercial operations. They overcame the millions of dollars in cost for technology and equipment by modeling themselves after *negociant* winemakers in the industry's European past who had created what wine buffs referred to as "wineries without walls."[25] As a group they shunned commercial, formulaic production techniques and emphasized the role of the winemaker as the one who oversees and controls all aspects of the winemaking process. They were a generation of what wine writer Dennis Schaefer referred to as a new breed of "active" winemakers. Many ignored the old vintner's adage that "nature makes the wines" and portrayed winemakers as more than "just the caretaker."[26] Their wines were commonly mentioned in *Wine Enthusiast* and *Wine Spectator.* Santa Barbara's entrants in this independent category included the labels of Chris Whitcraft, Jim Clendenen, Bob Lindquist, Rick Longoria, Lane Tanner, and John Kerr, to name a few.[27]

Chris Whitcraft converted his wine expertise as a radio wine-show host to that of Pinot Noir winemaker in the late 1970s. In 1973 Whitcraft, a native of Long Island, graduated from California State University, Fullerton, and took a job as manager for Mayfare Wine and Spirits in Santa Barbara. His local recognition for wine expertise started in 1978 when he helped establish the Santa Barbara Wine Festival and began a radio talk show focusing on wine. The wine bug bit him, and between 1978 and 1985 he made wine under the bond at Santa Barbara Winery and moved to Brander's bonded facility in 1988 and 1989. By 1990 his passion led him to the Miller Brother's Central Coast Wine Warehouse and Bien Nacido Vineyard.[28]

Jim Clendenen's fame among wine followers came from his purist Burgundian winemaking approach. After graduating from the Law and Society program at UC Santa Barbara in 1980, he accepted the assistant winemaker position at Zaca Mesa winery. He resigned the position in 1981 to work in Australia and Burgundy. In 1982 he returned to Santa Barbara, where he joined Adam Tolmach, former Zaca Mesa oenologist, and produced Au Bon Climat, traditional Burgundian Pinot Noir and Chardonnay wines. He started with a press and then leased equipment from Los Alamos Vineyards, owned by Santa Monica lawyer Sam Hale.[29] He produced 1,600 cases of Chardonnay and Pinot Noir in 1982.

The elite wine community took notice of Clendenen's Burgundian-style wines. In order to produce "signature wines" he mimicked the Burgundian winemaker's philosophy and attitude toward life and took on their demeanor. Clendenen felt no need to own vineyards because he saw grapes as "merely the raw materials, the blank canvas that we imprint or stylize."[30] He purchased grapes from selected vineyards with low yield production and used the Burgundian techniques of barrel fermentation, malolactic fermentation, and extended cellaring.[31]

Robert Lindquist followed Clendenen into Santa Barbara's artisan category of winemaking. His name recognition came from his use of "all the modern technology that is appropriate" within the bounds of traditional production techniques.[32] He established the Qupé label and described his style of winemaking as production in "a modern Stone Age winery." Lindquist entered the industry in 1979 as a twenty-two-year-old college social science graduate when he took a job as the manager of John Ream's wine shop in Los Olivos. After nine months at the shop he was fired, but he landed on his feet as John's father, Marshall Ream, hired him to be Zaca Mesa's first tour guide.[33] Over the next five years he trained under winemakers such as Ken Brown, Jim Clendenen, and Adam Tolmac.

Rick Longoria moonlighted his Longoria label while acting as the winemaker for the Gainey Vineyard. Longoria used intensely flavored winegrapes to produce naturally flavored fruity wines in the best California style. He began his career in the spring of 1974, one year after graduating from UC Berkeley with a degree in sociology. As a student at Berkeley he became familiar with regional Sonoma Valley wines while working at Buena Vista Winery in Sonoma, where he met and mentored with Andre Tchelistcheff. With Tchelistcheff he visited the new Firestone vineyard and in 1976 became the cellar foreman for Firestone. Two years later Longoria took the job of cellar master with Chappellet Winery in Napa. It was during this time that he realized that what appealed to him was the "diversity of the job," because "during the making of the wine, you become a chemist and craftsman combined."[34]

Longoria realized that he missed Santa Barbara County—he was born and raised in Lompoc—and in 1979 he took a job as winemaker at the new J. Carey Winery. Beginning in 1982 he slowly established his private Longoria label. In 1985 Longoria, who now had a young family, sought the job security of an established winery, and he accepted the winemaker position at Gainey Vineyard. Over the next decade he was active in helping found the SBCVA, serving as Gainey winemaker, maintaining his personal label, and consulting for numerous small local wineries. In 1996 he reached a new level of recognition when *Playboy* ran a photograph of his Cuvee Blues blend of Cabernet Franc and Merlot wine and commented that it had the "kind of energy you feel when B. B. King is cooking with Lucille or when Buddy Guy is wailing on his ax."[35] He received calls from as far away as Connecticut asking for a bottle of this wine.[36] Longoria resigned from Gainey in 1997 and opened a new winery with partner Iris Rideau next to Buttonwood Farm and Foley Winery (previous Curtis Winery) on Alamo Pintado Road in Santa Ynez.

Lane Tanner proved that a woman could also achieve status as an independent winemaker. Tanner specialized in Pinot Noir and claimed to be "a real old traditionalist." She believed that technology was good up to a point and that "winemaking is a simple process that machines can only refine so much."[37] She did everything herself and believed that her Pinot Noir was the most feminine, finicky, fickle, and incredibly responsive of all grapes. She said that "grapes want to become wine," and she accepted the responsibility of being "the keeper of the grapes."[38]

John Kerr also followed a circuitous route to becoming a winemaker. Upon returning from Vietnam in 1971 Kerr supported his college studies with a tasting-room job at Brookside Winery in Ventura.[39] In 1980 he followed his wife's archaeological career to Monterey and took jobs with Chalone Vineyard, Jekel Winery, and Ventana Vineyards. During this time he developed a winemaking philosophy that was a blend of traditional Burgundian styles, new university knowledge, and gut feelings.

Kerr reestablished his Santa Barbara wine career when his wife accepted a permanent archaeological position with the U.S. Forest Service in Santa Barbara County. He landed a consultant job with the newly established Babcock Winery and worked at Houtz and Brander Wineries. From 1984 to 1995, while serving as assistant winemaker at Byron Vineyards and Winery and using the Byron bond, he produced wines under his J. Kerr label. Kerr specialized in Chardonnay and Syrah wines, and by 1993 his production had grown grew to 1,300 cases. During this time his Chardonnays took numerous awards in Orange County and the Central Coast Winegrowers Association. After a long and arduous start-up struggle Kerr received recognition in 1994 when his 1991 J. Kerr Chardonnay took first place (out of 390 entries) in the American Wine Competition with a score of 98 and a platinum medal.[40] Like Longoria he eventually settled for the prestige and security of a corporate winery and accepted the title of winemaker for the Carey Winery in 1996.

Marvin Shanken, editor of *Wine Spectator,* fully believes in the cult of the celebrity as a moving force in the industry. Many people credit Shanken's publication with helping to develop this new focus and cite the fact that 85 percent of the magazine's covers feature personalities, not a wine bottle. One local beneficiary of *Wine Spectator* celebrity status was financier William Foley. Touted as an up-and-coming Pinot Noir producer, the businessman was featured in a full-page story and color photograph chronicling his $20 million quest for "peace, quiet, and Pinot Noir in Santa Barbara."[41] Foley, CEO of Fidelity National Title Inc. and CKE Restaurants, moved to Santa Barbara in 1994. He amassed his wine empire by purchasing the Santa Ynez Winery (renamed Lin Court after daughters

John Kerr in 1988 while assistant winemaker at the Byron Winery. Kerr later established his own JKerr wine label. Photograph courtesy *Santa Barbara News-Press*

Lindsay and Courtney) in 1995 and the J. Carey Winery from Firestone Vineyards in 1997. The crowning acquisition for his enterprise came when he secured 1,100 acres of premium vineyard land in Santa Ynez and Santa Maria. *Wine Spectator* granted Foley star status when six of his new releases rated between 88 and 92 in the magazine.

By 1990 Santa Barbara County had established a flourishing wine industry, but its success proved to be a double-edged sword. Owners of the county's more than thirty wineries and 10,000 acres of winegrapes profited from protracted statewide grape shortages and continued consumer preferences for premium wines. Santa Barbara wines could be found worldwide and county wineries, winemakers, and wines had received numerous awards that brought international recognition. The continuing tumultuous market, however, pushed northern wineries back to Santa Barbara as a solution to their supply deficiencies for the second time in thirty years. In the 1960s and 1970s northern wineries resolved their premium-grape shortages in part by importing Santa Barbara winegrapes. But in the late 1980s and 1990s these same northern vintibusinesses sought to purchase the county's vineyard lands to secure their future supplies of high-quality winegrapes. Small local wine businesses, mainly in Santa Ynez, feared this Napa takeover in a grape-short industry and looked for a means to resolve this newest threat to their existence.

Chapter 7

The Business of Wine

1990s

> Excellent wine generates enthusiasm. And whatever you do with enthusiasm is generally successful.
>
> —Phillippe De Rothschild, French vintner (1902–1988)

Overall the late 1980s and early 1990s were good years for the California wine industry. Wine as a business not only survived a flurry of neo-Prohibition government labeling, taxation, and advertising policies but continued to grow an average of 5 percent annually. As a result growers and wineries statewide could not keep up with the demand. Domestic wine shortages and a strong American dollar, when compared to European currencies, resulted in increased importation of foreign wines and fierce international competition for the American wine market. In response the entire California wine industry attempted to increase production efficiency and lower prices by utilizing new scientific and business techniques. Santa Barbara growers and wineries, while not at the center of the national and international issues, eventually provided a partial solution to continuing premium winegrape shortages. For a second time in thirty years the economic and political policies of survival forced many northern wineries to look to Santa Barbara County for premium winegrapes.

Neo-Prohibition Creates Public Policy for the Wine Industry

One perceived threat for the continued profitable expansion of the California wine industry was the resurgence of Prohibitionist ideologies in the United States in the 1980s and 1990s. The fear that alcohol weakened families, increased crime, and lessened the productivity of the workforce troubled alcohol opponents. The repeal of Prohibition in 1933 had not resolved the ethics of American drinking habits, and by the twenty-first century alcoholism had become the eighth-largest killer of Americans. After repeal the issue was ignored for more than twenty years as federal officials, burdened with depression and war, washed their hands of the problem and shifted the responsibility for regulation of alcohol to local and state governments. Individual states created their own alcohol policies and laws that produced a quagmire of taxation issues and distribution nightmares. These alcohol questions plagued the wine industry into the twenty-first century as pro-alcohol and anti-alcohol citizen groups grappled to establish a national standard for alcohol consumption and morality.

In California the alcohol issue appeared on the ballot as Proposition 134, or the Alcohol Tax Act of 1990. The measure sought to raise taxes on all alcohol ($1.29 tax on a gallon of wine) and opponents nicknamed the voter initiative a "sin tax" or "nickel-a-drink" tax. In Santa Barbara County Jeff Wilkes, Bien Nacido general manager, and Lon Fletcher feared that such a tax would lead to the loss of 668 acres of vineyards and the possible layoff of about 150 Santa Barbara County agricultural workers. They projected that local low-yield vineyards and wineries would fall by the wayside and that the additional tax burden would serve to deliver small wine businesses into the hands of northern vintibusinesses.[1]

Many industry leaders believed the tax was a neo-Prohibitionist outburst and countered with their own tax initiative. John DeLuca, Wine Institute president, requested that Senator Alfred Alquist (D-San Jose) and Assemblyman Dominic Cortese (D-San Jose) sponsor a ten-cent-per-gallon wine tax. They felt that this middle-of-the-road compromise could bring a moderate approach to the issue. The wine industry proposal failed to make the ballot, but voters rejected Proposition 134 by 69 to 31 percent.[2]

As alcohol again became a national issue, its control threatened the entire U.S. wine industry as reformers lumped all alcoholic beverages and tobacco together as drugs. Arguing moderation for wine became a controversial ethical position.[3] The wine industry began to back the American Wine Alliance for Research and Education (AWARE), which catered to the health care and medical community with accurate and credible information on all the issues of alcohol and health. The program provided a speakers bureau and purchased a membership in the London-based Centre for Information on Beverage Alcohol.[4]

Opponents, on the other hand, utilized well-organized and well-funded groups to blame numerous societal ills on these substances and convinced government officials to create regulatory policies that would be enforced by the Treasury Department's BATF. As a result, Presidents Ronald Reagan and George Bush succumbed to political pressures and declared a "war on drugs" in the 1980s. Continued special-interest pressures pushed the federal government to favor drug-educational programs, such as Mothers Against Drunk Driving (MADD), Students Against Drunk Driving (SADD), and Drug and Alcohol Related Education (DARE), that favored total abstinence from all alcoholic beverages. The power of these groups manifested itself in various ways. Oakland Athletics franchise president Bobby Brown, for example, demanded that his 1990 league championship team celebrate their championship with carbonated, nonalcoholic apple cider. Brown concluded that it would be inappropriate for role-model athletes to be seen on national TV with champagne.[5] Support for neo-Prohibition reached a crescendo in the mid-1990s when anti-alcohol groups (utilizing both private and government funds) outspent alcohol advertisers by a ratio of 10 to 1.[6]

Many in the wine industry acted to separate themselves from the connection being made between alcohol and drugs, but it was easier for alcohol opponents to link wine with distilled spirits because of the ownership structure of the industry. In the early 1980s Seagram purchased Wine Spectrum, Monterey Vineyard, and Taylor California Cellars from Coca-Cola.[7] The tie of wine and alcohol deepened further in 1989 when Heublein distillers purchased the Christian Brothers winery and became Napa's largest vintner with 1,940 acres of winegrapes.[8] Ernest Gallo blamed the distilled-spirit industry for wine's tainted image as an alcoholic beverage and along with Robert Mondavi began efforts to educate the public in the ethics of wine moderation. Gallo, however, was also blamed for wine's negative perception. In 1989 extreme anti-alcohol proponents in Santa Barbara went as far as to lace twelve bottles of Gallo Port with broken glass in an attempt to curb drinking by homeless people in the city. Phyllis van Kriedt, *California Wineletter* editor, contended that the large bulk wineries and their "skid row oriented products made them an easy, if not a fair, target."[9]

Bringing wineries together to lobby for supportive governmental alcohol policies won only limited acceptance. The statewide Wine Institute had failed to support alcohol education. As Matanzas Creek Vineyards' Bill MacIver recalled, the "Wine Institute and the big wineries were running scared when the issue boiled up and wanted no part of any association with health and social issues related to wine."[10] A coalition of small wineries issued a concise circular to the BATF in August 1993 defending their stand on wine in moderation. The 655-word statement followed a BATF decision to stop distribution of the full text of an April 1993 *Alcohol Abuse* article that spelled out the pros and cons of alcohol consumption. Santa Barbara wineries like Babcock and Houtz Vineyards supported the coalition's pressuring of BATF regulators to permit the distribution, by wineries, of the balanced summary of the scientific and medical evidence.[11]

Wine Label Battles

In 1990 anti-alcohol forces won a major victory that forced stringent labeling requirements for all alcoholic beverages. Representative Joseph Kennedy (D-Mass.) pushed through Congress a law requiring alcohol disclaimers on labels to counter "this country's infamous prince of drugs." Proponents argued that alcohol cost the nation over $85 million per year in work absence and served as a factor in half of the nation's traffic accidents.[12] In Santa Barbara County Jennifer Armstrong, Gainey Vineyards public relations director, feared that these label requirements would add to staff expenses and drive small winery prices beyond consumer pocketbooks. Winemaker Anthony Austin thought it would cripple wine advertising if labels carried a negative message.[13]

Despite the negative campaigns, the image of wine as a healthy beverage, when consumed in moderation, slowly countered teetotalism. In 1991 *60 Minutes*'s "French Paradox" report by Morley Safer caught wide attention. Dr. Serge Renaud, director of research for the French National Institute of Health, presented a study suggesting that moderate consumption of red wine could reduce coronary heart disease.[14] Renaud's "Mediterranean diet pyramid" included moderate amounts of wine along with exercise and low-fat foods to combat high cholesterol and heart disease. Numerous researchers from UC Davis, Harvard, UC Berkeley, Rutgers, and Kaiser Permanente in Oakland, California, expanded Renaud's research and published articles in *Lancet, Circulation,* and the *New England Journal of Medicine* that corroborated the health benefits of wine in moderation.[15]

The theory that wine in moderation was good for one's health did not gain immediate acceptance. BATF officials refused to allow wineries to place claims on labels or advertise the positive health research because wine was considered a gateway drug.[16] Many doctors, fearing malpractice suits, refused to prescribe a glass of wine with dinner for their patients until *moderation* was defined: Should wine be a daily medicine for the heart and what should the prescription be—one glass, two glasses, or an entire bottle?[17] More outspoken wine advocates like David Whitten, physician and editor of *To Your Health,* blasted anti-wine advocates for being Puritans with a "nagging fear that someone, somewhere, may be having fun" and labeled their attacks as deliberate attempts to confuse the general public. It would not be until 1992 that wineries would be able to advertise winemaker's dinners, because of the wine-health issue.[18]

In 1998 the BATF moved to approve statements that instruct consumers where to find information about the potential health benefits of moderate wine consumption. The resulting neo-Prohibitionist uproar quickly nullified initial jubilation. South Carolina Senator Strom Thurmond's two-decade campaign against wine now zeroed in on the Wine Institute by labeling the group as conspirators working with friendly government officials to promote alcohol. The senator brought his considerable influence to bear and called on the Departments of Health and Human Services and Agriculture to investigate wine organizations. At the same time, Thurmond introduced legislation to ban health-statement labels, supported measures to nearly triple federal taxes on table wine (to finance studies of alcohol's effects), and encouraged switching oversight of wine labels from the BATF to the Food and Drug Administration. Thurmond became the lightning rod for anti-alcohol forces, and his picture made the 31 July 1999 cover of *Wine Spectator* with large bold print declaring "Strom Thurmond, Wine's Public Enemy #1."[19]

Wine marketers found themselves between the proverbial rock and a hard place. Anti-alcohol forces wanted tough advertising stands for wine like those developed for tobacco and beer. They felt that Joe Camel, the Budweiser Frogs, and Louie and Frank the lizards (also used in Budweiser ads) enticed underage youth to smoke and drink. Most within the industry had no intention of promoting underage drinking. Yet, in order to continue their sales, they had to make efforts to market wine to Generation X. The problem intensified as many wineries realized that legal-aged drinkers in their twenties watched shows on MTV, for example, that were also popular with teenagers.

A new group of wine marketers broke traditional non-youth wine advertising practices and began the process of developing future consumers. Darryl Roberts, editor and publisher of *Wine X*, aimed his magazine at the twenty- to thirtysomething market. In San Jose, Joel Quigley, Bacchus-X wine club organizer, began wine education tastings for the 25- to 35-year-old age group with disposable incomes. The group, with a growing number of chapters, sponsored field trips to bay-area wineries to further their wine education. A later survey of Bacchus-X club members found that there had been "a 10 percent shift from monthly to weekly wine drinking, meaning they have gone from one bottle a month to four bottles per month." Large wineries also joined the campaign. Kendall-Jackson began sending trained wine educators to top business graduate schools (whose students' future disposable income could support an oenophile's habit) and to Bacchus X clubs to illuminate future consumers. Cone Tech winery in Grafton, California, developed Touchstone 6, a reduced-alcohol wine (6 percent by volume) for novice wine drinkers.[20] Numerous introductory low-alcohol and alcohol-free wines began to flood the market.

Foreign Competition

As American wine consumption increased in the early part of the 1980s many consumers turned to more moderately priced European wines. In 1982 U.S. wine imports topped $750 million, compared with $38 million in wine exports.[21] The situation worsened in 1983 when California consumption of French wines rose 16 percent and consumption of Golden State wines decreased by 7 percent. Exacerbating the crisis were continued winegrape shortages that drove the price of American wines upward and plummeting prices for French wine as a result of the appreciation of the American dollar by 69 percent, compared to the franc.[22] Foreign competitors had a firm foothold in the American wine market, and California wineries realized that they needed to expand both the domestic and international markets.[23]

Wine industry officials complained that they could not compete with foreign wines supported by subsidies and high tariffs. Some wineries predicted that this unfair playing field would be the eventual downfall of the entire American industry. Industry insiders pointed out that in 1982 European nations spent more than $14 billion in subsidies for all exported agricultural goods. Even though wine only accounted for 2 percent of the total trade deficit, how could the wine industry compete?[24] American politicians and business people argued about how to resolve the unfavorable balance of trade.

As foreign competition increased many growers and vintners counted on the California Wine Commission and the Wine Institute to promote the state's $6 billion wine industry and help level domestic and international trade issues. As early as 1983 California wine officials, worried about international trade questions, sent John DeLuca to Washington, D.C., to seek support for the organization's 465 members. The institute sought government policies that would "reduce, and eliminate barriers to trade on a basis which assures substantially equivalent competitive opportunities for all wine moving in international trade."[25] With the help of U.S. representative William Thomas (R-Bakersfield) 340 members of Congress supported the Wine Equity Act, which leveled trade barriers.[26]

The Wine Equity Act failed, however, when institute members could not come to an agreement on the basic issues of the bill. Since its inception in the 1970s, the California Wine Institute had reeled from disagreements between large and small wineries. Smaller vintners alleged that larger corporations controlled the wine commission, manipulated market shares, and wielded political clout for themselves. In an attempt to seek equity on the commission many of the smaller vintners resisted the system of voting power, determined by production, and adopted the battle cry of "one winery one vote." Buena Vista Winery celebrated its 130th birthday in 1987 by sponsoring a conference called "Vintage 2000—A Challenge to the Future." Participant Robert Mondavi passionately admonished many of the big names in the California industry for not having "a single, simple program."[27] By 1990 the inability to come together resulted in numerous small wineries leading a vote (125 to 111) to dismantle the commission.[28]

In the end all sides backed down in the face of an international trade war that could have extended to all agricultural goods.[29] Most realized that the Reagan and Bush administration threats to establish up to a 200 percent reciprocal tariff on European wine industries could only end in disaster for vintners seeking European export sales. Trade regulation proponents backed down even more after the death of the Wine Commission. In the long run, the real loss was the failure to establish a unified international trade plan. For the time being, the state's grape shortage persisted and domestic wine prices soared even further.

Another plan to deflate the escalation of wine imports revolved around improving consumer confidence in the quality of American wine and its price value. Most California wineries sought to define and regulate wine quality by defining new appellations. Larger wineries wanted broadly defined AVAS so they could blend grapes from numerous viticultural areas for their large-production premium wines. Small wineries wanted precise AVAS so consumers could tie premium wine to specific geographic locations. Some wineries began to push to amend the 85 percent rule, which allowed 15 percent of the grapes to be blended, to a 100 percent rule, which would not necessarily ensure better-quality wines, just more authentic wines.[30]

Santa Barbara County wineries fought the appellation battle when the BATF approved a Central Coast Appellation that included seven California counties from Alameda to Santa Barbara. Local growers feared that their quality winegrapes would be lost in a sea of mediocre fruit that would lower their wine quality and recognition. The local appellation struggle continued when Wine World petitioned the BATF for the creation of a

Santa Barbara Coast Appellation, which would include Santa Barbara County (including both Santa Ynez and Santa Maria Appellations) and San Luis Obispo County. Michael Moone of Wine World argued that a common viticultural region would aid in the marketing of wines on the national and international market. Rick Longoria failed to see how it would enhance the region's reputation. In June 1990 the SBCVA voted 11 to 2, with three abstentions, to oppose the measure.[31]

Bay-Area Expansion Plans Falter

Notwithstanding neo-Prohibition and foreign competition, consumption of California wines rose and northern wineries attempted to meet consumer needs by increasing vineyard acreage. Planting of more vineyards had always been the solution to the industry's winegrape shortages, but expansion efforts in the bay area faltered as large northern wineries and growers encountered land-use problems that stifled development of new vineyard lands. By the late 1980s Napa tourism had risen to 2.5 million visitors per year, and dozens of new wineries sprang onto the scene. It seemed as if everyone wanted to share in the good life as embodied by the wine industry.[32] The region's single-family-home value rose to $176,000 and home sales increased 23 percent. Fearing the impact of the flood of people and wineries on the area's agriculture, Napa County planners curbed growth of wineries by requiring that 75 percent of all grapes processed had to originate from Napa vineyards. Since land values had risen 58 percent to more than $55,000 per acre between 1987 and 1990 new vineyard planting had become cost prohibitive. Thus wineries had no hope of expanding local production through massive vineyard planting. A similar problem occurred in the adjoining Sonoma County, where land prices doubled to about $35,000 per acre.

The Scientific Solution

As Napa vineyard expansion possibilities dwindled many northern wineries intensified efforts to maximize vineyard production through science and technology. During the preceding hundred years American winery owners realized that science had played an important role in delivering an increased supply of consistently high quality and reasonably priced wines to a flourishing world market. They also grew accustomed to the fact that government agencies and universities normally financed this research and development.

Winegrape growers and vintners had learned over time that economic success for the wine industry was dependent upon continued viticultural research. The economic reality for winegrape growers and vintners fell within the "treadmill thesis" of Professor Willard Cochrane, which maintains that continuing agricultural education is required to keep up with technology and increased efficiency of the world marketplace. For California this tradition started in 1868 when the University of California began graduate studies in agriculture under the federal Morrill Act for agricultural education. Further state and federal money came from the Adams, Smith-Lever, and Smith-Hughes Acts, which allowed for the establishment of experimental vineyards and advanced enology and viticulture studies.[33]

Between 1868 and the 1990s UC Berkeley, and later UC Davis, trained professionals that shaped a post-Prohibition California wine industry capable of meeting the needs of expanding consumer markets. Winemakers educated in California earned a worldwide reputation for "book farming," and by 1991 UC Davis bragged that 75 percent of the people in the California industry had at least some training in their viticulture and enology programs.[34] As California's industry became increasingly successful more wineries turned to these trained winemakers. Vintners worldwide utilized the research and expertise of University of California's Harold P. Olmo (hybridizer), Ralph Kunkee (microbiologist), Vernon L. Singleton (wine biochemist), Carole Meredith (plant geneticist), Cornelius S. Ough (fermentation scientist), and Maynard Amerine (enologist). This created a shortage of wine experts, which in turn resulted in an expansion of viticultural studies from UC Davis to California State University at Fresno.[35] Many of these industry leaders, accustomed to supportive federal policies, failed to remember, however, that over time federal support for the wine industry wavered between tolerance and encouragement.[36]

Government support in the 1980s dwindled and growers and vintners faced a serious reduction in government research programs funded by state and federal governments. Governmental downsizing in the late

1980s and 1990s provided neo-Prohibitionists with an opportunity to pressure politicians not to fund research for alcohol-related industries. After six decades of federal agricultural price-support policies the 1990 Agricultural and Food Policy Act provided no direct support for the wine industry.[37] Dismayed over the loss of funds, Bob Hartzell, president of the California Association of Winegrape Growers, testified before the USDA subcommittee on Information, Justice, Transportation, and Agriculture about the need for increased funding for viticultural research. Hartzell pointed out to the committee that since Congress passed the 1990 excise tax (which raised wine taxes from 17 cents to $1.07 per gallon, a 529 percent increase) grape growers had contributed more to the U.S. Treasury than had any other agricultural group and therefore deserved research money. Governmental support never materialized and eventually most research programs and new technology costs fell to the resources of vintibusiness.[38]

Without government support vintibusiness leaders shifted their resources to support their own research and development. Large wineries like Mondavi and Gallo set up their own research programs and hired scientists for their private labs. Many smaller wineries joined to form the American Vineyard Foundation to fund public viticultural investigations. Yet, by the mid-1990s only one in six California wineries contributed to the foundation.[39]

University leaders and winery businessman fought over who should do the research and who should fund it. Washington State University agricultural economist Ray Folwell warned that "the industry is missing a golden opportunity to leverage its contributions through state-supported land grant universities." On the other side vineyard owner Andy Beckstoffer decried that university researchers saw wineries and growers as a "giant cash hog." Pete Opatz, Alexander Valley vineyard manager, sided with Beckstoffer and condemned the UC Davis viticulture department for wanting growers and wineries to just give "the money and we'll tell you what you want."[40] Such disagreements eliminated the possibility of a viticultural research program to reinvigorate and modernize the industry and alleviate winegrape shortages.

Although scientific investigation never occurred as a unified effort many individual vintibusinesses explored ways to protect and expand vineyards and reduce grape shortages. Common sense dictated that healthy vines produce more and better-quality grapes. Therefore improved plant health took on more immediacy in light of the protracted winegrape shortages. In the 1980s novelist Les Whitten, in his book *A Day Without Sunshine,* told the story of a plant louse destroying Napa. His predictions almost proved true until vintibusiness resources found new scientific solutions. By the end of the 1980s more than half of the vineyards of Napa needed replacement, since the old AxR#1 rootstock had lost its resistance, and industry economists estimated that it would cost more than $1 billion to replace acreage. Adding to the plant-health dilemma was the return of Pierce's Disease (a bacterium, *Xylella fastidiosa,* spread by insects that slowly kills the vine) in Sonoma and Santa Cruz Counties.[41] In the Santa Cruz Mountain's Livermore Valley Randall Graham watched his 30-acre Bonny Doon vineyard die from Pierce's Disease, as it had destroyed the Los Angeles industry almost one hundred years before.[42]

In an attempt to defeat phylloxera and ensure future winegrape supplies many large vintibusinesses utilized privately funded scientific research. Bob Steinhaur, Wine World vineyard manager, with his colleague Jim Frisinger, Beringer's Knight's Valley, set aside twelve acres for trial planting of five new resistant rootstocks.[43] Robert Mondavi formed a partnership with the National Aeronautics and Space Administration (NASA) to measure Napa phylloxera outbreaks through aerial satellite imaging. The three-year study in early plant disease identification from space cost Mondavi $150,000; NASA supplied the remaining $200,000. Still another ingenious method to finance research came from Dry Creek Vineyard with its specialty Bug Creek Vineyard wine. The Cabernet wine with the picture of a bug on the label and the phonetic Phil Awksira Cellars was meant to bring the plight to the general public.[44]

Other techniques used to alleviate grape shortages included micromanagement of vines and their growing environment to maximize peracre production. Proper irrigation of vines was one area where growers could maintain some control over vine production. Robert Mondavi employee Phil Freese, with the help of telecommunication engineers, utilized audio emissions equipment to identify grapevine water needs by monitoring the sound of bubbles exploding in leaf cells, caused by a lack of water. Bruce Cakebread, winemaker for Cakebread Cellars, borrowed a neutron gauge irrigation system from the Australian wine industry. In this system a computer monitors probes regularly spaced in the vineyard and irrigation can be administered to guarantee the best winegrapes.[45] Vintibusiness scientific trial and error also included the use of newly developed clonal selections, vine density, new canopy management techniques, and soil studies. Gallo reconstructed an entire landscape area to give it a rolling contour and perfect microclimate for desired varietals.[46]

Advanced scientific research moved many wineries toward space-age technologies by the mid-1990s. The creation of Global Information Systems (GIS) started a new era of satellite imaging to map and estimate plant health for vintibusinessess like Gallo, Beringer, and Mondavi. General advancements in computer technology by 1998 lead enology researchers at universities to perfect an artificial intelligence computer named ANN (Artificial Neural Networks) to supply wineries with data on soil, sunlight, weather, pH, elevation, canopy, grape varietal, brix, nitrogen levels, yeasts, and storage factors, among other capabilities. Wine researcher Paul Skinner designed "Vincula," a multivarietal modeling technique to enable wineries to track wines from vineyard to sale. Research was also under way to develop "Dr. Vine," a computer program to enable viticulturists to predict and detect the twenty-five most-damaging diseases and pests in their vineyards. Skinner's Napa-based firm, Terra Spase, created a "Terroir" program to inform growers how to select that rootstocks and clones best suited their needs for new plantings in Santa Barbara, Napa, and Sonoma.[47]

The environmental concerns and tighter state and federal standards of the 1980s and 1990s turned many growers to organic methods and integrated pest management (IPM) techniques.[48] Organic wines, common in Europe, entered the California market in 1980 when Frey Vineyards, in Mendocino County, joined the California Certified Organic Farmers (CCOF). Later, small, boutique wineries such as Husch, Hidden Cellars, and Olson joined with corporate wineries such as Wente Brothers, Mondavi, and Fetzer to form the Organic Grapes into Wine Alliance (OGWA), which by 1989 had grown to twenty-five members.[49] Santa Barbara's Buttonwood Organic Farms and Vineyard entered the organic field in 1993.[50]

Mechanization revolutionized common field and wine production tasks by keeping costs down and increasing production. Statewide skilled-labor shortages in the early 1990s forced wages and wine prices up. In order to compensate for the cost increases vintibusiness leaders invested in expensive new machines that picked, pruned, removed leaves, lifted wires, sprayed chemicals, planted cover crops, and fertilized. The new machines helped increase profits. A new picking machine could deliver 25 tons of grapes between 5 and 7 A.M. for $265 per acre. A field crew could not deliver this volume before 1 P.M., and its cost would be $625 per acre.[51]

Small wineries faced the age-old problem of cost-per-unit reductions with high-cost mechanization. The $80,000 to $250,000 cost per picker limited their use to large corporate wineries, cooperatives, or vineyard management businesses. Bob Steinhauer, senior vice-president of vineyard operations for Beringer Wine Estates, noted that terrain was the greatest limiting factor for machine usage, and Don Campbell, owner of El Pomar Vineyard Services in Templeton, California, believed that San Luis Obispo, Santa Ynez Valley, and the central coast are the best suited for mechanized pickers.[52]

Smaller wineries or regions requiring manual labor because of their terrain continued to rely on immigrant and alien workers. Unionization of California farm workers by the United Farm Workers (UFW) drove up the cost of wage-and-benefit packages, placing even more pressure on small vineyard operations and wineries.[53] Small wineries, resigned to higher wages, charged more for their wine and lobbied state officials to reinstitute the 1963 Bracero program to encourage guest worker programs from Mexico.

Market Quest for Quality Inexpensive Wine

Despite many innovations the failure of new science techniques to resolve grape shortages motivated wineries to seek cost-efficient methods to reduce premium-wine prices to remain competitive with cheaper imported wines. Many wineries explored the use of new synthetic corks and inexpensive closures to reduce the cost of high-priced corks used to seal and help age premium wines.[54] Researchers also experimented with the use of cheaper American oak barrels, higher quality yeasts, new horizontal fermentors, and beneficial vine fungi. Kendall-Jackson customized and integrated cooperage production into winery operations in an attempt to reduce French oak barrel costs by utilizing wood from forestlands purchased in France. Many wineries aggressively chased consumer taste preferences to stay ahead of the competition. Alison Green, Firestone winemaker, likened the efforts to the fashion industry, where "you have to plan a year ahead for what people want."[55]

Small premium wineries also began to investigate global markets where wealthy consumers preferred imported, handcrafted premium wines. California wines began to appear in Thailand, China, Hong Kong, Japan, Sweden, England, France, Germany, Italy, Spain, Canada, Mexico, and Australia. By 1996 California wine sales increased to $242 million as foreigners sipped 38.8 million gallons of U.S. wine—up from 7.3 million gallons in 1986.[56] Small artisan wineries in Santa Barbara also benefited from this international surge as wineries such as Zaca Mesa, Firestone, and Sanford found the global village anxious for their wines.

Retail tasting-room sales for wineries began to play a major role in overall marketing plans. Tasting rooms became major retail operations with sales managers and promotions. Winery general managers researched their prospective audiences and aimed and marketed their wines to the emotional level where customers would purchase wines.[57] Wine-tasting rooms grew to include gourmet food items, logo clothing, espresso coffee, tourist souvenirs, and deli lunch items, and featured a full array of events to draw people to their wineries and increase profit margins.

Chapter 8

Santa Barbara Vintibusiness

Napazation of Santa Barbara County

As we have seen, California wineries could not keep pace with domestic and international consumer demands.[1] Despite neo-Prohibition, consumption of premium wines increased and the industry continued to grow. Efforts to alleviate winegrape and wine shortages through science and efficient business practices failed to bridge the gap between consumer need (demand) and production (supply). This in turn forced many northern wineries to seek expansion possibilities outside of the bay area. By the mid-1980s more than 70 percent of California winery business plans projected an enlargement of their vineyards and facilities.[2]

Pressures to expand production outside Napa and Sonoma to the central coast intensified in 1988 when premium wine sales jumped 20 percent and accounted for 45 percent of the total domestic wine market. Eileen Fredrikson, wine consultant for and vice-president of the San Francisco–based Gomberg, Fredrikson and Associates, observed that cheaper land, recognized grape quality, and high profits drove wineries to the central coast. She said that "this is the market you want to be in." Michael Moone, president of Wine World, agreed with Fredrikson and believed that "we can produce a good value wine when we farm it ourselves."[3] In an attempt to overcome these shortages northern vintibusinesses looked southward to the less expensive Santa Barbara (Santa Maria Appellation) and San Luis Obispo County vineyard lands.[4]

As winegrape shortages forced vintibusinesses southward Santa Barbara County's reputation for high-quality winegrapes attracted many premium northern wineries. Wine writer Matt Kramer, in his book *Making Sense of California Wine,* described how the "best wines are revelations of place," or what he referred to as "Somewhereness."[5] Wine consumers who traditionally relied on the consistent quality of established regions recognized Santa Barbara labels. The large wine houses realized this and began the "napazation" of the Santa Barbara region. The county's twenty-three wineries and more than nine thousand acres of vineyards became the target for large wine corporations seeking stable supplies of premium winegrapes. Mondavi, Kendall-Jackson, and Wine World quickly purchased more than $36 million worth of central coast vineyards and wineries.

The move for ownership of Santa Barbara vineyard lands accelerated in 1987 when Tepusquet Vineyards fell on difficult financial times. After defaulting, previous owners Luis and George Lucas, with partner Al Gagnon, had not been able to negotiate their option to purchase from the Wells Fargo Bank.[6] Beringer Vineyards (Wine World Inc.), of Napa Valley, offered $12 million for the 2,700-acre ranch, including its 1,700 acres of developed vineyard. Michael Moone wanted the vineyard's 730 acres of premium winegrapes to upgrade its Napa Ridge Chardonnay label. Moone hoped to place Beringer in a position to knock S. Korbel & Brothers (Guerneville Sparkling Wine), Glen Ellen Winery, and Kendall-Jackson Winery out of the competition for the grapes. The Lucas brothers feared that Beringer would not give recognition to Santa Barbara County and would bury its quality grapes in their Napa Ridge second label. Their distrust of Beringer went back to 1978, when the winery breached (for rumored quality problems) grape contacts and both sides engaged in a series of lawsuits and countersuits.

With no love lost, Luis Lucas looked elsewhere for a partner or partners to help him execute his first right of refusal and strike down the Beringer offer.[7] He looked to other wineries that had grown dependent on Tepusquet fruit. First on the list was Kendall-Jackson Winery, which by 1985 produced 63,000 cases of Chardonnay per year from the region. Jess Jackson, San Francisco real estate lawyer and owner of Kendall-Jackson Winery and Vineyard, had also shown an interest in expanding his production to over 200,000 cases of Chardonnay, including a vintners reserve based on

Tepusquet Chardonnay grapes. Jackson recalled that he had "been pulling grapes out of this area since the seventies," and remembered that Santa Barbara County had an international wine reputation. He said, "I don't think they know how good they are."[8] The two formed a partnership that quickly dissolved when Jackson's Canadian financing failed to materialize.[9]

Jackson, not one to give up, found another partner for the deal and with his wife, Barbara Banke, purchased 1,200 acres of the Tepusquet vineyard. His new partner was another winery that had grown dependent on the premium grapes of the south coast viticultural area—Robert Mondavi Winery. Mondavi needed the Tepusquet Vineyard's Cabernet Sauvignon and Sauvignon Blanc grapes. The arrangement allowed Kendall-Jackson and Mondavi to secure their grapes while blocking Beringer's expansion efforts into the region.

Wine World Inc. (Beringer), a division of Nestlé S.A. of Switzerland, eventually found vineyard land in the county. In 1988 it purchased the 700-acre Cat Canyon vineyard near Santa Maria and in 1989 secured the 2,350-acre White Hills Vineyard. Wine World named its Paso Robles–centered enterprise Meridian Vineyards and hired Charles Ortman as winemaker. The 2,000 acres of Santa Barbara County vineyards became the centerpiece for the winery's Chardonnay program.[10] In 1990 the Wine Group of San Francisco joined Wine World in the county when it purchased the 330-acre Corbett Canyon Vineyards (formerly Los Alamos Vineyards) for $4 million.[11]

Napa Colonizes Santa Barbara County

Many locals began to gloomily refer to these northern purchases of Santa Maria vineyards as the "napazation" of the county. They predicted that these moves would eventually harm wine quality and reduce the profitability of Santa Ynez wineries. At the same time other locals felt that this influx of northern money would only strengthen and build the reputation of the region and would profit everyone in the long run.

Santa Barbara grape growers, while split on the issue of "foreign capital," benefited from statewide grape shortages that forced tonnage prices upward. Local grape prices jumped from $1,000 to $1,500 per ton, reflecting an overall minimum 20 percent increase. Anthony Austin, of Los Olivos Austin Cellars, felt that these escalated prices would "strengthen wine grape's role in the county's overall agricultural picture."[12] Lon Fletcher, on the other hand, felt that as Napa purchased Santa Barbara County vineyards they would "use us to pick up their quality," which would lead to lower grape prices as vineyard competition diminished. Barry Johnson, Gainey Vineyard general manager, agreed with Fletcher and warned that there were "a lot of award winners from Napa that use a great deal of Santa Barbara County fruit."[13]

Dale Hampton concurred with Fletcher and Johnson and acted to preserve an independent Santa Barbara wine industry. He realized that Napa's presence in the county helped secure the high prices for growers, but at the same time he feared the loss of local control over the industry. Hampton acted in 1988 when the Prudential Insurance Company decided to sell the 630-acre Sierra Madre Vineyard. He formed a partnership (the consortium included Hollywood producer Douglas S. Cramer and real estate developer John C. Cushman III) that purchased the vineyard for $8.5 million. Hampton felt that the acquisition was necessary "to protect the premium wine producers of the county" and that it was the only way to ensure "the continuing quality and reputation of the Pinot Noirs and Chardonnays produced from the local appellations."[14]

Hampton's fears intensified in 1990 when Robert Mondavi Corporation purchased 600 acres of Santa Maria land that included 175 acres of grapes and the 20,000-case Byron Vineyard winery. Byron's owner Ken Brown believed that the county produced the state's best Chardonnay and Pinot Noir grapes and that "in five or ten years" the local industry would "see double the acreage in the county."[15] Brown wanted to be part of this growth but lacked the capital to make it happen. The Mondavi buyout allowed him to remain as winemaker and expanded the facility's production to more than 50,000 cases.

Mondavi Corporation had more plans for the region. Tim Mondavi proclaimed that "you ain't seen nothing yet."[16] In early 1996 Mondavi Winery increased its county holdings to 1,500 acres, roughly equivalent to its Napa holdings, when it secured deals to acquire 1,100 acres adjacent to its other county lands. The purchases included 350 acres of unplanted land in Santa Maria and the Sierra Madre Vineyard.[17]

Not all participants in the Santa Barbara County wine industry feared the influx of northern vintibusinesses. Vineyard manager Jeff Newton believed that "the large wineries of Mondavi and Kendall-Jackson brought in the expertise and capital necessary to make the industry work."[18] Bryan Babcock added that "it is real healthy when people think enough of an area to come to the county and speculate in its soil and vineyards," and he believed that "it will only help in the long run."[19]

Between 1988 and 1996 California's fifteen largest winegrape growers created a "vineyard royalty" that increased their vineyard ownership by 75 percent. For Santa Barbara County this meant that Wine World, Robert Mondavi Winery, and Kendall-Jackson vintibusinesses assumed ownership of more than 6,300 acres of the county's nearly 10,000 acres of premium winegrapes. The top independent growers of Santa Barbara County dwindled to include Bien Nacido (589 acres), Firestone (448 acres), Rancho Sisquoc (408 acres), Zaca Mesa (224 acres), Carrari Vineyards (150 acres), Lucas Brothers (150 acres), Stolpman Vineyards (110 acres), Gainey Vineyards (85 acres), and small acreages maintained by wineries like Carey, Mosby, Buttonwood, Brander, Santa Ynez, and Santa Barbara.[20]

High industry demand and short supply encouraged the continued explosive growth in the county through the year 2000. Some began to consider Santa Barbara County to be the Silicon Valley of California's wine industry. County wine giants moved to further expand their facilities. Kendall-Jackson Vineyards secured county permission to build two compacted earthern reservoirs to store 39 million gallons of water for its vineyards. Beringer Wine Estates soon followed with four earthen reservoirs. Beringer also built a tasting room for its Meridian Vineyards wines in the downtown Santa Barbara Paseo Nuevo Shopping Center.[21]

The Local Business of Wine

Many independent Santa Barbara County wineries, mainly situated in Santa Ynez, secured alternative fruit supplies after their loss of Santa Maria grapes to northern wineries. Fears of the demise of the region's independent wineries subsided as local artisan wine businesses either sold their vineyard or winery, expanded their vineyard holdings and winery production, or adapted new marketing strategies. Funding for the expansion emanated from a strong U.S. and recovering California economy that permitted a new generation of professionals to retire to the wine lifestyle.

For some, survival came by selling the winery to an investor willing to modernize and expand the business. In 1986 Firestone Vineyards purchased the 25 acres of grapes and 7,000-case production facility of J. Carey Cellars. English industrialist Robert Atkin and his wife, Janice, wine collectors, committed their retirement to the wine lifestyle in 1990 when they purchased the Benedict Vineyard and 674-acre ranch for a reported $2.5 million.[22] This new influx of capital quickly expedited plans for a subterranean winery with a production of about 50,000 cases per year.

The Atkins, also partners in the Sanford Winery, then hired Sanford as the vineyard manager and reunited him with the vineyard. Sanford decided to retain most of the vineyard's Pinot Noir grapes and began plans to plant 150 acres of vineyards on his own 485-acre Rancho Rinconda. Capital for this multimillion-dollar vineyard would come from his newest partner, Robert Kidder, chairman of Borden Corporation and former chairman of Duracell Corporation.[23]

By the early 1990s Austin Cellars, faced with the necessity to recapitalize the winery, chose to sell to Art White, Napa and European wine researcher. In 1992 White and a silent partner formed the Santa Ynez Wine Corporation and purchased Austin Cellars. The niche for the small, vertically integrated enterprise would be centered on a converted home in the center of the Los Olivos tourist and art community. White said he was interested in "developing a close synergy between the businesses in Los Olivos, especially the restaurant, art galleries and our wines."[24] White, his wife, Nancy, winemaker Clay Thompson, and art gallery director Randy Viau created a two-room retail business that offered wine, gourmet snacks, Lenox china, tourist gifts, paintings, and sculpture.

The struggle to stand apart in a crowded premium-wine industry requires the development of a marketing image. For years Zaca Mesa had watched its wine image decline, and in 1993 general manager Jeff Maiken

Art and Nancy White in their Los Olivos tasting room. Photograph courtesy *Santa Barbara News-Press*

mobilized the quest for a new marketing vision. The winery hired Daniel Gehrs, Congress Springs winemaker, and introduced an "alumni winemaker" series, which featured 1,500 cases of wine from famous alumni winemakers like Clendenen, Lindquist, and Tanner.[25] Another marketing boost for the winery came when Zaca's 1993 Syrah was served at the White House during a visit by French president Jacques Chirac in 1996. When President Clinton ordered three cases for himself, owner John Cushman discovered that the winery was out of the wine and filled the order from his private stock.[26]

Ongoing supply limitations in the 1990s led many wineries to purchase premium bulk wines from other countries. Mondavi bought 600,000 gallons of wine from the Languedoc region of southwest France for prices from $4 to $8 per gallon. California bulk wine cost $10 to $20 per gallon. Other California competitors, including Fetzer, Sebastiani, Gallo, Wine World, Wente, Hess, Kendall-Jackson, and Mondavi, turned to South

American bulk wines. A joke circulating in the wine industry suggested that the best place to find large premium California winemakers was to stay at the Hyatt Hotel in Santiago, Chile. In 1996 Firestone Vineyard and Winery pursued this market, purchasing 20,000 cases of Merlot for its Prosperity Merlot label, and entered an agreement with Viña Santa Loria for a 300-acre vineyard in Colchagua, Chile.[27]

Locals also cashed in on the continuing wine merger boom. Fess Parker Winery and Vineyard purchased the 1,400-acre Camp Four Ranch near Santa Ynez for less than $7 million. In 1998 Joe Carrari sold his 196-acre Carrari Vineyards (off Highway 101) to the partnership of Royce Lewellyn of Santa Maria and Louis Lucas of Santa Ynez Valley. Carrari used his capital gains to acquire the 3,400-acre Ferrero family ranch just south of Highway 135 and planned to convert 600 acres to vineyards.

Limits and Restrictions on Winery Expansion

Wine consumption throughout the first part of the 1990s increased at an average rate just under 10 percent per year for high-end wines and stimulated the expansion of the number of Santa Barbara wineries and acreage. By the mid-1990s, however, the expansion was slowed by environmentalists and no-growth citizen groups empowered by home-rule ideals. Many Santa Barbara citizens feared that the county would become a tourist trap like Napa and Sonoma.

Bay-area wineries felt the environmental pinch first. Local environmental groups battled urban sprawl, traffic congestion, and water quality issues for decades. In Sonoma County, vineyards made up less than 5 percent of the total area while maintaining the highest community profile. During the 1960s through the 1990s people moved from urban areas to be near open space and to join in the fashionable trend of owning a winery. Many often disregarded "their surrounding neighbors, in pursuit of their hobby."[28] To check these developments, local residents formed groups like the Watershed Protection Alliance and the Sonoma County Conservation Action. In 1998 these Sonoma groups influenced local officials to create ordinances to oversee food service, special events (weddings, corporate parties, banquets, plays, entertainment), and retail sales on agricultural lands. Winery owners feared what this would do to their personal relationships and direct winery sales. Tourist-related industries (hotels, restaurants, boutiques) also worried about the effects of restrictions on their businesses.[29]

Local Santa Barbara County groups also acted to protect thousands of acres of undeveloped agricultural land while promoting local wines. Local planners, trying to avoid a Napa-like land-use fiasco, sought ways to protect the environment and agricultural character of the county while encouraging winery growth. Problems arose because much of the local acreage was registered under the Williamson Act. In response, Santa Barbara County Supervisor Bill Wallace led a group of agricultural developers in attempting to revise zoning laws that protected large-acreage ranches from "cookie cutting" developers and discouraged reasonable parceling for small- or medium-sized vineyard land.[30] In an effort to overcome the problem county planners developed a clustering program (based on the concept of transfer of development rights) that would allow farmers and ranchers to develop a small portion of their land while leaving the rest in agriculture for perpetuity. Owners of the 3,000-acre Rancho Todos Santos, east of Los Alamos, utilized this policy and removed 150 acres from preserve to build thirty-eight residential units and a winery.

As more and more wineries flourished and tourism expanded many local residents worried that the peaceful rural landscape they had escaped to would vanish. 3rd District Supervisor Gail Marshall began to receive numerous complaints through the Santa Ynez Valley General Plan Advisory Committee. Most dealt with the expanding number of winery events that brought hundreds if not thousands of visitors to the local community. The county had no set event policy, and the addition of twelve wineries in one year drove many citizens to call for a policy that would require each winery to apply for a permit for each event. Speaking at a citizens meeting, celebrity columnist Rona Barrett, Santa Ynez resident, told fellow citizens, "We are concerned about what will happen to the future of the valley." Another angry citizen responded, "Grapes do not need amplified music."[31]

Anti-growth environmentalists, on the other hand, organized to stop the county's acreage expansion. Since the 1969 Santa Barbara oil spill disaster the City and County of Santa Barbara have had a strong environmental community that has produced some of the strictest land-use laws in California and the United States.[32] At first glance wineries and vineyards seem compatible with open space, organic agriculture, and sustainable agriculture. The wine industry sells the ambiance of small towns, spectacular scenery, and outdoor activities—in short, it sells the environment. Yet, expansion of the industry to all available acreage destroys the very reason many tourists visit. Santa Barbarans carefully studied the effects on the northern California environment by tourism, wine industry expansion, and increased grape acreage.

Angered by what they saw happening in Napa and Sonoma, Santa Barbara environmentalists took action to stop winery expansion in the county. In February 1999 Jess Jackson's Cambria Winery received a fax from the Santa Barbara County Farm Bureau advising local wineries that Santa Barbara environmental group Earth First! was advocating sabotage of vineyards in Napa, Sonoma, and Santa Barbara. The group specifically targeted Jackson because he had cut down more than eight hundred oak trees to expand his vineyard plantings. The *Earth First! Journal* condemned industry officials in an article that militantly stated: "Perhaps we will join K-J for a little afternoon wine tasting at its Cambria wineries in Santa Maria, and if K-J doesn't remove their newly planted grapevines and irrigation pipes in a prompt and orderly fashion, perhaps some brave midnight warriors will have to do it themselves, the old fashioned way." The publication included a map indicating the location of seven other local wineries and the number of oak trees removed. Group members later stated that the map and statement were for "the identification and exact locations of these vineyards" and were "not intended to encourage the strategic destruction of any equipment on site."[33]

Moderate environmentalists, through the Sierra Club, encouraged more restrained actions. Local groups sued the county planning department, county supervisors, and Jackson for violating county land-use ordinances. Judge James Brown of Santa Barbara Superior Court struck down the suit as collateral (the Sierra Club never filed a complaint during the permit process) and ordered the environmental group to pay more than $17,000 to cover Kendall-Jackson's court costs.[34]

The important lesson for wineries all over the state was that vintibusinesses needed to proactively regain their image as stewards of the land and a cleaner environment. The Oregon wine region had already proved that wineries and grape growers could adopt sustainable agriculture techniques.[35] In an effort to rebuild citizen confidence local winegrape growers and wineries requested that the University of California Cooperative Extension Service sponsor a January 1998 seminar titled "How To Work Effectively with Regulatory Agencies." The seminar provided educational and practical advice on how to navigate the various permits required by county and state planners, U.S. Fish and Wildlife Service, California Department of Fish and Game, Regional Water Quality Control Board, and the ever-watchful eye of local environmental groups—Environmental Defense Council and the Community Environmental Commission. The ninety participants simulated the permit processes and various required public sessions.[36]

Overall the dampening land-use policies, along with a burgeoning American economy, tended to inflate prices of Santa Barbara agricultural land, and many winegrape growers looked elsewhere for cheap vineyard land. Dale Hampton opened new operations in Texas, where he quickly became the state's number one developer of winegrape lands. In 1995 and 1996 Hampton planted 360 acres of winegrapes just outside Austin.[37] Philippe Bieler, Swiss-Canadian businessman, hired Bob Lindquist of Qupé to be his consulting winemaker at Château Routas in France's Provence region. Lindquist oversaw production of a new wine labeled Cocqelicot, which means "poppy" in French, named as a tribute to his own label, Qupé, taken from a Native American word for "flower."[38]

Many of those who felt the pinch of county restrictions moved north on the central coast to nearby Paso Robles, along Highway 101 and Highway 46, on the north, and to San Miguel and Templeton on the south. Paso Robles contained huge parcels of inexpensive ($2,000 per acre) plantable vineyard lands with minimal land-use restrictions. Local winemaker Gary Eberle, of Eberle Winery, likened the moves to the Oklahoma land rush. The region's production jumped 72 percent in ten years as the county exploded from 6,500 acres of vineyards in 1991 to 15,000 acres in

1999.[39] Bay-area wineries like Gallo of Sonoma, Glen Ellen, Sebastiani, Robert Mondavi, Beringer, J. Lohr, Villa Mt. Eden, and Fetzer, to name a few, utilized Paso Robles grapes and acreage.

Despite restrictions and zero-growth proponents, small wineries persisted and continued to appear. By 1999 the county boasted an industry of more than fifty wineries and 20,000 acres of winegrapes.[40]

Marketing Problem

As Santa Barbara County developed its premium-wine industry competitive wineries sought ways to expand their market share. Premium-wine prices held steady at 10 percent growth per year, and many American and Santa Barbara artisan wineries relied overwhelmingly (up to 75 percent of total sales for many small wineries) on tourist and local retail sales and direct wine shipments to past customers. Marketing became an issue for these wineries as fifty sets of state laws regulated interstate shipments of wine.

Neo-Prohibitionists, fearing winery profiteering and sales to minors, joined with alcohol distributors, who feared loss of their three-tier marketing and distribution system (retailer, middleman, and wholesaler) and state governments, fearing tax revenue losses, to attempt to create policies against direct shipping policies in thirty-eight states and restrictive federal legislation. New state laws effectively blocked small California wineries out of direct trade with consumers in these states through laws that imposed stiff fines and imprisonment for exporting or importing California wines. Large wineries were somewhat unaffected by these policies because their large production capacity made it possible for distributors to legally deliver their wines to all states.

In response, groups such as the Family Winemakers of California, American Vintners Association, Coalition for Free Trade in Licensed Beverages, and the Wine Institute formed the Direct Shipping Coalition. The issue became more convoluted when Utah's Senator Orrin Hatch and Ohio's Senator Mike DeWine proposed federal legislation that would make it illegal for wineries, retailers, and wholesalers to offer Internet-based sales.[41] In California, U.S. Senator Dianne Feinstein and California governor Pete Wilson wrote to Hatch, arguing the cause for direct shipments.[42] As both the House and Senate worked on federal regulations (HR2031 and S557) to stop Internet and interstate sales many like Congressman Richard W. Pombo of Stockton, California, argued that "Teenagers are not going to order a $25 bottle of wine over the internet and then patiently wait for its arrival in the mail."[43]

Marketing attacks on small wineries did not stop with direct sales and Internet sales. In May 1999 Governor George Ryan of Illinois signed into law the Illinois Wine and Spirits Industry Fair Dealing Act of 1999. Sponsored by liquor distributors, the bill restricts a winery's right to fire its distributors without "good cause" and allows the state Liquor Control Commission to force wineries to continue their business relationships with distributors. Distributors claim the law was needed to protect them against foreign suppliers that arbitrarily dump wines in the American market. The first test of the law came in April 1999 when Kendall-Jackson winery ended its distribution agreement with Judge & Dolph and was ordered by the State of Illinois under the new law to continue doing business with the firm. Jess Jackson responded with a lawsuit.[44]

Despite the large array of neo-Prohibitionist attacks on wine, the industry flourished in California and Santa Barbara. By 1999 California total wine sales reached $33 billion of the state's total $1 trillion economy. The statewide industry employed 145,000 people full-time, paid $4.3 billion in gross wages, and grossed $12.3 billion in retail sales. Santa Barbara had similar impressive statistics as local sales increased by 35 percent since 1996.[45] That same year 54 percent of the county's 39,200 tons of winegrapes (from 16,500 acres of vineyards) found their way to wineries outside Santa Barbara County. The county's more than fifty wineries now produced 71,000 cases of wine, employed 589 people full-time, and paid out a total gross payroll of $22 million.[46] In June 1999 *Wine Spectator* featured the restaurants, wineries, and hotels of Santa Barbara in an eight-page photographic essay. The county had become a major player in regional vintibusiness and a first-class tourist wine destination.[47]

Chapter 9

Wine Is Here to Stay

Santa Barbara, California, and the United States

A Successful California and American Wine Industry

In the second half of the twentieth century American vintibusiness became a major player in the international wine trade. California wineries had been successful not only in recreating an American wine tradition but also in developing a new California style. Vintners aimed aggressive marketing programs at consumers with disposable incomes while educating a new generation in the benefits of premium wine. The downside to the massive growth of this market was the inability of wineries to match supply with increased demand. Thus, growers and producers spent three decades expanding acreage and production. This increased production lead to successful regional wine industries that quickly fell prey to a modern vintibusiness structure whereby larger wine corporations stabilized supplies of quality winegrapes (at low prices) through mergers and buyouts and smaller artisan wineries became dependent on agritourism and a healthy American economy that promoted luxury spending. Agricultural economic scholar James Harold Curry III recognized that the "internal systemic logic" of concentrating businesses in the American wine industry reinforced the growth of vintibusiness.[1] Thus, regional wine industries played a major role in the development and continued success of the modern American and world wine industry.

Throughout the 1990s wines become a major agricultural contributor to the American economy. By 1997 the American wine industry contributed about 207,000 jobs, paying $3.2 billion in wages, and directly contributed $12.4 billion to the gross domestic product. Average BATF taxes collected fell just under $500 million. The industry grew from 579 wineries in 1975 to a 1999 high of 2,081 American wineries. At that time only two states (North Dakota and Alaska) produced no wine. California led the pack with 1,056 wineries; New York, in second place, had only 136.[2]

Despite more wineries and continued increases in acreage and production (from the 1970s through the 1990s) American wineries failed to meet increased consumer demands. Wine wholesalers and vintibusinesses responded by importing larger amounts of New Zealand, Australian, Chilean, Argentinean, South African, French, Spanish, and Italian wines.[3] To combat the growth of imports American wineries boosted exports to these same nations to an all-time high of 10 percent of total wines produced ($262.5 million in 1998, up from $188.6 million in 1997).[4] This export market continued to be a boon as the 1989 Canadian–United States Free Trade agreement (CUSFTA) and the 1994 North American Free Trade Agreement (NAFTA) lowered the price of California wines for Canadians in particular. This expanded export program continued despite differences in U.S. and European Union laws on production practices and labeling. The problem was exacerbated by the fact that EU nations exported 12 percent of their product to America. This did not slow down the American export movement, and large vintibusinesses expanded exports as they practiced what agricultural economist David Scott Shaw identified as success by market persistence over a long period of time. Fellow agricultural economist Juan Solana Rosillo agreed that persistence is key but added the caveat that the marketing power of vintibusiness structures gave them the advantage of a "marketing subsidiary."[5] In other words, large American wineries needed to purchase small foreign wineries in order for each to use the other's distribution networks. The American vintibusiness industry proved that it was in the global industry for the long haul.

Throughout the 1990s long-term projections for continued growth never dimmed. John Love, World Agricultural Outlook Board (part of the USDA) predicted that "a robust economy—providing more discretionary income—is the key to continued growth in consumption." Love envisaged continued growth through 2010 at a rate of 2.5 percent, down slightly from 3 percent over the last half of the 1990s. Confident Wall Street investors viewed this growth as promising and continued to invest in vintibusinesses like Beringer Wine Estates, Brown-Foreman Corporation, Canandaigua Brands, Chalone Wine Group, Golden State Vintners, Ravenswood Winery, Robert Mondavi Corporation, and Willamette Valley Vineyards, to name a few.[6]

Santa Barbara's Regional Success

After three decades of development the Santa Barbara wine industry had become the largest and most important part of Santa Barbara County's agricultural sector. The local industry contributed $136 million is sales, accumulated $433 million in gross assets, employed 589 full-time and 2,200 seasonal employees ($31 million payroll), and spent $41 million in the county (taxes, goods, and services).[7]

As we have seen, the California industry's consumption-driven expansion in the later half of the twentieth century made Santa Barbara wines an industry success. Between 1960 and 1980—as U.S. table wine consumption increased from 22 million cases to 151 million cases—the industry grew an average of 10 percent yearly.[8] This rebirth of the modern California wine industry brought vintibusiness dependence on inexpensive regional winegrapes supplied by the expertise of local grape growers and vintners. During this period Santa Barbara contributed minor amounts of fruit to the expansion.

The crucial shift to increased dependence on Santa Barbara viniculture and viticulture came in the 1980s when American wine consumers developed a taste for the premium dry varietal wines found in the county. California premium-wine sales soared more than fivefold to more than 34 million cases, and the central coast played an important role in meeting this demand.[9]

As sales of premium California table wines continued to expand in the 1990s the region achieved international recognition for its quality grapes, premium wines, and talented winemakers. This success prompted the Santa Barbara County Vintner's Association to commission Gomberg, Fredrikson and Associates, wine industry consultants from San Francisco, to compile economic reports for the industry in 1992, 1996, and 1998. These surveys statistically demonstrated the explosive growth pattern for the county and confirmed that the local industry had made the transition from grape growers, to wineries, to vintibusinesses. The Santa Barbara wine industry moved from a grape-growing region with 1,840 acres of winegrapes and no commercial wineries in 1972 to a regional wine industry with 9,542 acres and more than thirty wineries in 1990. The evolution to vintibusiness was complete between 1992 and 1998 as wine industry investment in the county tripled to approximately $433 million, planted vineyard acreage increased from 9,500 acres to 16,500 acres, and the number of wineries jumped from 34 to 56. In 1998 local wineries passed the 1 million case production mark and industry revenues reached $136 million, up from $59 million in 1992 (an increase of 130 percent).[10]

The Santa Barbara County industry had truly benefited from ample capital provided by vintibusiness entrepreneurs and expertise from its local class of gentrified farmers (doctors, lawyers, dentists, retired CEOs, and businesses wishing to diversify). Together the two groups produced a lucrative industry whereby vintibusinesses owned just over 50 percent of the vineyard land and 78 percent of local grapes were used by county wineries or by wineries outside the county that owned local vineyards—including Beringer Wine Estates, Kendall-Jackson Vineyards, Robert Mondavi Winery, and Sutter Home Winery.[11] Two-thirds of the wineries were smaller, independent wine businesses with annual productions of up to 15,000 cases. The ten largest wineries accounted for about 80 percent of the county's annual production of 600,000 cases. In its 1999 economic update Gomberg and Fredrickson projected that "if all reported planting plans go forward as expected in 1999, county vineyards will exceed 20,000 acres by the year 2000."[12]

These optimistic predictions were not realized, however. The local industry only doubled in vineyard acreage to 18,000 acres in 2000, and the county's sixty wineries contributed $360 million to the local economy. The 2000 economic report by Motto Kryla Fisher, LLP (MKF), while reporting less acreage, touted the region for its extraordinary growth. Vic Motto, partner in MKF, emphasized the substantial increase in wine-related revenues, from $136 million in 1998 to $360 million in 2000. Motto called Santa Barbara County "one of the special, unique places in the world where world-class wines can be grown."[13]

Continued Success of Santa Barbara Artisan Wineries

The Santa Barbara County wine industry ended the twentieth century as a well-established and successful enterprise. Its continued success depended on the availability of inexpensive land, the accessibility of quality fruit, large-scale corporate capitalization, agritourism, and a consumer-based economy. As we have seen, the expansion and success of the wine industry helped inflate land prices between $5,000 and $10,000 per acre during the decade despite restrictions imposed by planners and environmentalists. Continued grape shortages encouraged out-of-county wineries to secure needed winegrape supplies by purchasing valuable Santa Barbara County vineyard lands.

For some, the county remained a place where wine avocations could be realized. Gerry Moro, retired Santa Barbara contractor, decided to invest all his time and capital into starting a winery. In 1989 he gave up luxuries, rented out his home and moved into a trailer, and began production of his Morovino label. A former Olympic decathlon competitor from Canada in the 1964 Tokyo and 1972 Munich games, Moro got advice and a start from Bill Wathen and Dick Dore while working a crush at Foxen Vineyard. His biggest concern was the county's shortage of quality winegrapes.[14]

A less-confident view of the county's ability to nurture a new generation of winemakers came from veterans Lindquist and Clendenen. Lindquist believed that

> there's going to be a saturation point because the wine market isn't really growing. Every case of wine extra that's produced in Santa Barbara County pretty much has to take a case of wine sale away from somebody else. Santa Barbara is on a growth curve, but there is going to be a saturation point, I think. You know, we all keep hoping that some miracle will occur and that Americans will stop drinking Coca-Cola with their meals, and start drinking a couple glasses of wine. And if that happens, then wine sales could boom. But I'm not holding my breath for it.[15]

When asked if he could start his winery operation in the 1990s Clendenen answered with a resounding no. In fact, he believed that young people out of college could not raise enough start-up capital unless they had personal contacts. Clendenen thought that if he were starting out now he would opt to be "the winemaker for some 50,000-case producer or 100,000-case producer," and then start his wine "on the side and let it grow to the point that I could live off it completely."[16]

As the first generation of Santa Barbara winemakers retired, many wondered who would be the county's second-generation leaders. Lessons from Napa had taught that second-generation California winemakers face more complex challenges than many of their pioneering parents. Robert Smiley, UC Davis Graduate School of Management, warned that American family businesses often fail when the second generation cannot succeed by using what was learned from their parents.[17]

The survival of small, independent wineries proved to be dependent upon their ability to recapitalize the winery on a generational basis. Many owners chose to sell because of health problems, estate considerations, divorce, capital shortfalls, retirement, and partner disputes. Others chose to sell because of the squeeze and competitiveness of large corporations, government regulations, and labor problems. To avoid inheritance taxes of up to 50 percent of an estate worth more than $600,000, many owners placed their wineries in a trust to protect the business for their heirs.[18] Some took advantage of a 1978 congressional decision that allowed inherited family businesses to amortize payment of the estate taxes over a ten-year period. This circumvented selling the company's stock to pay for taxes.[19] In Santa Barbara wineries like Firestone, Fess Parker, and Gainey faced this future challenge.[20]

The threat of a winery oligopoly continued throughout the 1990s. Although large northern corporate vintibusinesses controlled two-thirds of the vineyard land they did not totally control grape production or keep new entrants from the field. By 1996 local vintners, large and small, crushed 45 percent of locally grown grapes for Santa Barbara labels.[21] Most local industry leaders anticipated continued growth as long as consumer demand for quality wines stayed strong and government policies did not restrict growth.[22] In just thirty years Santa Barbara wine entrepreneurs had reestablished the county's wine industry by adapting Napa-like agricultural and business techniques. Between 1992 and 1996 winegrapes and wine sales increased 85 and 78 percent respectively, making local vintibusiness Santa Barbara's largest agricultural sector.[23]

Agritourism became a way of life for artisan wineries and remains the largest factor for success of these small wineries in the United States, particularly in Santa Barbara County. More than 75 percent of the county's wineries were small, family-owned businesses producing fewer than 15,000 cases of high-end premium wine annually. The destination allure of wineries, coupled with a strong economy that provides for ample disposable income, had made niche or artisan wineries successful. For these wineries continued growth depended upon American hyperconsumption of expensive wines, in what Cornell University professor Robert H. Frank called "Luxury Fever."[24]

Santa Barbara County had learned to entice agritourists from its position roughly midway between San Francisco and Los Angeles. Winery reports estimated that in 1998 almost 500,000 visitors flocked to tasting rooms along the industry's two "wine road" associations. County visitors when surveyed reported that 60 percent of their time was spent outside the city of Santa Barbara. This helped account for direct winery sales that reached a new high of 71,000 cases (up 41 percent from 1996) and winery event ticket sales of $2 million. Winery events and the Santa Barbara County Vintners' Association two festivals produced "induced tourist" spending in hotels and restaurants that reached $11 million in 1998.[25] These figures were proportional to Napa Valley's 4.9 million and Sonoma Valley's 2.5 million visitors.[26]

Good news for the premium wineries was the fact that jug-wine sales (wine priced below $3 per bottle) dipped to an all-time low of 47 percent of the total wine sales and accounted for only 21 percent of total winery revenue.[27] The lion's share of volume (53 percent) and total revenue (79 percent) belonged to vintibusiness wineries capable of producing large quantities of medium-priced, upscale wines. Jug-wine sales had dropped dramatically in the previous thirty years and modern consumers, with extra cash, were willing to spend a little more on better-quality wines.

Santa Barbara County wineries produced the majority of their wine for the premium-wine market—wine sold at more than $7 per bottle. By 1997 the average Santa Barbara wine retailed at $14 to $15 per bottle (with some as high as $40), and local wineries enjoyed a 4 percent share of the total California premium-wine market.[28] A closer look at Santa Barbara Pinot Noir and Chardonnay gives a better indication of the high-end value of these wines. In *Wine Spectator*'s 1999 review of Pinot Noir wines, 23 percent (42 of 182 wines tasted) were from Santa Barbara and had an average score of 87 out of 100 (low score, 79; high, 92) with an average price of $26 per bottle.[29] Chardonnay wines showed similar results: 10 percent of the wines tasted were from Santa Barbara (21 of 216 wines) with an average score of 89 and an average price of $23.30 per bottle.[30] Santa Barbara's two top wines securely place the county in the premium end of the wine marketplace.

For many the real question was the ability of wineries to continue to provide investors with favorable returns. *Baron's Dow Jones Business and Financial Weekly* predicted in the summer of 1998 that a wine glut of historic proportions was on the horizon. The magazine noted that more than half of American 21- to 24-year-olds never drank wine, and that over the next few years more than 100,000 new acres of vineyards would come into full production, an increase of 23 percent. Newcomers to the industry worried that high-priced land and wineries would fail to achieve profits over the long haul. Lewis Perdue, editor and publisher of *Wine Investment News,* predicted that "a lot of wineries that have become used to easily selling all they could make and raising prices whenever they wanted to are suddenly going to find they no longer have those luxuries. A lot of people who think they are immune to the coming glut will find they are not."[31]

In an economic down cycle, cheaper jug wines made by Gallo, Sebastiani, Almaden, Inglenook, and Franzia would suffer the greatest loss. People with less disposable income tend to move to alcoholic beverages with more punch for the dollar during hard times. Also at risk were wineries producing wines that sold for less than $20 a bottle. In good and bad times the rich will still purchase high-end wines. Pundits predicted the greatest market change would occur among middle-class consumers, whose pinched pocketbooks would force them to purchase wine priced at less than $10 per bottle. Thus, threats of depression or recession, like phylloxera, gnawed at the roots of the Santa Barbara niche industry, whose wines were predominately priced starting at $15 per bottle. An economic downturn could drive many of the county's wineries from the rural landscape.

There are those who do not believe the predictions of gloom and doom. Rick Beard, of Groezinger Wine Merchants, believed that "unless there's a serious market turnaround, something comparable to the 1987 crash, I don't think we'll see prices go back down." Beard went on to say, "I don't think we will ever see a glut of high-end, premium wines."[32] Many in the industry felt that wine pricing was more than a means to figure a return on investment. They believed that consumers linked price increases with higher-quality wine and that if consumers were to spend less in a glut, healthy wine businesses would lower their profit margins and survive just fine until the next boom.

For Santa Barbara County fears of a Napa-like urban and vintibusiness encroachment of the rural landscape persisted into the new millennium. On the bright side, however, Napazation of Santa Barbara County had created a successful vintibusiness industry that was well positioned to withstand future challenges.

Epilogue

A Backward Look Forward

According to the San Francisco Wine Institute the United States held its rank as the world's fourth-largest producer and third-largest consumer of wine between 1998 and 1999. The institute based its findings on a report from the Paris office of International de la Vigne et du Vin, which had surveyed forty-five member nations and gathered additional data from the Food and Agriculture Organization of the United Nations. American wine industry officials were initially pleased to see that their market share held strong at 534 million gallons produced, in comparison to the ever-persistent top three nations of Italy, France (1.5 billion gallons each), and Spain (863 million gallons). The report revealed that American wine consumption had risen 14 percent since 1998.[1] On the surface, the future looked good for the new American global wine industry.

Further investigation revealed that France, Italy, and Spain had suffered 3 to 11 percent declines in wine consumption over the same period of time. Many countries, including Australia, New Zealand, South Africa, Chile, and Argentina, also faced overproduction and falling prices and profits. More important for the American industry, this drop in consumption prompted these nations to increase exports to America. Additionally, other countries showed substantial increases in wine production—66 percent in China, 77 percent in Australia, 100 percent in Japan—which served to exacerbate the market glut and fierce global competition.[2]

While the exploration of the successful creation of vintibusiness and niche wineries in the Santa Barbara viticultural region illuminates the history of the American wine industry and its global presence, it fails to answer the pressing question of how this regional, national, and global American success will fare in the new era of world markets. Although no one can predict the future, one can learn from the past and, with history's lessons in mind, attempt to identify the problems that the American wine industry may face in the coming years. Wine historians can only hope that industry leaders will read and benefit from the narratives of past struggles.

Problems faced by oenophiles and people in the wine business have been consistent throughout the beverage's 7,000-year history. Recent trade publications, popular magazines, books, academic research, newspapers, and articles posted on the Internet reveal the staying power of a few key issues. During the twenty-first century most people in the wine industry were still worried that grape growers and winemakers could not continue to produce enough high-quality wines at acceptable prices for the ever-changing tastes of fickle consumers while ensuring profits for global vintibusiness investors.

The issues that worry people in the wine industry today have troubled grape growers and winemakers throughout wine's history. Viniculture's challenges fall under two areas: It is both an agricultural and an economic endeavor. As agriculture, viniculture faces the problems of combatting pests and diseases, finding new scientific techniques for improving quality and quantity, and discovering the means to overcome environmental issues. As an economic undertaking, viniculture challenges businesspeople to continuously search for possibilities to streamline and make their businesses efficient, using scales of size (consolidation through vertical and horizontal integration) that can soften the effects of boom-and-bust cycles. Throughout history viniculture has faced harsh obstacles during times of war, in economic recessions and depressions, and from the competitiveness of the global marketplace. Solutions have always emerged from improved vintibusiness practices that adapted the newest scientific and technological changes to an ever-increasing competitive national and global marketplace laden with vacillating government policies and changing health concerns.

Wine's story follows a geographic theme of movement to new places capable of quenching the thirst of an ever-changing global community. When wine first came to America vintners attempted for three hundred years to emulate the European wine industry. Yet, it was not until the twentieth century that the global quest for wine accommodated American domination of the industry. By the new millennium American wineries had become the model for global vintibusiness commerce. Many fear, however, that the American industry's international stature will be slowed, if not stopped, by the evolving globalization of wine production and marketing by multinational vintibusinesses.

For small wineries, which tied themselves to the imagery of the good life and the Jeffersonian yeoman farmer, survival depended upon their ability to adapt vintibusiness techniques to traditional marketing strategies. *New York Times* writer Elizabeth Becker astutely observed that the Jeffersonian yeoman farmer is a "straw man" and that the "real issues were 21st century questions of corporate interests, the environment, global trade, and budget constraints."[3]

Vintibusiness Practices

On September 11, 2001, the American age of innocence ended as terrorists leveled the twin towers of New York City's World Trade Center. The attack deepened the nation's ongoing recession. Wine industry spokesperson Vic Motto, partner in Napa consulting firm Motto Kryla Fisher, estimated that the industry lost more than $75 million in less than six months as wine sales in restaurants, hotels, and airlines plummeted and the California wine industry's growth slowed to a modest rate of 3 percent. The year 2001 marked the end of the wine industry's six-year double–digit growth as America faced a recession and increased global competition.[4] But the news was far from bad. Motto also cited figures showing that 90 percent of California wineries were profitable. Low-priced wines (under $8 per bottle) were hardest hit. Sales of mid-priced wines ($8 to $15 per bottle) increased 7 percent; premium wines (over $15 per bottle) were up 13 percent; and luxury wines (over $50 per bottle) showed no increase.[5] The mixed news was hard for industry leaders to interpret.

Most damaging to wineries, however, was the influx of wine from abroad. Imports grew to 23 percent of the U.S. wine market, the largest share since 1985. Vintners also faced increased competition from "ready-to-drink" beverages, such as Smirnoff Ice, that appealed to women and induced stores to reduce wine shelf space for these malt-flavored coolers. Major players like the Robert Mondavi Corporation ended 2001 with two straight quarters of reduced profits as net income fell 28 percent and sales dipped 6.7 percent, resulting in a downturn of almost 30 percent in the company's stock. Many industry watchers agreed with Paul Franson that "many wine producers are in denial about the economy and its impact on their business, at least publicly."[6] Retail sales remained strong for middle-end wines as consumers looked for values, and winery marketers took advantage of the new market by cutting prices and producing more mid-level wines. Complicating the American market downturn were wine trade tariffs of 6.3 cents per liter, some of the lowest in the world. San Francisco–based wine industry analyst Jon Fredrikson referred to the trend as "the era of the consumer."[7]

However, most agreed that premium wineries and high-end regions like Napa, Sonoma, and Santa Barbara would weather the downturn. Sonoma County's largest winery, Kendall-Jackson, boosted sales by 20 percent during this downturn and earned Fredrickson's award as the 2001 "winery of the year." Fredrickson believed "K-J is still strong and on fire."[8] Initial fears might have exaggerated the fallout from the terrorist attacks. Dave Andrew, Costco wine director, reported, "Wine sales were up 23 percent in October [2001], compared to the year before." Andrew credited the increase to the fact that "people are eating at home or gathering together with friends and family."[9]

Recession, depression, and war in a major wine-producing region can alter the profitably of the entire global wine industry; but because of its scale of operations, vintibusiness can withstand catastrophic political and economic events. Just as northern California wineries, such as Mondavi, Kendall-Jackson, and Beringer, for example, lessened the impact of boom-and-bust cycles by utilizing the Santa Barbara wine region in the 1980s and 1990s, wineries at the start of the new millennium seemed to be using vintibusiness consolidation at the international level to soften cyclic downturns and increase profitability.

Some of the most worried industry people were the vineyard owners who over the past decade aggressively planted new acreage to chase the market. Historically, the wine industry had suffered from boom-and-bust production and many had been warning for years that the next bust was just around the corner. As the wave of vineyards planted in the 1990s came "on line," many in feared that a glut of grapes and global competition would devastate the industry. Grape broker Barry Bedwell warned that vineyards planted in response to years of double–digit growth would flood the American market with grapes and wine. The problem worsened as Australian production tripled in a fifteen-year period and many growers picked only the best of their crops as they faced an Australian "wine lake." Australian wine insiders predicted the need for a 20 percent increase in exports to compensate for their glut.[10] Bedwell cited instances where Chardonnay grape prices dropped to $500 per ton, down from an average of $1,957 per ton the previous year. He warned, "It's a buyers market," adding, "The bottom line is, we shouldn't be planting anything right now."[11] Future periods of growth and stagnation for the Santa Barbara region will most likely be affected by the wavering vintibusiness need for their surplus winegrapes.

These gluts traditionally hit independent grape growers the hardest. More than ever, vintibusiness structures that integrated wineries and vineyards seemed to be the answer to stabilizing the cyclic market. Over time, large wine corporations managed up and down markets by simply reducing purchases and trimming contract prices paid for winegrapes. Many in the industry saw bust times as a natural process for weeding out marginal, low-end producers. Napa vintner Patrick Kuleto, a recent entrant to the industry, believed that "people who are weak will drop off" and that in the "long term, that makes the market better."[12] If one believes in the true market economy this natural process should be welcomed. After all, few would expect Congress to bail out wineries as it did the airline industry after the terrorist attacks of 11 September 2001. For small regional industries like Santa Barbara this could mean further consolidation as marginal small wineries and vineyards falter in periods of weak economic growth.

The depth of a glut effects local, regional, and national wineries. The real worry is that future global gluts could destroy many wineries that normally would have survived local downturns. Australia alone needs to sell an extra 98 million liters of wine in fiscal year 2003 to clear all of its export market stocks. As in the United States, vast new plantings in 2000 and record bumper crops compounded the Australian glut.[13] In order to achieve this export goal Australian producer BRL Hardy moved forward to create one of the world's largest vintibusinesses. The producer's chief executive, Stephen Millar, predicted that his wine empire "could be the Microsoft, McDonalds, or Coca-Cola of the wine industry." He went on to say that BRL would continue to purchase U.S.-based wine producers and take advantage of "the most profitable and biggest market in the world."[14]

Foreign entry into the American market did not stop there. In 2001 the U.S. government approved the $8.15 billion acquisition of Vivendi Universal's Seagram Spirits and Wine Group by Diago PLC and Pernod Richard SA. This merger placed California Seagram Chateau and Wine Estates, Sterling Vineyards, Mumm Napa Valley, Monterey Vineyard, Beaulieu Vineyard, Glen Ellen, MG Vallejo, and Blossom Hill under the same corporate and distribution family as Barton and Guestier Chateau and Estate (French wine importer) and the Guinness beer group. In order to handle its new wine dominance the Diago group placed its wine-marketing headquarters in Napa Valley.[15]

Since the end of Prohibition the American regional vintibusiness industry had created an organizational structure that responded to consumer preferences and integrated wineries and vineyards. In November 2001 Constellation Brands (Simi, Ravenswood, Franciscan Estates in Napa; Estancia in Monterey County; Covey Run, Paul Thomas, and Columbia in Washington; and Alice White in Australia) failed to take over Trinchero Family Estates (Sutter Home Winery), the fifth-largest wine marketer in America.[16] Despite the acquisition failure, Constellation stock registered a 50 percent gain in 2001, prompting John A. Faucher, J.P. Morgan analyst, to optimistically declare, "The company is well-suited for this type of economy" because most of its "brands tend to be lower end."[17] In January 2002 Jon Fredrikson at a told audiences at a Unified Wine and Grape Symposium, "If you are the biggest in the world, vertically integrated . . . you can get very aggressive against multinational competitors."[18]

Many in the Australian wine industry took to heart the call to vintibusiness and global competitiveness. Rick Allert, chairman of Southcorp, the world's largest listed wine company, warned Australians that "globalization has become a catch call for every political and economic ill" and that Australians should allow "mega–mergers between its major companies to reach critical mass or else risk being sidelined in the global economy." Wine leaders feared Southcorp more than they feared globalization. The company switched its corporate interest to wine after offloading its water-heater division to the Rheem Company for $540 million. For them the question is, Can industrial management handle a wine corporation?[19] By adopting American vintibusiness strategies global wineries were attempting to trump American wineries in their own market.

As foreign competitors learned to emulate American vintibusiness structures American wineries became more aggressive in the international marketplace. In Australia and New Zealand a flurry of alliances, acquisitions, and mergers positioned their industry to survive in the global wine economy,[20] prompting American observers to worry how the U.S. market would react if those two countries successfully flooded the market with cheap higher-quality wine.

For American wineries the lesson learned is that only a vintibusiness with multinational acquisitions and mergers can survive booms and busts of the global market. Continued market pressure of this sort could drive more of Santa Barbara's better small vineyards and wineries into the hands of northern megawineries, thus creating a situation in which more and more of the region's wineries will fall under the vintibusiness blankets of Mondavi, Kendall-Jackson, and others and become part of multinational wine production and marketing groups. As we have seen, larger Santa Barbara wineries like Firestone avoided this by adopting their own global presence by creating their own alliances with Chilean vineyards.

Science and Technology

Pest and disease agricultural economist Alejandro Waters believes that a successful wine industry must utilize "learning institutions" and their professional members' ability to develop new equipment, techniques, and marketing strategies to lure capital investors and provide future growth opportunities.[21] This simple premise has always driven successful wineries. As a result, most wine regions have tied themselves to university programs that train their employees, help in the continual fight against grapevine pests and diseases, devise machines to lessen dependence on expensive labor costs, provide techniques to improve quality in the vineyard and in the winery, and create and train business professionals to promote, sell, and distribute their product globally.

The Los Angeles wine industry fell prey to Pierce's Disease, spread by the glassy-winged sharpshooter, that choked the ability of vines to absorb water and nutrients. At the start of the new millennium the disease again threatened the California wine industry. In June 2000 the USDA declared that Pierce's Disease was an agricultural emergency after it caused more than $40 million of damage to the industry. According to William J. Lyons, secretary of the California Department of Food and Agriculture, "The glassy-winged sharpshooter has emerged as the most significant threat to California agriculture in 20 years."[22] One hundred years after its first appearance, the disease had returned and threatened to again destroy wineries in the Southern California region, specifically Rancho Cucamonga and Temecula, and had spread north to Kern County. A UC Riverside entomologist warned, "This is the type of thing that can put you out of business."[23]

Between 1995 and 2000 agricultural scientists spent more than $10 million on an estimated sixty projects to combat the disease, none of which were successful. Talk of the eventual destruction of the California wine industry prompted the U.S. Congress in November 2001 to approve $16.5 million for the USDA to begin a national battle against Pierce's Disease. California senator Barbara Boxer quickly announced that Congress was proud to "assist California's grape growers and vintners in protecting their crops from the deadly disease."[24] As part of the funding the USDA Animal and Plant Health Inspection Service received $8.5 million and the Agricultural Research Service (ARS) received $8 million to fund general grapevine research projects designed to find biological answers and better grape rootstocks.[25] One recipient of ARS funds was the Sunnyvale, California, Comtex Corporation, which agreed to design DNA primers and probes to detect the disease. In the words of Norm Schaad, phytobacteriologist with the USDA, "Detection is our best line of defense."[26]

Industry leaders and scientists alike agreed that this one-time influx of funding was a good start but would not eradicate the disease. Edwin L. Civerolo, plant pathologist with ARS, reminded all interested parties that cuts in agricultural research had left the United States without "the experience or infrastructure to do the work."[27] Some turned to the expertise of scientists at the University of Sao Paulo, Brazil, for a means to save the $2.7 billion California wine industry, since Brazilian scientists had cracked the genetic code of the Pierce's Disease bacterium (*Xylella fastidiosa*).

In September 2000 agricultural inspectors found a single glassy-winged sharpshooter in Santa Barbara County. All eighty-seven members of the Santa Barbara Vintners Association quickly began a vigilant watch.[28] In a global economy can a small regional winery in Santa Barbara afford to protect itself against new pest and disease threats and afford to replant if a disaster does occur?

In general, governmental funding for viticulture and viniculture steadily decreased in the second half of the twentieth century, and much of the funding for scientific research fell to large corporations. One of the California leaders in this private scientific development has been the Modesto-based E & J Gallo Winery. Its Gallo Technical Research Center employs chemists, microbiologists, and biologists to keep the corporation on the cutting edge of new techniques, machines, and agricultural science. In 2001 the center devised a computerized system to diagnose possible problems from the field to the finished product. In the past winemakers had to react to problems as they occurred. With this early detection system, which utilizes the genetic codes of harmful organisms, winemakers can react before major problems occur. Gallo owns the system's patent and has exclusive right to sell licenses to other wineries.[29]

Not all corporations had to create an in-house research and development team to take advantage of the new viticultural and vinicultural science. New scientific consulting firms appeared and offered, for a price, their services and discoveries to the wine industry. Leo McCloskey, chemist and one-time Sonoma winemaker, created Enologix, a biochemcial company that identified eighty-four chemical characteristics of taste, smell, and color of more than 35,000 award-winning wines. McCloskey believed that through the use of "reverse-engineered winemaking" he could help winemakers alter and consistently reproduce their best wines. This claim and method met with considerable resistance from winemakers such as Robert Mondavi (who had since 1965 boasted his use of traditional French techniques) and UC wine scientists such as Roger Boulton and Ann Noble. Wine consultant Larry Brooks remarked, "This is bullshit, this is impossible, this can't work." Jeff Morgan, former West Coast editor of *Wine Spectator,* commented, "When Jesus started preaching he didn't have any converts. But the more miracles he produced, the more people followed him." McCloskey responded to his detractors by reminding them that "a guy making wine in Napa wants to think he's this French wine farmer, but he's not. He's driving a Porsche 911, and the guy in France is driving a truck."[30]

How will consumers respond to scientific wines? Will these keep American wines at the cutting edge of the global market? How can boutique Santa Barbara wineries that tout their use of traditional winemaking and the mystique of wine artistry compete with the possibility of consistently high-quality, scientifically produced cheaper wines? More important, can small Santa Barbara wineries afford the price tag attached to cutting edge technology offered by people like McCloskey and Gallo?

Other scientific changes for the wine industry also attacked the old mystic of wine and connoisseurship. Most agreed that cork was the best closure for premium wines, which are designed to age. Yet, many were beginning to question the value and use of cork on cheaper table wines because of increasing cork taint problems and escalating cork prices. Screwtop wine bottles had until this time been considered a sign of low-quality, skid row products. Despite the poor image, worldwide problems in securing good quality inexpensive corks drove many winemakers to experiment with synthetic corks. In 2001 the industry reeled with the announcement that many Australian and New Zealand wineries (Jacob's Creek, Wyndham Estates, Goldwater Estate, and Giesen Wine Estate, to name a few) along with a few American wineries (such as Sonoma-Cutrer Vineyards and Napa PlumpJack) experimented with screw caps on premium wines. Screw tops were cheaper and there was no evidence that they would affect the quality of the wine. As to consumers' reaction to the screw caps, Sonoma-Cutrer winemaker Terry Adams believed that "once they pour [the wine] in their glass and taste it, it's a moot point."[31] Again the advantage belonged to larger wineries that could afford to experiment with wine. Can small Santa Barbara County vintners afford to experiment and face one or two years of losses in order to achieve long-term profits?

Vintibusiness quickly realized the need to educate and train the ever-increasing collection of midlevel professionals responsible for business management, marketing, and distribution of their wine. The UC Davis Graduate School of Management and the Department of Viticulture and Enology started a wine executive program aimed at these new industry managers. The professional development program, for middle- and senior-level staffs in wineries, vineyards, industry suppliers, distributors, financial institutions, and service providers, prepared participants for success in the global marketplace.[32]

UC Davis also launched a thirteen-month MBA program in cooperation with the business school in Bordeaux, France. Alyson Grant, French program director, predicted that the executive-level program would teach "everything from vine to wine with an emphasis on the world market."[33] Participants studied at universities and wineries in California, France, and Chile and, most important, made industry contacts around the world. Other business schools, such as the UC Berkeley Haas School of Business, began to provide training for winery consultants. Their goal was to help MBA candidates understand the global economics of the wine industry and make contacts in California, France, Spain, and Portugal.

Education for wine-marketing professionals became high tech when VinPro Vineyard Consultation Services, Agri Informatics and NETGroup Solutions in Johannesburg, South Africa, began offering wine-business executives computer software to trace the distribution paths of their product and avoid distribution bottlenecks. Aidan Morten, viticultural consultant for VinPro, believed their computer program would "be able to look at the barcode on a bottle, and identify the exact vineyard block from which it was produced, the climatic conditions, and the cultivation practices that were followed."[34] Can small artisan or family-run wineries in regions like Santa Barbara afford to utilize expensive software and hire well-trained middle-level managers and executives to remain competitive in the global market?

It's All in the Image

Prohibitionists have often attempted to lump wine with alcohol and destroy the beverage's food relationships. Many wine industry people have done little to combat this effort and in many cases have strengthened the anti-alcohol movement. Large wine corporations, with lines of both premium and cheap wines, have not been affected as much as have smaller middle- and high-end wineries, which are dependent on wine's symbolism as artistic, upper class, and fashionable. Wealthy wine drinkers will always purchase their product; but middle-class consumers buy the greater portion of high-end wine, making the product's profitability dependent upon economic good times as well as on social and religious beliefs—the same intangibles that lead governments to waiver in their support of the wine industry. For boutique wineries survival in the future will depend on their ability to uplift and maintain wine's public image as a means to promote premium-wine sales and maintain the governmental support necessary for the industry's survival.

Environment

As the California wine industry expanded its use of rural landscapes over the last half of the twentieth century it became the target of numerous environmental groups and governmental land-use planners. By the 1990s many environmental groups, determined to save and preserve the natural beauty of the earth, viewed vintibusinesses as just another corporate entity destroying the environment for profit. The result was a surge of local, state, and federal environmental policies that limited the growth of the industry and restricted both planting of vineyard acreage and placement of winemaking facilities (seen as wine factories by some) and threatened winery tourism, which brought hordes of people and supported profitable subsidiary services and facilities.

During the decade of the 1990s some Californians battled to protect older native oak trees that shared climatic similarities with grapevines. Most vintibusiness vineyard planters, wishing to utilize new equipment and planting techniques, usually recommended clearing a location of all indigenous vegetation and supported recreating a landscape perfect for the new vineyards and for maximum production. Environmentalists, wishing to save older trees and conserve habitats for endangered species, fought vigorously to change this business practice. First came a battle over how to define what is an old tree. The State of California had defined an "old tree" as any tree over 200 years old. Many environmentalists wanted to have the definition changed to include any tree growing before California became a state in 1850.[35]

Environmental issues became more complicated for the wine industry as local, state, and federal regulators enforced the Wetlands Protection Act and environmental groups, through judicial review, convinced judges that steelhead trout, a relative of the Coho salmon, should be covered under the act that originally protected salmon along Sonoma County's Russian River.[36] Vast acreages were shielded from further development, and wineries that wanted to expand faced long and expensive environmental impact processes.

For Sonoma County vintibusinesses the story became more complicated as environmental groups again enlisted judicial review to place the California tiger salamander on the endangered species list. This move substantially diminished the amount of land for vineyard and winery expansion and development of subsidiary businesses and homes for workers. Charles Carson, executive director of local governmental affairs for the Home Builders Association of Northern California, warned that "for all practical purposes, this will stop everything southwest of Santa Rosa until Fish and Game does a multiyear study." Many feared that the study eventually would expand to cover the thirty other counties with salamander habitats and halt plantings of new vineyards by Kendall-Jackson, Robert Mondavi, and Beringer. Mike Falasco, Wine Institute spokesman, worried that the new ruling would limit "the ability to find new land to plant vineyards" in the foothills and coastal valleys of California.[37]

The story spiraled further downward as a federal judge accepted for consideration a case to protect frogs in Calaveras County made famous by Mark Twain's story. The courts declared that the red-legged frogs, found in twenty-eight counties in a habitat covering 4.1 million acres, also fell under the protection of the federal wetlands act.[38]

Large individual vintibusinesses became embroiled in the wetland controversies. In a response to environmentalists and a settlement of a 1996–1997 Army Corps of Engineers permit violation, E & J Gallo agreed to create a 37.5-acre wetland wildlife preserve. Gallo had, without permits, constructed a holding reservoir and altered land to stop gully erosion on a wetland preserve. After five years of legal briefs and courtroom appearances Gallo lawyers agreed to pay a $95,000 fine, grant a conservation easement, create the wetland preserve, and pull out thirteen acres of grapevines.[39]

Gallo was not the only winery to come into conflict with environmental planners. In 2001 Sonoma-Cutrer Vineyards, subsidiary of Kentucky whiskey maker Brown-Foreman, ran into problems when it attempted to build a new winery near Forestville, California. Local conservationists feared that the winery's projected use of 2.1 million gallons of local underground water would destroy the marsh habitat of an endangered lily. As a result the Sonoma County Board of Supervisors ordered Sonoma-Cutrer to conduct a hydrologic study before a permit would be considered. In Napa County the Sierra Club filed legal opposition to the use permit granted to Beringer Wine Estates by the Napa County Planning Commission. The Napa County Sierra Club feared that the project would destroy the wetland habitat of the endangered, one-inch-long fairy shrimp that lived in pools for a few weeks after winter rains.[40]

Not all wineries battled over the environment. In 2001 two of the industry's largest trade groups promoted sustainable agriculture with environmentally responsible grape growing and wine production. Based on an earlier set of guidelines developed in central coast regions of California the proposed code attempted to establish levels of acceptable pesticide use, soil management techniques, winery energy conservation, and community outreach.[41] The first plan, founded in 1995 by Robert LaVine, grower-relations representative for Robert Mondavi Winery, organized the establishment of the Central Coast Vineyard Team to investigate sustainable practices in San Luis Obispo, Santa Barbara, and Monterey Counties. Utilizing a state grant the team created formal guidelines for central coast growers wishing to become environmentally friendly. By 2002 UC Davis encouraged the movement by hosting a workshop, sponsored by the California Association of Winegrape Growers, designed to educate small wineries and vineyard owners on how to become nature friendly and navigate state and federal laws dealing with vernal pools, oak woodlands, and riparian habitats.[42]

For small regional wineries in Santa Barbara County the wetlands act, oak tree controversy, and anti-growth conservationists played an important role in the development of the county. Santa Barbara County is a strongly pro-environmental community and considered by many to be the birthplace of the modern environmental movement. Near Los Alamos, the Kendall-Jackson Winery's Barham Ranch became a model for wineries wanting to improve their image in this environmentally friendly region. In 1997 the winery bulldozed 843 oak trees to make room for the 540-acre vineyard and unleashed a public furor that threatened to stop all winery development in the county. In response, the Jess Jackson enterprise established an oak tree regeneration program, in conjunction with the University of California Cooperative Extension Service, that earned them recognition from the California Live Oak Foundation for their "enlightened efforts." Project and vineyard director Bob Johnson said, "Our goal is to plant 8,000 oaks."[43]

Santa Barbara land-use restrictions are some of the toughest in the state and evolved over the years in part to protect the region from a Napa-like overdevelopment. New projects faced years of environmental review, and citizens' input frequently forced developers to scale back and add costly items to their projects. In December 1999 Beringer Wine Estates unveiled a fifteen-year plan to build a 555,000-square-foot winery near its White Hills Vineyard. Fruit grown on more than 8,300 acres in Santa Barbara County would be processed near the vineyards, thus avoiding the need to truck grapes seventy miles north to Beringer's Meridian Vineyards winery in Paso Robles.[44] This project to build the county's largest winery structure faced years of planning commission meetings. The proposed twelve-acre facility exceeded the five-acre limit established by the state's Williamson Act. In 2000 environmental groups forced wineries to reconsider proposals on projects at the Royal Oaks Winery in Santa Ynez Valley and for a winery by Fess Parker in Lompoc. Winery expansion also promoted development of additional service industry projects that included a twenty-five-room Country Gardens Inn by Fess Parker and a fifteen-room Santa Ynez Inn in Los Olivos, planned by Douglas and Christine Ziegler of Los Alamos.[45]

Some people in the county still felt the review processes and redesigns were not stringent enough. In the last half of 2000 Santa Barbara County Supervisor Gail Marshall lead a campaign to keep tasting room visitors and winery events limited to commercial areas in Los Olivos and Los Alamos, keeping rural roads free of traffic. Marshall firmly warned wineries, "It is not necessary for successful wine marketing to have a tasting room and entertainment events" at a winery.[46] Established wineries on rural roads faced closure of established tasting rooms and events if Marshall's proponents prevailed.

Large vintibusiness structures can afford to protect the environment, and many worry that small wineries and grape growers cannot survive and expand with these strict and very expensive environmental requirements. Whether environmental protection evenutally will foster or destroy small regional wineries and vintibusinesses is to be seen. More important, one wonders if federal and state governmental officials will continue to vacillate between a passion for the environment and using the environment as a playing piece in party politics and campaign promises.

Many believed an environmentally responsible image would help future sales and protect the wine region's fragile environment. Santa Barbara winemakers such as Richard Sanford and county wineries such as Cottonwood and Buttonwood had moved in this direction in the past. In 2001 the Central Coast Wine Growers' Association and the Santa Barbara Environmental Defense Center sponsored a public seminar to discuss means to reduce pesticide and herbicide use.[47] Many believed environmental friendliness could also provide the business niche needed by boutique wineries for their economic survival.

As county planners become more protective of the Santa Barbara wine region northern wineries will no longer have cart blanche access to new vineyard land. For agribusinesses, therefore, the most inexpensive and only secure way to obtain winery space in the county would be to buy up existing wineries and their vineyards.

Global Trade

In the long run the modern global wine industry thrives on educating and creating wine images to influence consumer tastes and provide market needs for their products.[48] Simply put, the success of the industry is heavily tied to educating each generation of consumers on the benefits and pleasures of wine drinking.[49]

Empires and nations, since the time of the ancient Greeks and Romans, have competitively traded wine. As winegrape growers and producers looked for markets to sell wines that exceeded local and regional uses they established wine as an international trade commodity. Wine's prestige increased as a result of its use as a food, religious image, and social construct. Countries like France, Italy, Spain, Portugal, and Germany developed wine cultures and rose to the top of the Old World industry. For centuries they created systems of small local and regional growers and vintners who in turn formed cooperatives to compete in export markets. This system worked well until two world wars and a worldwide depression devastated their industries. Economic historian Olivier Zunz showed how America entered the post–World War II era as the economic leader and helped rebuild world economies and industries, including wine. Through a study of the Santa Barbara wine region, we have seen how northern California wineries created a particular style of growing, making, marketing, and, most important, organizing their wine businesses into vintibusinesses. Old and new global wine industries quickly learned to accept the new business style and modeled their industries after the successful American industry. Competition for global wine sales became a challenge for the future American wine industry.

Many American industry leaders have failed to follow key postwar social, economic, and political trends in Europe. Since the end of World War II, Europe's expanding middle class has learned to consume luxury goods and services. Surprisingly, this has not always benefited the European wine industry, as producers faced declines in local sales and wine consumption. From the 1980s to the present, per capita consumption of wine has fallen 60 percent in France and by 45 percent in Italy. Most industry followers attribute this decline to consumption of better-quality, higher-

Bottles of Santa Barbara County Foxen Vineyards Chardonnay line shelves of the Majestic Wine Shop in Wales, England. Author 2001 photograph.

priced wines (less, but better, wine is being purchased), changes in social traditions that downplay the daily importance of wine, and an increased consumption of bottled water. Europeans cultures now tend to view drinking during the workday as problematic. In pre-World War I France, for example, there were 500,000 cafés; today, there are fewer than 160,000 such establishments.[50] The neighborhood society has given way to the home for private and social entertainment.

The problem of decreasing consumption became complicated by the fact that growers, chasing markets, overplanted, and grape production increased while consumer demand fell, creating what many labeled a European "wine lake" as production exceeded consumer demand.[51]

This imbalance in supply and demand is not new. Santa Barbara, California, and European growers faced the issue in the 1980s. In American many growers let fruit drop and rot in an attempt to keep prices up. EU policies encouraged distillation of excess wine juice and helped finance the removal of 10 percent of Europe's vineyards. Over a five-year period these methods reduced production from 210 million to 154 million hectoliters and eliminated the European surplus. Other nations like New Zealand, Argentina, and some Australian regions also promoted vine-pull plans. In South Australia the government subsidized pulling out old, inefficient vineyards and helped to replant with new, commercially viable varieties. These government-planning schemes helped save their industries and secured future supplies of quality wines for consumers and profits for the industry. Can American vintibusiness compete with global businesses that receive government subsidies, national industry planning, and price protections? Only time will tell as the global market weeds out marginal wine businesses. The good news for consumers was that the quality of wine steadily increased and prices held steady or dropped.

The obvious business conclusion is to export what cannot be sold locally. France, Italy, Spain, Portugal, Australia, New Zealand, Chile, and Argentina have all stepped up exports and are aided by the formation of the trade partnership benefits of the European Economic Community and the creation of vintibusiness structures to rival the American model.

Government Policies

In order to maintain its viability in a global marketplace the American wine industry must continue to educate and train the general public in the wine life-style and simultaneously lobby state and federal legislators for favorable policies that provide money for research and development, open up interstate distribution systems, make wine a food and not an alcohol commodity, and support and protect America in the global marketplace.

The struggle to shape federal farm policies took an unusual turn in the latter half of 2001. Traditional agribusiness interests in Congress braced themselves to argue against President George W. Bush's administration and its stance of reducing subsidies. The Bush administration released a 120-page farm policy paper that supported reducing commodity payments in favor of programs supporting global trade, the environment, and all farmers large and small. Disagreements centered on saving the current system of supporting commodities or saving the family farm. Proponents from urban constituencies argued that the money only benefited agribusiness farmers. These urban legislators asked, "Are farmers more noble than plumbers, or the welfare mother who has to go back to work and isn't qualified for a dime?" During a program aired on farm radio network Agrinet, Secretary of Agriculture Ann M. Veneman criticized the old commodity programs and stated, "We believe a farm bill needs to help all rural America, not just a few farmers who receive commodity payments."[52] She urged farmers to find profits in the global marketplace and not in commodities.

In a more surprising political move many environmentalists backed the Bush plan, hoping that more money for small farmers and ranchers, whom they see as stewards of the environment, would do more to protect wildlife, open spaces, and clean air and water. In the end, however, it may be up to the World Trade Organization to decide whether commodity programs violate trade limits. As vintibusiness structures learn to navigate the new global economy they have also learned to maximize their presence in their regional and national economies. This places more pressure on small artisan wineries to be more efficient in the domestic marketplace. Can they compete with scientifically increased quality and falling prices of the large corporate giants in liquor and grocery stores?

Many believe that further pressure from nonagriculture governmental agencies will threaten the viability of the wine industry. The new millennium brought a recession that decimated state budgets. Several states immediately considered increasing the "sin taxes" on tobacco and alcohol. Eight states moved to raise taxes on wine, beer, and distilled spirits, and Washington and North Carolina boosted a surcharge on alcohol sales and a liquor tax.[53] Could wine become a target like cigarettes and face a situation whereby product taxes approach or exceed the actual cost of the item and thus serve as a deterrent to product use? Can small wineries with small scales of efficiency stay competitive with vintibusinesses' prices after taxes are added? Small regional wineries will be forced to either lower or fix prices to keep after-tax prices down. Will their scale of operation allow for reduced profits?

As history has shown, a competitive marketplace turns many wineries, large and small, to cost-cutting measures that effect quality and truth in advertising. In 2001 Rabbit Ridge Winery (Healdsburg) paid a record settlement of $810,000 after a six-month BATF investigation revealed that between 1994 and 2000 the winery mislabeled 17,000 cases of wine with erroneous vintage dates, geographical information, and brand names. Agents found an additional 28,000 cases with no records to back up the information on the labels. Winery owner Erich Russell also settled an unfair business practice suit with Sonoma County when he was accused of constructing seven buildings without permits and producing 400 percent more wine than he was allowed. That firm was not the only one to pay mislabeling fines. In 2000 Bronco Wine Company paid $750,000 and C. Mondavi & Sons of St. Helena paid $300,000.[54]

Quality and standards become difficult for marginal wineries to maintain in markets faced with fierce competition and oversupply. Consumers have not always known where their wine came from. Under present laws wineries cannot create misleading names for their wines. In Napa Valley 85 percent of the grapes must come from that location to qualify for a label citing Napa Valley. To qualify as Napa County 75 percent of the grapes must be from the county. Yet a loophole exists for geographic brand names used before 1986—e.g., Napa Creek, Napa Ridge.[55]

Splits between small regional wineries and larger vintibusinesses doing blending from many regions deepened the labeling controversy. Big winery names like Tim Mondavi, Jess Jackson, and Phil Wente argued for a new California Coast label to include a 14-million-acre stretch of the California coast from San Diego to Mendocino. They argued that this would keep wineries from using cheap, low-quality wines in the coastal blended labels. Many worried that regional high-quality grapes like those found in Santa Barbara County could be lost in the coastal blending of the sixty-eight existing American Viticultural Areas, thus lessening the region's premium designation. Patrick T. Will, Solvang importer and former Firestone employee, warned, "This is going backwards." Wes Hagen, vineyard manager and winemaker at Clos Pepe Vineyard near Lompoc, agreed: "It's too broad," and "it would not educate the wine consumer."[56] For regions like Santa Barbara it is important to regulate the use of Santa Barbara, Santa Maria, or Santa Ynez on its labels. These names promise consumers a quality and taste only to be found in that region. Heavy regulations can benefit both small and large wineries.

The cyclic nature of the wine industry is in part due to the changing tastes and social acceptance of wine as a beverage. In order to level out sales the wine industry must advertise its products and train the next generation of wine connoisseurs. Wineries should not forget, however, how tobacco advertising, event sponsorship, and youth-oriented programs ended as government authorities regulated their sales and advertising. The wine and distilled spirits industries had voluntarily banned their advertising on radio and television, but this changed in 1996 as manufacturers and distributors of distilled spirits began buying advertising on cable networks and local television broadcasts. In 2001 NBC established a nineteen-point guideline for alcohol advertising that included a minimum of four months of messages with social responsibility themes, followed by advertising that was 20 percent dedicated to themes such as designated drivers, moderation, and health issues. The ads were to be run only during prime time (9 P.M. to 11 P.M.) and could not portray drinking as being a mark of adulthood or a "rite of passage."[57] Depending on public and government responses to the new advertising the other networks (CBS, Fox, ABC) would most likely follow suit, to be able to share in liquor advertising revenues.[58] This mass advertising benefits the low- and middle-level wines that compose the products of giant vintibusinesses. How will wineries respond? Many argue that small boutique wineries will benefit from a lifted image and presence of wine in the society as consumers move up the scale to better, premium wines.

For small boutique wineries advertising consists of attracting tourists and local visitors to their wineries. When the visitors return home they find that the only way to receive their favorite vacation wines is to order directly from the winery or join the winery's wine club. More than half of the states, however, have banned direct shipments and many states have moved to make such shipments a felony enforced by federal regulations. These restrictions are an extension of post-Prohibition laws that gave the states free reign to regulate alcohol within their respective boundaries. Consumers in New York, Maryland, Virginia, Florida, and Tennessee, to name a few, challenged state regulators in state and federal courts. They argued these laws were attacks on the Constitution and its guarantee of free trade. Charles W. Ehart, National Conference of State Liquor Administrators executive secretary and Maryland Alcohol and Tobacco Division tax administrator, responded, "It's an intoxicating product. It's a drug. It's a controlled drug," and producers and distributors "knew what kind of product it was when they got their license." In Ehart's opinion, "If they wanted to operate uncontrolled, they should have started up a hardware store."[59] The real battle seemed to be between small wineries and large wine and alcohol distribution businesses that feared the loss of their middleman profits. Adding to the issue were the fears of lost state and federal taxes at a time when state revenue was shrinking. Illustrating the adage that politics makes strange bedfellows, neo-Prohibitionists sided with tax collectors and wholesalers to secure strict regulation of the wine domestic marketplace.

One of the biggest obstacles to wine health and lifestyle education was a BATF regulation blocking mention of wine's health benefits on labels. Throughout most of written history winemakers have touted the health values of their product, and recently numerous medical studies have backed these claims. For American health proponents the battle peaked in what became known as the "French paradox." Americans, worried about what *Toronto Star* columnist Frank Jones called the "twentieth century plague"—heart disease, high cholesterol, obesity—began to seriously investigate the Mediterranean diet. Study after study, conducted in the United States, the Netherlands, England, France, and Italy, alleged the health qualities of moderate wine consumption. Most studies on heart health claims were again supported in 2001 when a research group in the United Kingdom isolated compounds (polyphenols) in red wine that they claim battle a protein linked to heart disease.[60]

Numerous other studies showed other beneficial side effects from moderate wine drinking. Professor Dr. Giuseppe Zuccala, Catholic University of the Sacred Heart in Rome, completed a study of 15,807 Italian men and women aged 65 and older. His study showed that 19 percent of drinkers (8,700 participants) and 29 percent on nondrinkers (7,000 participants) showed signs of mental impairment. Zuccala believed that his study "shows that among older persons, moderate alcohol intake protects from the development of cognitive impairment."[61] In Sardinia, 112-year-old Antonio Todde, an Italian shepherd, made the Guinness Book of Records in 2000 when he was recognized as the world's oldest man. Todde's recommendation for longevity was "just love your brother and drink a good glass of red wine every day."[62]

Industry leaders battled to be able to advertise the good health news as the BATF continually ruled to eliminate the use of pro-health labels and advertising. In 2001 the Competitive Enterprise Institute filed an appeal to the BATF's ban on advertising the medical benefits of moderate alcohol consumption. The public policy watch group argued that scientific support for this relationship is so extensive that it is even cited in the federal government's own dietary guidelines. The group's argument was based on the concept of the public's right to know.[63]

The industry as a whole needed to be more protective of its public image. In November 2001 the Copia: American Center for Wine, Food, and the Arts, a brainchild of Robert Mondavi and funded with $74 million in taxpayer money, opened to angry reviews by many Catholics. The museum displayed ceramic figures, entitled "Poetical Gut," by Spanish artist Antonio Miralda. The thirty-five *caganers* (figurines), done in eighteenth-century Spanish Catalonian peasant style, showed popes and nuns defecating. Copia executive director Peggy Loar defended the display, saying, "These figures symbolize the cycle of eating and fertilization of the earth."[64] William Donohue, director of the 350,000-member Catholic League, replied, "When it's degrading, everybody knows it except the spin doctors who run the museums."[65] The industry needs to aggressively address its history and image against more conservative groups attempting to codify their moralities.

Looking Forward

The Santa Barbara wine industry must not lose track of the lessons of history—its own and the industry's. Can the region continue to produce enough high-quality wines at acceptable prices for the ever-changing tastes of fickle consumers while ensuring profits for vintibusiness investors and local niche wineries? Can this regional, national, and global American success thrive in the new era of world markets?

Many believe that "wine is king and wine grapes are queen in Santa Barbara County." In his 2000 Santa Barbara wine industry report wine consultant Vic Motto predicted, "The future looks very good because the local wine industry is well-positioned." Motto reported a strong, 26 percent increase in sales (more than 18.5 million bottles with Santa Barbara County on the label) as a result of a recent four-year investment of $150 million and 10,000 acres of plantings. The fervent regional spokesman believed these "facts are in our favor" and reminded skeptics, "The region's rapid economic growth is twice the pace of California's wine industry as a whole."[66]

Not everyone shared Motto's absolute faith in the wine industry royalty. Some believed that the boom of the 1990s, during which local wineries tripled to 60 and vineyards grew to 140, outpaced the growth in worldwide wine consumption. Many forgot that Santa Barbara County's production accounted for less than 2 percent of overall California production and that overall California production was only 7 percent of the global wine industry. How will global market gluts affect local small growers and producers? Tom Beckman, president of the Santa Barbara County Vintners Association, worried about this worldwide competition and warned, "Like any business it becomes survival of the fittest." In Santa Barbara County three-quarters of the wineries are small (producing fewer than 5,000 cases), family-owned businesses that charge more than $20 per bottle for their wine. When prices drop during a wine glut, how will they compete with large wineries that can absorb losses? Beckman believed, "We really have to think about the world as our market," but added, "As much as we want to aggressively compete abroad, we have to aggressively compete at home." Lewis Perdue of Sonoma, editor of *Wine Investment News,* cautioned that increased planting by large wineries in recent years would enable them to overcome a glutted market by reducing or terminating grape purchases from small independent growers. Perdue further warned, "You can't depend on exports because there's a worldwide glut."[67]

Los Alamos grower Joe Carrari sided with Perdue and warned Santa Barbara growers, "I think there is going to be a shaking-out on grapes," adding, "The demand will level off and drive prices downward." Dale Hampton, founder of Hampton Farming Company in Santa Maria, "told everyone who's called me that if you go into the grape market without a contract in your hand then you're not being a very smart individual." Hampton tempered his statement with the prediction that "it will be a small shakeout," because "we're growing really exceptional, great fruit, and that's going to be the key to being successful." Both these men remembered the glut of the 1980s and what it took to survive in Santa Barbara County. Jeff Newton, co-owner of Coastal Vineyard Care, agreed with Carrari and Hampton that the county had insulated itself "to the greatest extent possible by growing ultra-quality premium fruit and perhaps choosing varieties that are kind of niche varieties."[68]

Like Zorba the Greek many feared the ever-increasing complexity of the world and held out great hopes for wine's ability to ease this tension. With that in mind it becomes important for wine lovers to take an interest in the future of their favorite beverage and understand the problems presented by globalization of the wine industry and how that could benefit or interfere with their personal enjoyment of wine.

Notes

Introduction

1. The term *vintibusiness,* coined by the author, refers to the agribusiness phenomenon whereby vertical integration of grape farming, wine production, and wine distribution falls with in the control of an agricultural corporation.

2. Olivier Zunz, *Why the American Century?* (Chicago: University of Chicago Press, 1998); Alfred D. Chandler Jr., *The Visible Hand: The Managerial Revolution in American Business* (Cambridge: Harvard University Press, 1977); Olivier Zunz, *Making America Corporate, 1870–1920* (Chicago: University of Chicago Press, 1990).

3. For descriptions of the American merger tradition see Naomi R. Lamoreaux, *The Great Merger Movement in American Business, 1895–1904* (New York: Cambridge University Press, 1985). For descriptions of the California wine business tradition see Vincent Carosso, *The California Wine Industry: A Study of the Formative Years* (Berkeley: University of California Press, 1951); Charles L. Sullivan, *Napa Wine: A History from Mission Days to Present* (San Francisco: Wine Appreciation Guild, 1994); James T. Lapsley, *Bottled Poetry: Napa Winemaking from Prohibition to the Modern Era* (Berkeley: University of California Press, 1996); Ernest Gallo and Julio Gallo, with Bruce Henderson, *Ernest and Julio: Our Story* (New York: Random House, 1994); Robert Mondavi, with Paul Chutkow, *Harvests of Joy: My Passion for Excellence* (New York: Harcourt Brace and Company, 1998).

4. Alan L. Olmstead, "Induced Innovation in American Agriculture," *Journal of Political Economy* 101 (February 1993): 100–18.

5. Economic Research Division of Security First National Bank, *Ventura, Santa Barbara, and San Luis Obispo Counties* (Los Angeles: Economic Research Department, Security First National Bank, July 1966), 34, 25–29.

6. Victor W. Geraci, "Grape Growing to Vintibusiness: A History of the Santa Barbara, California, Regional Wine Industry, 1965–1995" (Ph.D. diss., University of California, Santa Barbara, 1997), 101–40.

7. Ibid.

8. Raymond J. Folwell and Mark A. Castaldi, "Economies of Size in Wineries and Impacts of Pricing and Product Mix Decisions," *Agribusiness: An International Journal* 3 (fall 1987): 281–92; Tim Unwin, *Wine and the Vine: An Historical Geography of Viticulture and the Wine Trade* (New York: Routledge, 1991), 25.

9. Leon Adams, interview by Ruth Teiser, in *California Wine Industry Affairs: Recollections and Opinions* (Berkeley: Regional Oral History Ofice, Bancroft Library, University of California, 1990).

10. Geraci, "Grape Growing to Vintibusiness," 101–40.

11. Rich Cartiere, "1995: U.S. Vintners 'Worst Best Year Ever,'" *Wine Business Monthly,* March 1996, 1–2); M. L. Hilton, Rich Cartiere, and Christian McIntosh, "Capacity and Demand Debate," *Wine Business Monthly,* July 1996, 1, 4, 6.

12. Kathleen Sharp, "Big Wineries Head South," *Santa Barbara News-Press,* 19 June 1988.

13. Kathleen Sharp, "Northern Operations Expand Southward," *New York Times,* 17 June 1990; Mike Dunn, "Vintners' Great Expectations," *Sacramento Bee,* 22 March 1989. Santa Barbara agricultural land averaged about $15,000 per acre, or 65 percent of Bay Area grape land.

14. Rich Cartiere, Teri Shore, and Marshall Farrer, "Calif.'s 'Vineyard Royalty' Doubles Holdings," *Wine Business Monthly* 3 (May 1966): 1–6.

15. Mark Van De Kamp, "Report Predicts Boost for Economy," *Santa Barbara News-Press,* 31 July 1997, sec. B, p. 1; Gomberg, Fredrikson and Associates, *The Wine Industry's Economic Contribution to Santa Barbara County: Based on the Santa Barbara County Vintners Association 1996 Economic Survey* (San Francisco: Gomberg, Fredrikson and Associates, 1997); Anthony Gene White, "State Policy and Public Administration Impacts on an Emerging Industry: The Wine Industry in Oregon and Washington" (Ph.D. diss., Portland State University, 1993), 97–104.

16. Gomberg, Fredrikson and Associates, *Wine Industry's Economic Contribution to Santa Barbara County: 1996.*

Chapter 1 | Northern European Roots and the First American Wine Culture

1. Nikos Kazantzakis, *Zorba the Greek,* trans. Carl Wildman (New York: Simon and Schuster, 1981), 80.

2. "Wine Truly a Drink of the Ages," *Los Angeles Times,* 6 June 1996; Paula Harris, "Wine's Medicinal Nutritional Roots Traced Back to Stone Age," *Wine Business Monthly* 3 (July 1996): 29–30; Kim Marcus, "New Tests Find Evidence of Wine at the Dawn of Civilization," *Wine Spectator,* 31 July 1996, 8.

3. Unwin, *Wine and the Vine,* 3.

4. Carlo Cipolla, "European Connoisseurs and California Wines," *Agricultural History* 49, no. 1 (spring 1975): 294–310. Discussions of the "chicken or egg" argument for the beginning of American agricultural capitalism can be found in Allan Kulikoff, *The*

Agrarian Origins of American Capitalism (Charlottesville, Va.: University of Virginia Press, 1992), and James A. Henretta, *The Origins of American Capitalism: Collected Essays* (Boston: Northeastern University Press, 1991).

5. Isadore Kaplan, "The First Recorded Case of Alcohol Abuse—Noah's Alcoholism," *Maryland Medical Journal* 42, no. 5 (May 1993): 444–45. A good discussion of the interplay between wine and religion can be found in Robert C. Fuller, *Religion and Wine: A Cultural History of Wine Drinking in the United States* (Knoxville: University of Tennessee Press, 1996).

6. Jack Pickleman, "A Glass a Day Keeps the Doctor . . ." *American Surgeon* 56, no. 7 (July 1990): 395–97.

7. Unwin, *Wine and the Vine.*

8. Ibid., 59.

9. Richard Hakluyt, *The Principal Navigations, Voyages, Traffiques, and Discoveries of the English Nation* (1589; rpr. Glasgow: J. MacLehose and Sons, 1903–1905), 8:430, 221, 51–56.

10. Robert Johnson, "Nova Britannia," in *Tracts Relating Principally to the Origin, Settlement, and Progress of the Colonies in North America,* ed. Peter Force (Washington, D.C., 1836–1846), vol. 1, nos. 6, 16.

11. W. Elliot Brownlee, *Dynamics of Ascent: A History of the American Economy,* 2d ed. (New York: Alfred A. Knopf, 1979), 37. Because North America had native vines, vine diseases and pests that existed in the New World immediately attacked imported vines. Fungus diseases like powdery mildew (*Uncinula necator*), downy mildew (*Plasmopara viticola*), and black rot (*Guignardia bidwelli*) had a long history of destruction of native vines. Vines also had to withstand onslaughts of extreme weather, flying insects, and *Phylloxera vastatrix.* A. J. Winkler et al., *General Viticulture,* rev. ed. (Berkeley: University of California Press, 1974), 445.

12. Michael R. Best, "The Mystery of Vintners," *Agricultural History* 50 (April 1976): 362–76. Practical winegrape growing guides in English existed as early as 1658. *Journal of the Commons House of Assembly, 1742–1744,* ed. J. H. Easterby, in *Colonial Records of South Carolina* (Columbia, S.C., 1954), 553.

13. Thomas Pinney, *A History of Wine in America: From the Beginnings to Prohibition* (Los Angeles: University of California Press, 1989), chap. 3.

14. Leon D. Adams, *The Wines of America* (San Francisco: McGraw-Hill, 1990), 17; Pinney, *History of Wine in America,* 84–85.

15. Ibid., 18.

16. Ian R. Tyrrell, *Sobering Up: From Temperance to Prohibition in Antebellum America, 1800–1860* (Westport, Conn.: Greenwood Press, 1979), 147, 11.

17. Ibid., 232–33.

18. Stanton Peele, "The Conflict Between Public Health Goals and the Temperance Mentality," *American Journal of Public Health* 83, no. 6 (June 1993): 805–10.

19. W. J. Rorabaugh, *The Alcoholic Republic: An American Tradition* (New York: Oxford University Press, 1979), ix.

20. Ibid., 41.

21. Ibid., 61–89.

22. Peele, "The Conflict Between Public Health Goals and the Temperance Mentality."

23. Rorabaugh, *Alcoholic Republic,* 104.

24. Tyrrell, *Sobering Up,* 137, 150.

25. Joni G. McNutt, *In Praise of Wine: An Offering of Hearty Toasts, Quotations, Witticisms, Proverbs, and Poetry Throughout History* (Santa Barbara, Calif.: Capra Press, 1993), 108.

26. Paul Lukacs, *American Vintage: The Rise of American Wine* (New York: Houghton Mifflin, 2000). Lukacs's book makes a good case for the rise and eventual prominence of the American wine industry.

27. Pinney, *History of Wine in America,* 107–14.

28. Ibid., 121–25.

29. Ibid., 139–49.

30. Ibid., 150–55.

31. Lukacs, *American Vintage,* 15.

32. Ibid., 35, chap. 7.

33. Rorabaugh, *Alcoholic Republic,* 105.

34. Flagg quotation in Lukacs, *American Vintage,* 35.

35. Don Kladstrup and Petie Kladstrup, with J. Kim Munholland, *Wine and War: The French, the Nazis, and the Battle for France's Greatest Treasure* (New York: Broadway Books, 2001), 240.

Chapter 2 | Boom and Bust: Birth and Death of the First California Wine Industry

1. Spanish explorers and settlers in South Carolina, Florida, and North Carolina, like their English colonial competitors on the East Coast, had also met limited local success because of the sour-tasting wines fermented from native species of *Vitis californica* and *Vitis girdiana.*

2. It is not known what grapes were used for this industry, but many historians have labeled them the Mission grape. In 1986 more than 1,800 acres of Mission grapes were still used in California for the production of sweet wines. Pinney, *History of Wine in America,* 234.

3. C. W. Hackett, ed., *Historical Documents Relating to New Mexico, Neuva Vizcaya, and Approaches Thereto, to 1733* (Washington, D.C., 1923–1937), 3:406, in Pinney, *History of Wine in America.*

4. Pinney, *History of Wine in America,* 233–38.

5. Ibid., 243–58.

6. James V. Mink, "The Santa Ynez Valley: A Regional Study in the History of Rural California" (Master's thesis, University of California, Los Angeles, 1949), 2–20; Ralph Auf der Heide, "The Vineyards," *Santa Barbara Magazine,* winter 1977, 6–14.

7. Paul W. Gates, *California Ranchos and Farms, 1846–1862, Including the Letters of John Quincy Adams Warren of 1861, Being Largely Devoted to Livestock, Wheat Farming, Fruit Raising, and the Wine Industry* (Madison: State Historical Society of Wisconsin, 1967), ix; Walker A. Tompkins, *Santa Barbara History Makers* (Santa Barbara, Calif.: McNally and Loftin, 1983), 9–12.

8. Gary L. Peters, "Trends in California Viticulture," *Geographical Review* 74 (October 1984): 463; Gates, *California Ranchos and Farms,* ix; Robert G. Cowan, *Ranchos of California: A List of Spanish Concessions, 1775–1822, and Mexican Land Grants, 1822–1846* (Fresno, Calif.: Academy Library Guild, 1956).

9. Gates, *California Ranchos and Farms,* xix; Cowan, *Ranchos of California;* Beverly Bastian, "Imperfect Titles, Invalid Claims: The California Land Commission and the Californios" (Ph.D. diss., University of California, Santa Barbara, in progress).

10. Vada F. Carlson, *This Is Our Valley* (Santa Maria, Calif.: Santa Maria Historical Society, 1959), 1–100. Carlson discusses the agricultural viability of growing wheat, grapes, olives, walnuts, and vegetables on the Santa Maria–area ranchos. He describes the Los Alamos Valley, drained by an arroyo, as possessing "a land of marvelous fertility and beauty, with magnificent timber, principally live oak, excellent water, with golden grain waiving from hill to hill" (94). "On the Rancho Tepusquet Abraham Pacifico Ontiveros converted cattle ranch lands and planted 2,000 acres in walnuts, olives, grapes, grain and vegetables" (24). Tompkins, *Santa Barbara History Makers.* Tompkins mentions that Don Gaspar Orena, the last of the Spanish bluebloods, or *gente de razon,* purchased the Mexican ranchos of La Zaca, Alamo Pintado, and Corral de Quati. In 1791 José Francisco de Ortega planted vineyards and claimed squatters' rights to the Refugio Cove lands and received the Nuestra Señora del Refugio Rancho in 1833.

11. Gates, *California Ranchos and Farms,* ix.

12. Mink, "Santa Ynez Valley," 80.

13. Missouri state entomologist Charles V. Riley identified the insect and suggested that the French graft to American rootstock in order to save their industry. Missouri was to take the lead in furnishing the rootstock that saved the French wine industry.

14. Pinney, *History of Wine in America,* 373–81.

15. Gates, *California Ranchos and Farms,* 64; Charles L. Sullivan, *A Companion to California Wine: An Encyclopedia of Wine and Winemaking from the Mission Period to the Present* (Berkeley: University of California Press, 1998), 298–99, 168, 171–73. Carosso, *California Wine Industry,* 7–8; Irving McGee, "Jean Paul Vignes, California's First Professional Winegrower," *Agricultural History* 22 (July 1948): 176–81.

16. Gates, *California Ranchos and Farms,* 66.

17. Lukacs, *American Vintage,* 63, 69.

18. Adams, *Wines of America,* 20; Carosso, *California Wine Industry,* 86–102.

19. Eric E. Lampard, *The Rise of the Dairy Industry in Wisconsin, 1820–1920,* (Madison: State Historical Society of Wisconsin, 1967).

20. Lukacs, *American Vintage,* 57.

21. Maynard A. Amerine, "The Napa Valley Grape and Wine Industry," *Agricultural History* 49 (January 1975): 289–91.

22. Lukacs, *American Vintage,* 169.

23. Victor W. Geraci, "The El Cajon, California, Raisin Industry: An Exercise in Gilded Age Capitalism," *Southern California Quarterly* 74 (winter 1992): 329–54.

24. Lukacs, *American Vintage,* 47–57, 58, 59.

25. Pinney, *History of Wine in America,* chaps. 11–13.

26. Doris Muscatine, Maynard A. Amerine, and Bob Thompson, eds., *The University of California/Sotheby Book of California Wine* (Los Angeles: University of California Press, 1984), 383, 414, 419; Pinney, *History of Wine in America,* 374.

27. Lukacs, *American Vintage,* 87.

28. Ibid., 77.

29. Stella Haverland Rouse, "Pioneer Family Preserved Early Goleta Winery," *Santa Barbara News-Press,* 4 October 1984, sec. D, pp. 4, 9; Richard S. Whitehead and Mary Louise Days, "San Jose Winery: A Landmark of Mission Times," in *Those Were the Days: Landmarks of Old Goleta,* ed. Gary B. Coombs (Goleta, Calif.: Institute for American Research, 1986), 79–88. The Cavaletto family has preserved the structure by constructing a shed around the original winery, which has been designated California State Historical Landmark #25.

30. Tompkins, *Santa Barbara History Makers,* 127–30; Stella Rouse, "1865 Was a Vintage Year for Santa Barbara Winery," *Santa Barbara News-Press,* 11 October 1986, sec. B, p. 5.

31. Tompkins, *Santa Barbara History Makers,* 127–30; Rouse, "Vintage Year"; Elias Chiacos, "Westside Was a Huge Estate Winery," *Santa Barbara News-Press,* 18 July 1990, sec. B, p. 1. Albert Packard emigrated to Mexico in 1840 because of his anti-American sentiment and came back to San Francisco in 1850 for the gold rush. He moved to Santa Barbara in 1852 and became partners with Lewis T. Burton and the Jesus Maria rancho (Vandenberg Air Force Base) and acquired 250 acres of Santa Barbara Westside land when he married Manuela Burke Ayres.

32. Colman Andrews, "Wine Country Gambler: Brooks Firestone's Southern California Strategy Pays Off," *Los Angeles Times Magazine,* 19 July 1987, 8–13; Mink, "Santa Ynez Valley," 52–55; "Olden Days: Pioneer Settler Tried Many Crops," *Santa Barbara News-Press,* 14 September 1969.

33. Helen Caire, "Santa Cruz Vintage," *Noticias* 35 (spring/summer 1989): 142–51.

34. Jesse D. Mason, *History of Santa Barbara County, California* (Oakland, Calif.: Thompson and West, 1883), 422.

35. Hubert Howe Bancroft, *The Works of Hubert Howe Bancroft*, vol. 34, *California Pastoral, 1769–1848* (San Francisco: History Company, 1888), 194.

36. Mason, *History of Santa Barbara County*, 301.

37. Mink, "Santa Ynez Valley," 2; Otis L. Graham Jr., Robert Bauman, Douglas W. Dodd, Victor W. Geraci, and Fermina Brel Murray, *Stearns Wharf: Surviving Change on the California Coast* (Santa Barbara, Calif.: Graduate Program in Public Historical Studies, University of California, Santa Barbara, 1994), 25.

38. Muscatine, Amerine, and Thompson, eds., *University of California/Sotheby Book of California Wine*, 383, 414, 419; Pinney, *History of Wine in America*, 374.

39. Charles M. Gidney, *History of Santa Barbara, San Luis Obispo, and Ventura Counties* (Chicago: Lewis Publishing Co., 1917), 128. Gidney writes that Lompoc's deed provided that "no vinous, malt, spirituous, or other intoxicating liquors shall ever be sold or manufactured upon any portion of the Lompoc and Mission Vieja Ranchos purchased by this corporation."

40. Otis L. Graham Jr., Sarah Harper Case, Victor W. Geraci, Susan Goldstein, Richard P. Ryba, and Beverly J. Schwartzberg, *Aged in Oak: The Story of the Santa Barbara County Wine Industry* (Santa Ynez, Calif.: Cachuma Press, 1998), 8–11. This publication came from a contract between the Santa Barbara County Vintners Association and the University of California, Santa Barbara, Public History program and served as the basis for the author's Ph.D. dissertation.

41. For general readings on the after-effects of Prohibition, see: Thomas M. Coffey, *The Long Thirst: Prohibition in America, 1920–1933* (New York: Norton and Company, 1990); David E. Kyvig, *Law, Alcohol, and Order: Perspectives on National Prohibition* (Westport, Conn.: Greenwood Press, 1985); David E. Kyvig, *Repealing National Prohibition* (Chicago: University of Chicago Press, 1979); Gilman M. Ostrander, *The Prohibition Movement in California, 1848–1933* (Berkeley: University of California Press, 1957); Clark Warburton, *The Economic Results of Prohibition* (New York: Columbia University Press, 1932); John C. Burnham, "New Perspectives on the Prohibition Experiment of the 1920s," *Journal of Social History* 2 (fall 1968): 51–68; and John C. Burnham, *Bad Habits: Drinking, Smoking, Taking Drugs, Gambling, Sexual Misbehavior, and Swearing in American History* (New York: New York University Press, 1993).

42. Muscatine, Amerine, and Thompson, eds., *University of California/Sotheby Book of California Wine*, 50, 51.

43. Ibid., 62; Peele, "The Conflict Between Public Health Goals and the Temperance Mentality."

44. Lukacs, *American Vintage*, 106.

45. Ibid., 107.

46. Burnham, *Bad Habits*.

Chapter 3 | The California Wine Revolution

1. Zunz, *Why the American Century?;* Lukacs, *American Vintage,* 7–8.

2. Letter, Seymour Berkson to T. V. Ranck, Rome, 11 December 1932, in Than Van Ranck Collection, box 9, Yale University Sterling Memorial Library, New Haven, Conn.

3. Lukacs, *American Vintage,* 103.

4. Adams interview in *California Wine Industry Affairs.*

5. Sullivan, *Napa Wine,* chaps. 11, 12, pp. 234–305; Alan E. Fusonie, "John H. Davis: His Contributions to Agricultural Education and Productivity," *Agricultural History* 60 (spring 1986): 97–110.

6. Lukacs, *American Vintage,* 111. In the California wine industry, agribusiness manifested itself in what this author has termed *vintibusiness.*

7. Gavin-Jobson Publication, *The Wine Marketing Handbook, 1972* (New York: Gavin-Jobson, 1972), 14–15; Catherine Gilbert Murdock, *Domesticating Drink: Women, Men, and Alcohol in America, 1870–1940* (Baltimore: Johns Hopkins University Press, 1998), 161.

8. "Pop Wines . . . Something for Everyone," *Los Angeles Times Home Magazine,* 15 October 1972; "U.S. Wineries Savor Success at Home," *Los Angeles Times,* 23 February 1979.

9. Richard Bunce, "From California Grapes to California Wine: The Transformation of an Industry, 1963–1979," *Contemporary Drug Problems* (spring 1981): 57.

10. Adams, *Wines of America,* 31–34, 37–38.

11. Bureau of Alcohol, Tobacco, and Firearms Records for the Bonded Winery Number 3577, Umberto Dardi, in Special Collections Archives, University of California, Davis. Local sources allude to the fact that Dardi fell into a vat while punching down the cap of homemade wine and that his daughter succumbed to the fermentation gases while attempting to save her father.

12. Bureau of Alcohol, Tobacco, and Firearms Records for the Bonded Winery Number 4228, Benjamin Alfonso, ibid.

13. Lin Rolens, "When the Magic Was on Mountain Drive," *Santa Barbara Magazine,* January/February 1992, 40–47; Elias Chiacos, ed., *Mountain Drive: Santa Barbara's Pioneer Bohemian Community* (Santa Barbara, Calif.: Shoreline Press, 1994); Stanley Hill, interview by Teddy Gasser, Santa Barbara, Calif., 10 January 1987, collection of the Santa Barbara Historical Society.

14. Lukacs, *American Vintage,* 85.

15. Frank J. Prial, "Wine Talk: A Coda to the 1976 France vs. California Rivalry That Changed Some Attitudes," *New York Times,* 22 May 1996, sec. B, p. 5; "20 Years Ago . . . a Taste of History," *Wine Enthusiast,* June 1996, 45.

16. Lukacs, *American Vintage,* 86.

17. Terry Robards, "History of Wine Repeats Itself: '76 Paris Tasting Recalled at Smithsonian," ed. Ben Giliberti, *Wine Enthusiast,* July 1996, 8; Matt Kramer, "Slipperiness at the Smithsonian," *Wine Spectator,* 31 August 1996, 29.

18. K. S. Moulton, "The Economics of Wine in California," in *University of California/Sotheby Book of California Wine,* ed. Muscatine, Amerine, and Thompson, 380–405.

19. Gavin-Jobson Publication, *The Wine Marketing Handbook, 1980* (New York: Gavin-Jobson, 1980). Using a Gallup Poll as their source, Gavin-Jobson built a profile of American wine drinkers as under 50, well educated, and ethnically and regionally concentrated. Results pointed out that 79 percent of college graduates drank wine, compared to 41 percent of grade school graduates, and that 74 percent of those between the ages of 18 and 49 drank wine. Pollsters also showed that wine drinking followed ethnic and regional lines. Poll results indicated that 83 percent of Catholics drank wine, compared to 59 percent of Protestants, and that 75 percent of people from the Western and Eastern states drank wine, compared to 55 percent from Southern states. Gender differences were not that great: 74 percent of men and 64 percent of women drank wine. The survey also showed that the percentages of people who drank alcoholic beverages averaged around 64 percent of the total population.

20. Fuller, *Religion and Wine,* 8–9.

21. Nathan Chroman, "Wine: What the Doctor Ordered," *Los Angeles Times,* 11 May 1972, sec. 6, p. 18.

22. Gavin-Jobson Publication, *Wine Marketing Handbook, 1972,* 14, 89. As Americans' incomes increased, so did their expenditures on wine. It became apparent in 1971 that consumption increases in 1970 and 1971 were in part generated by youth-market "pop" wines (wines with low alcohol content). Young adults, who had formerly emulated their elders, now followed the examples of the younger generation and reversed the "dad and lad syndrome." Frank Braconi, *The U.S. Wine Market: An Economic Marketing and Financial Investigation* (Merrick, N.Y.: Morton Research Corporation, April 1977), 4–5.

23. Lukacs, *American Vintage,* 91.

24. George Alexander, "Wine Making: An Old Art Is Now a Science," *Los Angeles Times,* 20 September 1973.

25. Ibid. Large food-processing and alcoholic-beverage companies found that investments in the industry provided an edge on inflation, and they began to purchase and vertically integrate marginal wineries. Typical of these ventures was Heublein's 1969 purchase of Beaulieu and Inglenook and Nestlé Corporation's 1971 purchase of Beringer.

26. Irving Hoch and Nickolas Tryphonopoulos, *A Study of the Economy of Napa County, California,* Giannini Foundation of Agricultural Economics Research Report no. 303 (University of California, Davis, Agricultural Experiment Station, August 1969).

27. Sullivan, *Napa Wine,* 234–305.

28. "High Costs Squeeze out Local Wine Industry," *San Diego Union,* 23 January 1966; James D. Hofer, "Cucamonga Wines and Vines: A History of the Cucamonga Pioneer Vineyard Association" (Master's thesis, Claremont University, 1983).

29. Donald Joseph de la Peña, "Vineyards in a Regional System of Open Space in the

San Francisco Bay Area: Methods of Preserving Selected Areas" (Master's thesis, College of Environmental Design, University of California, Berkeley, 1962).

30. Rebecca Ann Conard, "The Conservation of Local Autonomy: California's Agricultural Land Policies, 1900–1966" (Ph.D. diss., University of California, Santa Barbara, 1984), vi; Dean Brown, interview by Victor W. Geraci and Jeff Maiken, tape recording, Santa Ynez, Calif., 25 October 1995, Special Collections, University of California, Santa Barbara. In his interview Brown described how many investors saved agricultural acreage through a system of depreciation on full costs of vineyard investment and three years of zero income tax write-offs (while waiting for vine production to begin) and established vineyard investment as a tax loophole for a hedge against increasing rates of inflation faced by large landholders, cattle ranchers, and agribusiness during the 1970s.

31. Wine Institute Statistical Survey, 1974. Total of all wine marketed in 1964 was 175,918,000 gallons; by 1974, this figure had doubled, to 349,403,000 gallons (26). Braconi, *U.S. Wine Market,* 14–18, 37–57, 89–98.

32. Leonard Greenwood, "Italian-Brazil Colony Wine Uses California Grapes," *Los Angeles Times,* 2 April 1972, sec. H, p. 1.

33. Ibid.; Hoch and Tryphonopoulos, *A Study of the Economy of Napa County.*

34. Greenwood, "Italian-Brazil Colony Wine Uses California Grapes." In Caxias Do Sul, Brazil, the government looked to California for expertise, cuttings, marketing strategies, and technology in an attempt to help fill this worldwide need for winegrapes.

35. The Bank of America released wine industry reports from its agricultural economics division in 1970, 1973, and 1978. The data were readily available for and used by Santa Barbara pioneers.

36. Olmstead, "Induced Innovation in American Agriculture."

37. Economic Research Division of Security First National Bank, *Ventura, Santa Barbara, and San Luis Obispo Counties* (Los Angeles: Economic Research Department, Security First National Bank, July 1966), 34.

38. Lynn Samsel, Diane I. Hambley, and Raymond A. Marquardt, "Agribusiness' Competitiveness for Venture Capital," *Agribusiness* 7 (July 1991): 401–13.

39. Ibid., 25–29. Between 1960 and 1965 Orange County grew at a rate of 64.5 percent and Ventura at a rate of 52 percent.

40. The Santa Barbara County Department of Agriculture's yearly crop reports support this position of a prosperous agricultural economy in Santa Barbara. Between 1925 and 1952 Santa Barbara County agricultural lands averaged more than 750,000 acres and showed constant growth in total crop values to a high of more than $67 million. Starting in 1953 the total number of acres decreased to around 550,000 yet maintained crop values above $60 million, supporting statewide fears of lost croplands and of the new, efficient commercial agriculture. During the 1960s croplands stabilized at an average just over 675,000 acres while crop values continued to climb, topping $92 million in 1969. New land tax incentives (Williamson Act) began to take effect, and the 1970s saw

more than 900,000 acres farmed and an ever-increasing total crop value: more than $248 million in 1979. Winegrapes appear on these county reports starting in 1973 with a report of 5,555 acres and a total value of $558,700.

41. University of California Agricultural Extension Service, *The Climate of Santa Barbara County: Plantclimate Map and Climatological Data* (Santa Barbara, Calif.: University of California Agricultural Extension Service, 1965). The report was prepared cooperatively with C. Robert Elford, state climatologist in San Francisco; Marston H. Kimball, extension bioclimatologist from the University of California, Davis; and George E. Goodall, Marvin J. Snyder, and Jack L. Bivins, Santa Barbara County farm advisers.

42. Ibid., 6.

43. Ibid. Charts in the report include table 4, "Heating Degree Days" (20); table 5, "Effective Heat Summation, Degree Days for Grapes" (23); table 6, "Average Monthly and Seasonal Precipitation" (23); table 8, "Annual Precipitation Totals, 1931–1960" (27); table 10, "Computed Evapotranspiration" (29); table 12, "Surface-Wind Summary" (31); table 13, "Percentage of Time with Fog, Precipitation, of Low Visibility" (32).

44. Table 5, ibid. Based on H. E. Jacob and A. J. Winkler, "Grape Growing in California," California Agricultural Extension Service Circular no. 116, November 1950. Santa Barbara's index was 2,977 and Santa Maria's was 2,151. A. J. Winkler, "The Effect of Climatic Regions," *Wine Review* 6 (1938): 14–16.

45. Maynard A. Amerine and A. J. Winkler, *Grape Varieties for Wine Production,* University of California, Berkeley, Division of Agricultural Sciences pamphlet no. 154, March 1963. The Santa Ynez Valley is a cool region II on the Winkler/Amerine Scale. Solvang, in the valley's center, averages 2,680 degree-days, contrasted by 1,970 degree-days for Lompoc (region I), and 2,820 degree-days for Santa Barbara. On the scale, region I has fewer than 2,500 degree-days; region II has 2,501 to 3,000 degree-days. Varieties classified as high quality for Santa Barbara County include Chardonnay, Sauvignon Blanc, White Reisling, and Cabernet Sauvignon.

46. None of the winegrape pioneers who were interviewed recalled seeing the Agricultural Extension Service's *Climate of Santa Barbara County: Plantclimate Map and Climatological Data,* but the data were available for deciding whether to plant winegrapes in the county during the late 1960s.

Chapter 4 | Santa Barbara Pioneers Plant Winegrapes

1. This was the same project that produced the University of California, Davis, Heat Degree Day Index that established five types of viticultural growing regions in the state. This system measures the cumulative average daily temperatures above 50° F in California's grape-growing regions and is used as a gauge in selecting grape varietals for regional microclimates. A good, detailed discussion of this heat summation system can be found in Muscatine, Amerine, and Thompson, eds., *University of California/Sotheby Book of California Wine,* 98–105.

2. Stephan Bedford, interview by Victor W. Geraci, tape recording, Santa Maria, Calif., 24 February 1994, Special Collections, University of California, Santa Barbara. Bedford, along with Katie O'Hara, Fess Parker Winery public relations director, gathered this information in an interview with Nielson prior to his death. The transcript and recording from the interview could not be located.

3. Bedford interview.

4. Pacific Gas and Electric Company, *Finest Dry Wine Grapes: New Tepusquet Vineyard Blessed with Ideal Climate* (hereafter, PG&E report).

5. Ibid.

6. Ed Holt, interview by Richard P. Ryba, tape recording, Santa Maria, Calif., 21 April 1995, and Harold Pfeiffer, interview by Richard P. Ryba, tape recording, Santa Maria, Calif., 21 April 1995, both in Special Collections, University of California, Santa Barbara.

7. Becky Sue Epstein, "Way with Wines," *Santa Barbara News-Press,* 1 December 1988, sec. E, pp. 1, 10.

8. Holt and Pfeiffer interview; Bedford interview. Pfeiffer also shared with the interviewer unpublished personal notes dated 1 July 1989.

9. "Major Grape Venture Announced for Region," "1200-Acre Vineyard Slated for Tepusquet Mesa," undated news clippings, *Santa Maria Times,* in Dale Hampton personal files.

10. Bob Miller, interview by Richard P. Ryba, tape recording, Santa Barbara, Calif., 15 September 1994, Special Collections, University of California, Santa Barbara.

11. Dale Hampton, interview by Victor W. Geraci and Susan Goldstein, tape recording, Santa Maria, Calif., 10 February 1994, Special Collections, University of California, Santa Barbara.

12. Bank of America Economics Department, *Outlook for the California Wine Industry.*

13. Louis Lucas, interview by Richard P. Ryba, tape recording, Santa Maria, Calif., 29 June 1994, Special Collections, University of California, Santa Barbara.

14. Ibid. The vineyard was named for the Dalmatian Islands off Yugoslavia, from whence the Lucas family came and where relatives continue the family's four-century tradition of grape farming.

15. Dalmatian Vineyard Associates Performa, undated news clipping, in Dale Hampton personal files.

16. Hampton interview; Lucas interview.

17. Ibid.

18. Lucas interview. Those involved in the endeavor projected that within four years the company would establish a winery and eventually produce 4.8 million fifths (400,000 cases) of wine from the operations.

19. Coastal Farming Company Limited Partnership Agreement, in Dale Hampton personal files. The corporation was located at 106 North Conception in Santa Maria, California, 93454. Joe Tucker had a B.S. degree in production management and engi-

neering. He had worked for Rainmaker Pipe Company between 1956 and 1962 and then served as field superintendent in charge of a 6,000-acre irrigated farm property for Sinton and Brown Company. In 1970 he designed the Tepusquet irrigation system. Garth Conlan received a B.S. degree in agriculture from California State Polytechnic College and worked as an agricultural power engineer for the Pacific Gas and Electric Company between 1958 and 1971.

20. Tad Weber, "1986 Called a Vintage Year," *Santa Barbara News-Press,* 2 October 1986, sec. B, p. 1. By 1986 the firm managed 4,900 acres in Santa Barbara County. For his role in organizing the growth Hampton was named the 1986 California Central Coast Wine Grape Growers Association "Man of the Year."

21. Bob and Jeanne Woods, interview by Richard P. Ryba, tape recording, Santa Maria, Calif., 12 April 1995, Special Collections, University of California, Santa Barbara.

22. By the 1990s both vineyards belonged to the Cambria Limited Partnership under the Kendall-Jackson label.

23. The ranch lies at the intersection of Telephone and Betteravia Roads in Santa Maria.

24. Woods interviews; "Receiver Appointed to Preserve Assets of S.M. Vineyards," *Santa Barbara News-Press,* 10 April 1975; "Prudential Insurance Sells Sierra Madre Vineyard," *Los Padres Sun* (Santa Ynez, Calif.), 17 August 1988.

25. Jeff Wilkes, interview by Susan Goldstein, tape recording, Santa Maria, Calif., 3 March 1994, Special Collections, University of California, Santa Barbara.

26. Miller interview.

27. Ibid.

28. Wilkes interview. The virus-free plants were purchased from UC Davis and are inspected twice yearly in order to maintain their certified nursery status.

29. Miller interview. Miller estimated that in the past twenty years the Bien Nacido Vineyard has sold $4 million to $5 million in certified grape cuttings.

30. Barry Johnson, interview by Susan Goldstein, tape recording, Santa Ynez, Calif., 28 January 1994, Special Collections, University of California, Santa Barbara.

31. Cork Millner, *Vintage Valley: The Wineries of Santa Barbara County* (Santa Barbara, Calif.: McNally and Loftin, 1983), 95. Mrs. Bettencourt's family bought the property in 1923 and ran a dairy for more than fifty years.

32. Boyd Bettencourt, interview by Beverly Schwartzberg, tape recording, Santa Ynez, Calif., 8 April 1994, Special Collections, University of California, Santa Barbara.

33. Carol Caldwell-Ewart, "Sanford Winery: Managing Costs Profitably," *Pacific Wines and Vines,* November/December 1993, 40; Richard Paul Hinkle, "Searching for the Holy Grail," *Wines and Vines,* July 1993.

34. Richard Sanford, interview by Victor W. Geraci and Otis L. Graham Jr., tape recording, Santa Barbara, Calif., 7 March 1995, Special Collections, University of California, Santa Barbara; Hinkle, "Searching for the Holy Grail."

35. Dean Brown interview.

36. A. Brooks Firestone, interview by Richard P. Ryba, tape recording, Santa Ynez, Calif., 18 February 1995, Special Collections, University of California, Santa Barbara.

37. T. Hayer, interview by Richard P. Ryba, tape recording, Santa Ynez, Calif., 29 June 1994, Special Collections, University of California, Santa Barbara.

38. Dan Berger, "Firestone's Family Values," *Los Angeles Times,* 20 January 1994.

39. Bob Wiedrich, "Firestone's Tire-to-Vine Trek Not So Implausible," *Chicago Tribune,* 12 March 1990, business section. Brooks's concerns proved to be correct: The company was sold to Bridgestone Corporation of Japan in 1988.

40. Hayley Firestone Jessup, interview by Victor W. Geraci, tape recording, Santa Ynez, Calif., 3 February 1994, Special Collections, University of California, Santa Barbara; Catherine Boulton Firestone, interview by Victor W. Geraci, tape recording, Santa Ynez, Calif., 3 February 1994, ibid.

41. Millner, *Vintage Valley,* 109–14.

42. Jeff Maiken and Sheryl Duggan, interviews by Sarah Case and Victor W. Geraci, tape recording, Santa Ynez, Calif., 27 January 1994, Special Collections, University of California, Santa Barbara.

43. Wesley Mann, "Vintner's Grape Plans Back on Track," *Santa Barbara News-Press,* 7 May 1982, sec. B, p. 10; Joe Shoulak, "A Heady Time for Vintners," *Santa Barbara News-Press,* 27 September 1987, sec. E, pp. 1, 2, 3.

44. Mann, "Vintner's Grape Plans Back on Track," 10, 11.

45. Bob and Jeanne Woods interview.

46. Geraldine Mosby, interview by Susan Goldstein, tape recording, Santa Ynez, Calif., 28 January, 1994, Special Collections University of California, Santa Barbara, Santa Barbara, California.

47. Bryan Babcock, interview by Susan Goldstein, tape recording, Santa Ynez, Calif., 2 February 1994, Special Collections, University of California, Santa Barbara; Robert Lawrence Balzer, "Young but Mature: Babcock Wines Bear out the Promise They Showed in '87," *Los Angeles Times Magazine,* 5 March 1989, 36.

48. Donna Marks, interview by Beverly Schwartzberg, tape recording, Santa Ynez, Calif., 8 March 1994, Special Collections University of California, Santa Barbara.

49. Mary Anne La Pointe, "County Grape-Growing Operations Now a Source of Premium Wines," *Santa Barbara News-Press,* 23 May 1977, sec. B, pp. 1, 2; "Winery Operations Allowed in Farmland Preserve Areas," *Santa Barbara News-Press,* 28 June 1977, sec. B, p. 1; Braconi, *U.S. Wine Market.* This report predicted that per capita wine consumption in the United States would increase to 2.7 gallons per adult by 1985 and that the rate of population growth would also continue to increase.

50. Braconi, *U.S. Wine Market.* Between 1967 and 1972 premium wine consumption jumped an average of 10.7 percent per year. By 1972 Americans consumed 337 million gallons, up from 203 million gallons in 1967.

51. Ibid.; Kenneth R. Farrell, "The California Wine Industry: Trends and Prospects" (testimony presented at a public hearing to consider amendment of the State of California Marketing Order for Wine, San Francisco, Calif., 2 March 1966). Farrell projected that a 2.5 percent increase in per capita income would yield a 1.0 percent increase in per capita consumption of table wine.

52. Farrell, "California Wine Industry," 3. From table "Wine Entering U.S. Distribution channels, According to Origin, 1960–1980."

53. Jerry Belcher, "Wine Upstaging Other Libations," *Los Angeles Times*, 3 June 1980.

54. Braconi, *U.S. Wine Market*, 37–57. Consumption of wines with less than 14 percent alcohol doubled from 1960 (36 percent) to 1973 (72 percent).

55. Farrell, "California Wine Industry," 5–6 (source: U.S. Department of Commerce, Bureau of the Census); Braconi, *U.S. Wine Market*, 4–23. The number of adults 21 and over began to increase in the second half of the 1960s. During the 1970s, an average of 3.9 million persons per year reached the legal drinking age. By 1980, the adults in this age group (21 to 44)—the group associated with higher wine consumption—made up about 36 percent of the total population of the United States. Wine consumption also increased as many states lowered the legal age for alcoholic beverage consumption. In 1973 twenty-two states with 53 percent of the total population retained 21 as the legal age, while fifteen states lowered their legal ages to between 18 and 20. California still maintained an age limit of 21.

56. Ibid. Wineries developed marketing strategies that utilized wine festivals, wine classes, and wine-tasting parties and in 1971 spent more than $32 million for television advertising, up from $10 million in 1969. A growing body of literature also brought more people to the world of wine. In 1967 only 90 books were in print on the subject of wine and winemaking, most copyrighted before 1960. In 1972 there were 151 such books, of which about 30 were published in 1972.

57. Ibid., 8–10. Imported wines were predicted to rise from 6.6 percent of the market in 1960 to 14 percent in 1972 and to 20 percent in 1980. Imports from France, Italy, Spain, Portugal, and West Germany increased to 40 million gallons, up by 27.7 million gallons per year over 1967. Wine shipments from other states (New York, New Jersey, Arkansas, Georgia, Michigan, Ohio, Washington) doubled between 1960 and 1972. These states accounted for 15.4 percent of the national market. Braconi, *U.S. Wine Market*, 37–57.

58. Ibid., 11. Italy led the world with 1.7 billion gallons; France produced 1.6 billion gallons; the United States produced 362 million gallons, of which California produced 307 million gallons. The United States also lagged behind Spain (625 million gallons), Russia (759 million gallons), and Argentina (583 million gallons).

59. A. Brooks Firestone interview.

60. Braconi, *U.S. Wine Market*, 71.

61. Sullivan, *Napa Wine*, 399.

62. Ibid., 20.

63. Braconi, *U.S. Wine Market,* 71.

64. Carl Cannon, "A Favorable Wine Projection Should Not Cloud the Heads of Investors," *Los Angeles Times,* 14 May 1978, p. 7, col. 3; "Enthusiasm Chills for U.S. Wines," *Los Angeles Times,* 22 May 1984.

65. Carl Cannon, "Coke Unveils Wine Plan and It's a Corker," *Los Angeles Times,* 19 November 1978, p. 6, col. 1.

Chapter 5 | Santa Barbara Develops Wineries: 1970s–1980s

1. Nora K. Wallace, "A Tipple of the Hat to the Economy," *Santa Barbara News-Press,* 1 December 1992.

2. Hampton interview; Bedford interview.

3. "Wineries Warned on More Planting," *Santa Barbara News-Press,* 30 June 1978.

4. Catherine Boulton Firestone interview.

5. John Fredrikson, "The 80s Didn't Deliver as Forecast," *Wines and Vines,* June 1990, 32–35.

6. Jay Stuller and Glen Martin, *Through the Grapevine: The Real Story Behind America's $8 Billion Wine Industry* (New York: Wynwood Press, 1989), 24; Kirby Moulton, "The Changing Face of the Wine Economy," *Wine Institute News,* September 1991, 6–7.

7. A. J. Winkler, interview by Ruth Teiser, 1973, for *Wine Spectator,* California Winemen Oral History series, transcript in Regional Oral History Office, Bancroft Library, University of California, Berkeley.

8. Many sources in the industry refer to these small wineries as boutique wineries. In a 5 March 1997 conversation with the author, wine maker Rick Longoria recommended that the term *artisan* be used to describe these smaller wine businesses. Longoria said *artisan* connotes a skilled craftsman of wines, whereas *boutique* refers to a small retail shop of specialty wines.

9. Folwell and Castaldi, "Economies of Size in Wineries."

10. Unwin, *Wine and the Vine,* 25.

11. Leon Adams, interview by Ruth Teiser, 1986, for *Wine Spectator,* California Winemen Oral History series, 2–5, transcript in Regional Oral History Office, Bancroft Library, University of California, Berkeley.

12. Cheryll Aimee Barron, *Dreamers of the Valley of Plenty: A Portrait of the Napa Valley* (New York: Scribner, 1995), 24.

13. Joan Dew, "Wine Country's Rising Star: Region Achieves New Recognition," *Los Angeles Herald Examiner,* 18 May 1989; Samsel, Hambley, and Marquardt, "Agribusiness' Competitiveness for Venture Capital."

14. "Planners Consider Rules for County's Wineries," *Goleta Valley Today,* 30 September 1974; Santa Barbara County Environmental Quality Commission, *Environmental Quality Report 74-EIR-15, for the Santa Ynez Winery, Santa Ynez, California* (Santa Barbara, Calif., 1974), 1.

15. Mary Anne La Pointe, "County Grape-Growing Operations Now a Source of Premium Wines," *Santa Barbara News-Press,* 23 May 1977, sec. B, pp. 1, 2; "Winery Operations Allowed in Farmland Preserve Areas," *Santa Barbara News-Press,* 28 June 1977, sec. B, p. 1.

16. "Winery Operations Allowed in Farmland Preserve Areas."

17. Ibid.

18. "Area Growers Resist Curbing Outside Grapes," *Santa Barbara News-Press,* 26 May 1982; Robert Sollen, "Planners Oppose Proposal on Mobile Home Tract Sale," *Santa Barbara News-Press,* 28 May 1982, sec. C, p. 1; "Tepusquet Canyon Winery Proposal," *Santa Barbara News-Press,* 4 July 1982, sec. D, p. 2.

19. Santa Barbara Planning Commission, meeting minutes from 6 January, 25 May, 27 May, 9 June 1982; Sollen, "Planners Oppose Proposal."

20. Santa Barbara County Department of Resource Management, *Agricultural Planned Development and Transfer of Development Rights* (Santa Barbara, Calif.: Santa Barbara County Department of Resource Management, September 1985).

21. David Baum, "These Golden Vineyards: How Did Santa Barbara Get So Good So Fast?" *Santa Barbara Magazine,* July/August 1992, 30–35.

22. Folwell and Castaldi, "Economies of Size in Wineries," 281–92.

23. Lukacs, *American Vintage,* 217.

24. A. Brooks Firestone interview.

25. Paul Gilster, "Style and Substance," *Wine Spectator,* 16–22 November 1989.

26. Chet Holcombe, "First Firestone Wine Delivered," *Santa Barbara News-Press,* 2 June 1976, sec. A, p. 12; Marshall Berges, "Kate and Brooks Firestone," *Los Angeles Times Home Magazine,* 8 October 1978; Colman Andrews, "Wine Country Gambler: Brooks Firestone's Southern California Strategy Pays Off," *Los Angeles Times Magazine,* 19 July 1987, 8–14; Bob Wiedrich, "Firestone's Tire-to-Vine Trek Not So Implausible," *Chicago Tribune,* 12 March 1990, business section.

27. Maiken and Duggan interview.

28. Kathleen Sharp, "Zaca Mesa Owner Sets Sights on World Market," *Santa Barbara News-Press,* 18 October 1987, sec. G, pp. 1, 3.

29. Maiken and Duggan interview.

30. Linda Berberoglu, "Zaca Mesa Consolidates; Assets Exceed $11 Million," *Santa Barbara News-Press,* 2 February 1983, sec. A, p. 7.

31. Millner, *Vintage Valley,* 110–11; "Valley Winery Beginning Project to Triple Production," *Santa Barbara News-Press,* 26 July 1981; "Zaca Mesa Winery King of the Grapes," *Santa Barbara News-Press,* 21 July 1982, sec. B, p. 5.

32. Lucas interview.

33. Fess Parker, interview by Victor W. Geraci, tape recording, Santa Ynez, Calif., 17 April 1995, Special Collections, University of California, Santa Barbara. Parker was involved with the development of Disneyland, Six Flags over Texas Enterprises, and Fess Parker's Red Lion Inn.

34. Ibid.

35. Ibid.

36. Ibid.

37. Parker interview.

38. Gallo and Gallo, *Ernest and Julio Gallo,* 146–49.

39. Ibid., 148.

40. Bettencourt interview.

41. Jonathan Gold, "California's New Wave Winemakers Rockin' Vines in the Santa Maria Valley," *Elle,* January 1992, 76; Baum, "These Golden Vineyards"; James Laube, "Trivial Pursuits in California," *Wine Spectator,* December 15, 1995, 15, 25; Jeff Morgan, "California's 'Other' Coast," *Wine Spectator,* 15 May 1996, 58–59.

42. Barron, *Dreamers of the Valley of Plenty,* 23–24.

43. Bob Senn, "J. Carey," *Santa Barbara News-Press,* 30 October 1985, sec. D, p. 1.

44. Millner, *Vintage Valley,* 56.

45. Mosby interview.

46. Ibid.

47. David and Margy Houtz, interview by Sarah Case, tape recording, Santa Ynez, Calif., 28 January 1994, Special Collections, University of California, Santa Barbara.

48. Babcock interview.

49. Dennis Schaefer, "Smart as a Foxen," *Santa Barbara Independent,* 19 April 1993, 36.

50. James Laube, "Rising Stars of Cabernet: Foxen Breaks out of a Mediocre Pack in Santa Barbara," *Wine Spectator,* 15 November 1992; Schaefer, "Smart as a Foxen"; Mark Winters, "Nouveau Vintners Break Ground in Santa Ynez," *California Law Business,* 17 July 1989, 9.

51. "San Luis Obispo Firm Buys County Vineyard," *Santa Barbara News-Press,* 15 December 1988, sec. B, p. 17.

52. The property is located in the northern part of Santa Barbara County, near Santa Maria, east of 101 between Betteravia and Clark Roads.

53. Biographical sketch of C. Frederick Brander, provided by the Brander Winery. Brander has also published an article in the *American Journal of Enology and Viticulture* and is said to be fluent in French, Spanish, and English.

54. C. Frederick Brander, interview by Beverly Schwartzberg, tape recording, Santa Ynez, Calif., 16 February 1994, Special Collections, University of California, Santa Barbara.

55. Alton Pryor, "Tasty Marketing Twist: A Gourmet Wine Tour," *California Farmer,* 11 August 1984, 53. At that time the cost of purchasing land and establishing a vineyard averaged around $16,000 per acre. The Gainey vineyard planting cost averaged $10,000 per acre.

56. "Ranch Building Winery with Direct Marketing Approach," *California-Arizona*

Farm Press, 26 May 1984, 8; "Panel to Consider Rezoning Ranch for Winery Use," *Santa Barbara News-Press,* 5 December 1983; "Grapes to Be Grown Locally: Planners OK Santa Ynez Winery," *Santa Barbara News-Press,* 8 December 1983; Tad Weber, "Wine Harvest Pressed for Time," *Santa Barbara News-Press,* 15 September 1985, sec. A, pp. 1, 3. In 1983 the planning commission voted to allow winery building on the condition that half the grapes used for wine would originate in the Santa Barbara or San Luis Obispo Counties over a five-year period.

57. Larry Walker, "A Napa Valley Quiz Show," *Wine Enthusiast,* June 1996, 59.

58. Pryor, "Tasty Marketing Twist," 53; "Ranch Building Winery with Direct Marketing Approach"; "Gainey Vineyard Sets Grand Opening Sunday," *Santa Ynez Valley News,* 22 November 1984.

59. Dan Berger, "For Wine Makers, Image Is as Important as Grapes," *San Diego Union,* 16 December 1984, sec. D, p. 4. During this same period Chateau Julien in the Carmel Valley designed a similar marketing technique on a smaller scale.

60. Millner, *Vintage Valley,* 89–94; Stella Haverland Rouse, "In Old Santa Barbara," *Santa Barbara News-Press,* 7 November 1990, sec. B, p. 3.

61. Pierre Lafond, Laila Rashid, Bruce McGuire, and Craig Addis, interviews by Beverly Schwartzberg, tape recording, Santa Barbara, Calif., 28 January 1994, Special Collections, University of California, Santa Barbara; Robert Lawrence Balzer, "Deliciosa: An Ideal Climate and a Master Hand Contribute to a Most Unusual Wine," *Los Angeles Times Magazine,* 23 April 1989, 42.

Chapter 6 | Santa Barbara Gains Recognition

1. Ken Sternberg, "Gold Medals Lead to Golden Sales: Winning Small Wineries Get a Boost," *Wine Business Monthly* 6 (January 1999): 23–28.

2. Abby Sawyer and Jim Hammett, "American Appellations Earn Distinction as a Marketing Tool: Growers and Vintners Weigh Merits of Tying Appellation to Varietal," *Wine Business Monthly* 5 (June 1998): 1, 13–19.

3. Ibid., 19.

4. Department of the Treasury, Bureau of Alcohol, Tobacco, and Firearms, Rules and Regulations, "Santa Maria Viticultural Area," 46:150 (5 August 1981): 39811–12, chart E, Map of the Santa Barbara County Wine Industry.

5. Department of the Treasury, Bureau of Alcohol, Tobacco and Firearms, Rules and Regulations, "Santa Ynez Valley Viticultural Area," 48:74 (15 April 1983): 16250–51. Amerine and Winkler, *Grape Varieties for Wine Production,* University of California, Berkeley, Division of Agricultural Sciences pamphlet no. 154.

6. Bob Barber, "Winegrowers' Group Director Optimistic on County Grapes," *Santa Barbara News-Press,* 11 September 1986, sec. D, p. 7.

7. Tad Weber, "Growers, Wine Makers May Team Up," *Santa Barbara News-Press,* 13 March 1987.

8. "Area Wines to Be Judged Saturday in Santa Maria," *Santa Barbara News-Press,* 15 July 1981, sec. C, p. 4; "County Wineries Healthy," *Santa Barbara News-Press,* 15 September 1985, sec. A, p. 9; Jenny Perry, "Sipping in the Summer Sun: Wine Festival Benefit," *Santa Barbara News-Press,* 26 August 1986; Jenny Perry, "Wine Harvest Festivals Mean Merrymaking," *Santa Barbara News-Press,* 17 September 1986; Santa Barbara County Vintner's Association, "SBCVA Mission and Policies," from membership form, May 1993.

9. Laura Madonna, "Making the Consumer Connection: The Importance of Tourism to the Wine Business," *Wine Business Monthly* 6 (May 1999): 1, 11–14.

10. Graham et al., *Aged in Oak.*

11. Joe Shoulak, "A Heady Time for Vintners," *Santa Barbara News-Press,* 27 September 1987, sec. E, pp. 1, 2.

12. Unwin, *Wine and the Vine,* 359–60; Rosalind Kent Berlow, "The 'Disloyal' Grape: The Agrarian Crisis of Late Fourteenth-Century Burgundy," *Agricultural History* 56 (April 1982): 426–38.

13. Hugh Johnson and Bob Thompson, *The California Book of Wine* (New York: William Morrow, 1976), 122.

14. Frank J. Prial, "A Winery in the Making," *New York Times,* 23 July 1978, 36, 44.

15. Bob Thompson, *California Wine Country* (Menlo Park, Calif.: Lane Books, 1969, 1977, 1979).

16. Malcolm R. Hebert, "The Pick of the Vines," *Los Angeles Times,* 14 October 1979; "Pinot Noir: Put to a Rigorous Test," *Los Angeles Times,* 5 October 1980; "Area Wines to Be Judged Saturday"; "County Wineries Are Big Winners," *Santa Barbara News-Press,* 20 July 1981; Harvey Steiman, "Scouting the Wine Country of the Future from San Diego to the Sierra," *San Francisco Examiner and Chronicle,* 18 November 1981; "Zaca Mesa Winery King of the Grapes," *Santa Barbara News-Press,* 21 July 1982, sec. B, p. 5; Bill Griggs, "Summer of '84 Grape Production Could Bring Forth an All Star Cask," *Santa Barbara News-Press,* 30 September 1984, sec. D, p. 2.

17. "New Releases," *Wine Spectator,* 1–16 November 1983, recommended Sanford's 1982 Santa Maria Chardonnay. Zaca Mesa advertisements were found in *Wine Spectator,* 1–15 June 1981, 16–31 July, 1–15 September 1983. The winery's 1982 Toyon wine was listed as a recommended buy in *Wine Spectator,* 16 October 1983.

18. Larry Roberts, "Masters of Wine on First California Tour," *Wine Spectator,* 1–15 June 1981, 19. The honored title requires that the applicant be 25 years old, have served five years in the English wine trade, and pass a comprehensive written exam and three tasting exams. From 1954 to 1981, only 108 people had passed the exam.

19. "County Vintners Take High Honors," *Santa Barbara News-Press,* 22 June 1987.

20. Frank Prial, "Wealth of Winners Tarnishing Gold of Wine Competitions," *Santa Barbara News-Press,* 31 August 1986, sec. C, p. 1.

21. Bill Griggs, "Vintner Bubbles About Capital Business," *Santa Barbara News-Press,*

12 February 1981, sec. B, p. 1; Jerry Rankin, "Winemaker Forgets Political Wrath, Offers Reagan a Case of His Best," *Santa Barbara News-Press,* 3 April 1986, sec. A, pp. 1, 11.

22. Barney Brantingham, "Pieces of Paradise," *Santa Barbara News-Press,* 3 April 1979, sec. B, p. 1; Shoulak, "Heady Time for Vintners"; Matt Kramer, "Gone with the Wind?" *Wine Spectator,* 31 July 1996, 31; Morgan, "California's 'Other' Coast."

23. Gomberg, Fredrikson and Associates, *The Wine Industry's Economic Contribution to Santa Barbara County, 1998 Survey Update: An Assessment of the Industry's Economic Dimensions* (Santa Barbara, Calif.: Santa Barbara County Vintner's Association, June 1999), 6–7; Mark Van De Kamp, "Santa Barbara Called California's Hottest Region," *Santa Barbara News-Press,* 12 July 1999.

24. Judy Kimsey, "Winemakers, the Next Superstars: Individuals Lend Focus to Advertising," *Wine Business Monthly* 6 (July 1999): 26–28.

25. Cliff Carlson, "Case Study: Emergence of 'Escargociants,'" *Wine Business Monthly* 3 (June 1996): 51–52.

26. Dennis Schaefer, *Vintage Talk: Conversations with California's New Winemakers* (Santa Barbara, Calif.: Capra Press, 1994), 7–9.

27. Bob Senn, "Touring the Wine Belt: The Definitive Guide!" *Santa Barbara Independent,* 15 May 1997, 27–31. Senn includes Byron "Ken" Brown, Bruno D'Alfonso, Bill Mosby, Bryan Babcock, Bill Wathen, Dick Dore, Bruce McGuire, Andrew Murray, Kathy Joseph, and Craig Jaffers in this wine artist category.

28. Chris Whitcraft, interview by Beverly Schwartzberg, tape recording, Santa Ynez, Calif., 3 February 1994, Special Collections, University of California, Santa Barbara.

29. Jim Clendenen, interview by Richard P. Ryba, tape recording, Santa Maria, Calif., 10 February 1994, Special Collections, University of California, Santa Barbara.

30. Schaefer, *Vintage Talk,* 56.

31. Dan Berger, "Winemaker of the Year," *Los Angeles Times,* 31 December 1992, sec. H, p. 18.

32. Schaefer, *Vintage Talk,* 210.

33. Robert Lindquist, interview by Sarah Case, tape recording, Santa Maria, Calif., 24 February 1994, Special Collections, University of California, Santa Barbara.

34. Tad Weber, "Wine Making," *Santa Barbara News-Press,* 27 September 1987, sec. A, pp. 1, 11.

35. "Pour Us Some Blues," *Playboy,* August 1996, 161.

36. The author took this call in July 1966 while serving as Gainey Vineyard tasting room manager.

37. Mark Van De Kamp, "Local Vintners Sample the Taste of Technology," *Santa Barbara News-Press,* 21 April 1996, sec. A, pp. 1, 2.

38. Lane Tanner, interview by Susan Goldstein, tape recording, Santa Maria, Calif., 3 February 1994, Special Collections, University of California, Santa Barbara.

39. John Kerr, interview by Sarah Case, tape recording, Santa Ynez, Calif., 9 February 1994, Special Collections, University of California, Santa Barbara.

40. J. Kerr Winery press packet release.

41. Jeff Morgan, "The $20 Million Quest: Financier William Foley Looks for Peace, Quiet, and Pinot Noir in Santa Barbara," *Wine Spectator,* 15 September 1999, 125.

Chapter 7 | The Business of Wine: 1990s

1. Karen White, "Ag Community Voices Opposition to Wine, Beer Tax Hike," *Santa Maria Times,* 18 July 1990; Bob Senn, "A Noble Beverage Nickel-a-Drink Sin Tax Unfair Burden on Vintners," *Santa Barbara News-Press,* 30 September 1990.

2. Dale M. Heien, "The Impact of the Alcohol Tax Act of 1990 on California Agriculture" (position paper sponsored by the United Agribusiness League, Irvine, Calif., July 1990); "Putting the Squeeze on the Grape," *Los Angeles Times,* 28 April 1989; White, "Ag Community Voices Opposition to Wine, Beer Tax Hike"; Senn, "A Noble Beverage"; Herbert A. Sample, "Alcohol Tax Measure Losing," *Santa Barbara News-Press,* 7 November 1990, sec. A, p. 5.

3. Dan Berger, "Defining the Legal Limit," *Wine News,* December/January 1993–1994, 12.

4. Phyllis van Kriedt, "A Welcome New Focus for AWARE," *California Wineletter,* 24 September 1992, 1.

5. John Elson, "A Golden Age for Grapes," *Time,* 10 December 1990, 88–92.

6. Lewis Perdue, "It's the Alcohol, Stupid!" *Wine Business Monthly* 4 (April 1997): 6. The anti-alcohol organization Join Together estimated that dry groups spent $10 billion in 1995, compared to just over $1 billion by alcoholic beverage businesses. They believed that the American public was far more likely to receive the message that all alcohol consumption is bad. One must also consider that the wine industry as a whole had adhered to a voluntary moratorium on wine advertising during most of the 1980s and 1990s.

7. Mort Hochstein, "Seagram Reveals Its Strategies," *Wine Spectator,* 16–31 July 1984, 4–5.

8. "They Will Sell No Wine," *Time,* 29 May 1989, 75; Sally Lehrman, "Investors Try to Squeeze More out of Grapes," *Santa Barbara News-Press,* 10 July 1989, sec. B, p. 4.

9. Ernest Gallo, "Gallo Jabs at Distillers," *Wine Spectator,* 16–31 July 1984, 5; "Ernest Gallo Calls for Action," *California Wine Tasting Monthly,* October 1993, 4; Heron Marquez, "3 Wine Bottles Containing Glass Found in the Area," *Santa Barbara News-Press,* 20 July 1989, sec. B, p. 1; Victor W. Geraci, *Santa Barbara New House: The First Forty Years, 1955–1995* (Santa Barbara, Calif.: Santa Barbara New House, 1995); Phyllis van Kriedt, "W.I. Tries to Pull a Fast One," *California Wineletter,* 2 September 1993; "Gallo Halts Sale of Fortified Wines," *Santa Barbara News-Press,* 21 September 1989, sec. B, p. 2.

10. Van Kriedt, "W.I. Tries to Pull a Fast One."

11. Phyllis van Kriedt, "BATF Issues a Landmark Industry Circular," *California Wineletter,* 2 September 1993.

12. "Wine Industry Continues Battle Against Regs, Taxes," *California Wine Tasting Monthly,* June 1993, 6.

13. Millicent Lawton, "Talk of Label Vexes Vintners," *Santa Barbara News-Press,* 20 July 1990, sec. B, pp. 1, 2.

14. Jennifer Coverdale, "Alcohol and Heroin: Schools Say They Are the Same," *Wine Business Monthly* 3 (June 1996): 1, 4–7; Per-Henrik Mansson, "The Father of the French Paradox," *Wine Spectator,* 15 March 1994, 45; E. B. Renaud, "Wine, Alcohol, Platelets, and the French Paradox for Coronary Heart Disease," *Lancet* 339, no. 8808 (20 June 1992), 1523–26.

15. "Wine Industry Fights Health Tax, Opposes Perception of Wine as Sin," *California Wine Tasting Monthly,* April 1993, 5; Thomas Matthews, "Wine: Prescription for Good Health," *Wine Spectator,* 15 March 1994, 37–44; Robyn Bullard, "The Power of the Paradox," *Wine Spectator,* 15 March 1994.

16. Dan Berger, "The BATF Label Fable," *Wine News,* February/March 1992, 10–11; Dan Berger, "Freedom of Speech," *Wine News,* April/May 1992, 9; "Wine Industry Fights Health Tax," 5.

17. Steven O'Hara, "Afraid to Prescribe Wine," *Wine News,* December/January 1993–1994, 14; Ellen Alperstein, "Savoring South Australia: Touring the Country's Wine-Producing Region," *Relax: The Travel Magazine for Practicing Physicians,* August 1993, 16–18; Jane Shufer, "Good Medicine: How Doctors Incorporate Wine in Their Lives," *Wine Spectator,* 15 March 1994, 46–47; Laura Shapiro, "To Your Health," *Newsweek,* 22 January 1996, 52–54; Kim Marcus, "In a Dramatic Shift, New Federal Guidelines Say It's OK to Drink Moderately," *Wine Spectator,* 29 February 1996, 8–9; Thomas Matthews, "Britain Raises Safe Drinking Limits," *Wine Spectator,* 29 February 1996, 9.

18. David Whitten, "Fighting Puritans," *Wine Spectator,* 31 March 1996, 36; Phyllis van Kriedt, "Free Run," *California Wineletter,* 14 August 1992.

19. "Thurmond Calls for Wine Institute Investigation," *Wine Business Monthly* 6 (April 1999): 8; Kim Marcus, "Strom Thurmond's Crusade Against Wine," *Wine Spectator,* 31 July 1999, 38–44.

20. Cassandra Larson, "Is the Wine Industry Slacking in Its Efforts to Market to Generation X?" *Wine Business Monthly* 6 (July 1999): 14, 1, 12–15.

21. Jeff Mapes, "Reagan Tells Congress No on Wine Equity Act," *Wine Spectator,* 16–31 December 1983, 19.

22. Wesley Mann, "Area Firm Sips French Wine Market," *Santa Barbara News-Press,* 6 March 1983, sec. D, p. 2.

23. Carl Cannon, "U.S. Wineries Hope to Crack French Market," *Los Angeles Times,* 22 February 1979; Paul Taylor, "Growers Fear for Some French Wine," *Los Angeles Times,* 13 September 1979.

24. Mapes, "Reagan Tells Congress No."

25. James Suckling, "Wine Legislation Attempts to Curb Tariff Barriers," *Wine Spectator,* 1–15 June 1983, 2.

26. Mapes, "Reagan Tells Congress No."

27. Stuller and Martin, *Through the Grapevine,* 50.

28. Philip Hiaring, "*Wines and Vines* Revisits Santa Barbara County," *Wines and Vines,* April 1991, 29–32; "Rapid Changes In Wine Commission Legal Dispute," *Wines and Vines,* April 1990, 14; Dan Berger, "Small Wineries Beat Giants, Kill Marketing Power," *Los Angeles Times,* 25 May 1990; Lawrence M. Fisher, "Smaller Wine Makers Gain Clout," *Los Angeles Times,* 16 June 1990.

29. "Wine Tariff War Could Aid California Vintners," *Advertising Age,* 9 November 1992, 8.

30. James Laube, "Blending Bends the Rules Too Far," *Wine Spectator* 24 (15 September 1999): 35.

31. Jerry Cornfield, "Area Winemakers Discuss Thirst for a New 'Coast' Label," *Santa Barbara News-Press,* 23 August 1990; Jerry Cornfield, "Area Vintners in Ferment over Label," *Santa Barbara News-Press,* 28 August 1990, sec. B, pp. 2, 3.

32. Marc Frons, "Tasting Wines at Their Scenic Sources," *Business Week,* 15 May 1989, 157.

33. Harold F. Breimyer, "The Economic Returns of Agricultural Education," *Agricultural History* 60 (spring 1986): 65–72; Margaret W. Rossiter, "Graduate Work in the Agricultural Sciences," *Agricultural History* 60 (spring 1986): 37–57.

34. Richard Steven Street, "Wizards of Wine," *Wine News,* June/July 1991, 14–17.

35. Sally McMurray, "Who Read the Agricultural Journals?" *Agricultural History* 63 (fall 1989): 1–19.

36. Carosso, *California Wine Industry,* 145–59. Between 1880 and 1919 state and federal support for the wine industry came in the form of tax support, tariff protection, pure-wine laws, formation of the National Viticultural Association, and support of viticultural research and education. Between 1919 and 1933 Prohibition halted governmental support for the industry.

37. R. G. F. Spitze, "A Continuing Evolution in U.S. Agricultural Policy," *Agricultural Economics* 77 (1990): 126–39.

38. Phyllis van Kriedt, "Hartzell Explains the Consequences of the 1990 Excise Tax Increase," *California Wineletter,* 2 September 1993; Phyllis van Kriedt, "Research at Risk," *California Wineletter,* 14 August 1992.

39. Mike Winters, "U.S. Wine/Grape Researchers Decry Money Woes," *Wine Business Monthly* 4 (May 1997): 1, 14–18.

40. Ibid., 15.

41. "Infestations and Tight Money Will Shake out Wine Industry," *California Wine Tasting Monthly,* April 1993, 7.

42. Martha Groves, "Scourge Threatens State's Wine Producers," *Los Angeles Times*, 29 September 1996, sec. A, pp. 1, 32.

43. Lyn Farmer, "Beringer on the Offensive," *Wine News*, February/March 1993, 7.

44. Phyllis van Kriedt, "NASA Joins the Fight Against Phylloxera," *California Wineletter*, 23 April 1993; Phyllis van Kriedt, "Phylloxera Update," *California Wineletter*, 7 September 1993; Phyllis van Kriedt, "A New Wine from Phil Awksira," *California Wineletter*, 14 August 1992.

45. Paula Harris, "Harvest Preparation Case Study: Neutron Probe to Gauge Irrigation Comes of Age," *Wine Business Monthly* 3 (August 1996): 29–32.

46. Brian St. Pierre, "Getting Great Grapes," *Decanter*, 1990, 2–10.

47. Anne Eisenberg, "A Pleasing Bouquet, A Hint of Silicon: Seeking the Perfect Vintage, Winemakers Turn to Laptops, Digital Sensors, and Even Satellites," *New York Times*, 31 December 1998, sec. G, pp. 1, 6; Cyril Penn, "Grape Growers Gravitating Toward Space Age Technologies," *Wine Business Monthly* 6 (February 1999): 53–56; Judy Kimsey, "2001: A Wine Odyssey: Forget HAL— Meet ANN," *Wine Business Monthly* 5 (June 1998): 35–39; Paul Franson, "Terra Spase Creates Its Place in Viticulture," *Wine Business Monthly* 5 (June 1998): 40–46.

48. Thane Peterson, "A Glass of White—Hold the Pesticides," *Business Week*, 14 September 1992, 116; Jane Hulse, "Organic Farming: A Growing Concern," *Santa Barbara News-Press*, 24 December 1989, sec. A, pp. 1, 7.

49. Larry Walker, "Wineries Are Trying Organic Techniques," *Wines and Vines*, June 1989, 59–60; Elizabeth Christian, "More Vintners Going Green as Consumers Press for Organic Wine," *Los Angeles Times*, 26 August 1990, sec. D, pp. 1, 3; David Adair, "Defining Organic Wines," *Wines and Vines*, March 1991, 23–24. The movement was helped when the sulfite issue was resolved. (Sulfite, added to wine as a preservative, is sulfur in the form of SO_2.) OGWA allowed the addition of sulfur dioxide to wine.

50. "New Tasting Room," *California Wine Tasting Monthly*, April 1993, 7.

51. Paul Franson, "Looming Labor Shortages Drive Mechanization in Vineyards," *Wine Business Monthly* 5 (November 1998): 437–53; Ken Sternberg, "Mechanization in the Vineyard: Predicted Labor Shortages Lead Trend Towards Machine Harvesting," *Wine Business Monthly* 6 (July 1999): 51.

52. Franson, "Looming Labor Shortages."

53. Mike Winters, "Rested and Ready, Labor Predicts a New Dawn for Field Workers," *Wine Business Monthly* 4 (November 1997): 30–35.

54. Bob Smith, "The Long and Short of Wine Corks," *Santa Barbara News-Press*, 18 January 1989; Lyn Farmer, "The Quirks of Cork," *Wine News* February/March 1994, 10.

55. Tad Weber, "Wine Making," *Santa Barbara News-Press*, 27 September 1987, sec. A, pp. 1, 11.

56. Martha Groves, "The Road to Grapeness: California Wineries Pour Their Efforts

into Building Reputation Overseas," *Los Angeles Times,* 26 June 1996, sec. D, pp. 1, 6; Frank Prial, "In France, a Rumble Is Heard: 'Vive Gallo,'" *New York Times,* 2 July 1999.

57. Steve Heimoff, "Gay Wine Marketing Slowly Follows Beer and Spirits Lead," *Wine Business Monthly* 3 (March 1996): 15–17.

Chapter 8 | Santa Barbara Vintibusiness

1. Cartiere, "Vintners 'Worst Best Year Ever.'"

2. Hilton, Cartiere, and McIntosh, "Capacity and Demand Debate."

3. Kathleen Sharp, "Big Wineries Head South," *Santa Barbara News-Press,* 19 June 1988. The county's twenty-three wineries used less than 40 percent of the grapes grown.

4. Kathleen Sharp, "Northern Operations Expand Southward," *New York Times,* 17 June 1990; Mike Dunn, "Vintners' Great Expectations," *Sacramento Bee,* 22 March 1989. Santa Barbara agricultural land averaged about $15,000 per acre, or 65 percent of bay-area grape land. Santa Maria land sold for $4,000 to $6,000 per acre, and Santa Ynez land sold for $21,000 to $25,000 per acre.

5. Matt Kramer, *Making Sense of California Wine* (New York: William Morrow and Company, 1992), 7–10.

6. Dan Berger, "Major County Vineyard May Be Sold," *Santa Barbara News-Press,* 14 April 1987, sec. B, p. 1; Dan Berger, "Sale of Vineyards Hits Snag," *Santa Barbara News-Press,* 13 June 1987.

7. Barbara Banke and Jess Jackson, interview by Richard P. Ryba, tape recording, Santa Maria, Calif., 11 February 1994, Special Collections, University of California, Santa Barbara.

8. Ibid.; Mike Raphael, "Winery Hopes for Planners' OK," *Santa Barbara News-Press,* 30 December 1989, sec. B, p. 3; Dan Berger, "Santa Maria Area Vineyards Are Sold," *Santa Barbara News-Press,* 4 May 1987, sec. B, p. 1; Dan Berger, "Tepusquet Vineyard Sold in Joint Deal," *Santa Barbara News-Press,* 3 July 1987.

9. Dan Berger, "Sale of Vineyards Hits Snag."

10. Robyn Bullard, "One Part Chuck Ortman, Three Parts Vineyard," *Wine Spectator,* 15 April 1994, 31; James Laube, "Napa Valley's Beringer Vineyards in Play: Investor Group May Pay $300 Million for Wine World," *Wine Spectator,* 15 December 1995, 11; James Laube, "Sonoma's Chateau St. Jean Appears Headed to Wine World," *Wine Spectator,* February 29, 1996, 10; James Laube, "Wine World's New Treasure," *Wine Spectator,* 15 May 1996, 25. Wine World itself became victim of centralization in 1995 when Texas Pacific purchased the corporation and then added Suntory's Chateau St. Jean to its Beringer Vineyards, Chateau Souverain, Napa Ridge Winery, and Meridian Vineyards family.

11. Sharp, "Northern Operations Expand Southward."

12. Tad Weber, "Area Growers See Green: Vintage Prices Are Toasted," *Santa Barbara News-Press,* 14 October 1988, sec. B, pp. 1, 2.

13. Raymond Estrada, "The Grapes of September," *Santa Barbara News-Press,* 17 September 1989, sec. F, pp. 1, 3.

14. "Prudential Insurance Sells Sierra Madre Vineyard," *Los Padres Sun* (Santa Ynez, Calif.), 17 August 1988; Kathleen Sharp, "Vineyard Sold for $8.5 Million" *Santa Barbara News-Press,* 19 August 1988, sec. A, p. 19.

15. Nora K. Wallace, "Santa Maria Valley Touted as Emerging Wine Region," *Santa Barbara News-Press,* 23 August 1990, sec. B, pp. 1, 4.

16. "Mondavi Winery to Buy Byron Vineyard," *Los Angeles Times,* 9 December 1989; Barney Brantingham, "To Our Health," *Santa Barbara News-Press,* 24 December 1989; Wallace, "Santa Maria Valley Touted."

17. Jeff Morgan, "Mondavi Buys Key Santa Barbara Vineyard," *Wine Spectator,* 30 April 1996, 13.

18. Jeff Newton, telephone interview by Victor W. Geraci, 9 November 1994. Newton believed that the refusal of local wine businesses to use Davis-trained people or techniques for field management almost killed the industry between 1982 and 1988.

19. Weber, "Area Growers See Green."

20. Cartiere, Shore, and Farrer, "Calif.'s 'Vineyard Royalty.'" Between 1993 and 1996 Kendall-Jackson purchased Geoffrey's Cellars, Mission Trails, Battaglia, Longhar Grinding, and Jim Rice vineyards in Santa Barbara County. Robert Mondavi Corporation purchased the Garcey Ranch (360 acres) and Sierra Madre (750 acres). Fess Parker Winery purchased 80 acres of the Sierra Madre vineyard.

21. Mark Van De Kamp, "Santa Barbara Land Boom Continues," *Santa Barbara News-Press,* 3 August 1999; Jim Hammett, "Meridian Opens Santa Barbara Tasting Room," *Santa Barbara News-Press,* 7 April 1999.

22. Jerry Rankin, "Firestone Buys J. Carey Cellars; Owners' Wines Blend, Politics Don't," *Santa Barbara News-Press,* 26 January 1986, sec. A, pp. 1, 6; Dan Berger, "Collectors Are Now Owners of Benedict," *Los Angeles Times,* 9 August 1990, 35.

23. Bob Thompson, "Sorting Out the Sites," *Decanter,* 1991; James Laube, "Richard Sanford Starts Again in Santa Barbara with New Pinot Noir and Chardonnay Vineyards," *Wine Spectator,* 31 March 1996, 14.

24. Pat Murphy, "Austin Cellars Serving Fine Art with Its Wine," *Santa Barbara News-Press,* 6 December 1993, sec. B, p. 6.

25. Jay Stuller, "Hollywood and Wine: Making the Most of an Image," *Hemispheres,* January 1995, 89–90, 92, 95.

26. Kim Marcus, Jeff Morgan, Bruce Sanderson, and Daniel Thomases, *Wine Spectator,* 30 April 1996, 11. *Wine Spectator* scored the 1993 Syrah at a 94 and named it one of the top ten wines of the year.

27. Jeff Morgan, "'Mad Rush' to Chile by California and French Vintners," *Wine Spectator,* 31 May 1996, 8–9; Thomas Matthews, "Onward and Upward," *Wine Spectator,* 30 June 1996, 55–56.

28. Judy Kimsey, "Regulation: Growers and Environments Strive for Harmony in the Hills," *Wine Business Monthly* 6 (January 1999): 61.

29. Chris Finlay, "Wineries and Tourism: A Symbiotic Relationship," *Wine Business Monthly* 6 (May 1999): 8–9.

30. Mike Chase, "More Homes on the Range?" *Santa Barbara Independent,* 8 August 1996, 23–25.

31. Mark Van De Kamp, "A Double-Edged Sword in Santa Ynez Valley," *Santa Barbara News-Press,* 11 November 1998.

32. Graham et al., *Stearns Wharf.*

33. Cassandra Larson, "Vineyard Development Turns Environmentalist Heads: The Best Defense Against Possible Offense," *Wine Business Monthly* 6 (May 1999): 50 (48–53); Tim Tesconi and Randi Rossman, "Threat Against Vineyards Reported: Environmental Groups May Retaliate for Cutting Oak Trees," *Santa Roas Press Democrat,* 24 February 1999, sec. B, p. 1; B. W. Rose, "Threat Against Vineyards a Mix-up," *Santa Rosa Press Democrat,* 25 February 1999, sec. B, p. 1.

34. "Sierra Club to Pay K-J's Legal Costs," *Wine Business Monthly* 6 (July 1999): 10.

35. Mark Neal, "Agriculture Must Be in Front of Environmental Movement," *Wine Business Monthly* 5 (October 1998): 8–10; Lisa Shara Hall, "Oregon Takes a Leadership Role with Sustainable Agriculture," *Wine Business Monthly* 6 (August 1999): 43–47.

36. Renee Cashmere, "Current Issues: Central Coast Growers Strive to Stay One Step Ahead of Regulations," *Wine Business Monthly* 4 (December 1997): 41–43.

37. Mark Stuertz, "Texas Looks into 21st Century: California's Hampton Farming Helps Lead the Way into the Future," *Wine Business Monthly* 3 (July 1996): 10.

38. Thomas Garrett, Jeff Morgan, and Jane Shufer, "Grapevine," *Wine Spectator,* 30 June 1996, 9–12.

39. Dan Berger, "Paso Robles Finds Its Place in the Wine World," *WineToday.com,* 3 February 1999.

40. Ibid.

41. Cyril Penn, "Direct Shipping Issue Gains Increasing Visibility," *Wine Business Monthly* 6 (May 1999): 43–44.

42. "Feinstein and Wilson Get Involved in Direct Shipping Debate," *Wine Business Monthly* 5 (November 1998): 9.

43. Dana Nigro, "Home Delivery Crackdown Approved by Wide Margin," *Wine Spectator,* 15 September 1999, 12.

44. Ted Appel, "K-J Suit Takes on Illinois Law," *Santa Rosa Press Democrat,* 10 June 1999.

45. "Grapevine," *Wine Spectator,* 31 March 2000, 13.

46. Gomberg, Fredrikson and Associates, *The Wine Industry's Economic Contribution to Santa Barbara County, 1998 Survey Update: An Assessment of the Industry's Economic Dimensions* (Santa Barbara, Calif.: Santa Barbara County Vintner's Association, June 1999.)

47. Jean T. Barrett, "Santa Barbara: This City Promises a Wealth of Winery Day Trips, Along with Near-Permanent Sunshine and Warmth," *Wine Spectator,* 15 June 1999, 79–86.

Chapter 9 | Wine Is Here to Stay: Santa Barbara, California, and the United States

1. James Harold Curry III, "Agriculture Under Late Capitalism: The Structure and Operation of the California Wine Industry" (Ph.D. diss., Cornell University, 1994), abstract.

2. Kim Marcus, "U.S. Winery Total Grows at Fast Pace," *Wine Spectator,* 15 September 1999, 21.

3. Steve Barsby and Associates for Vinifera Wine Growers Association, "The Economic Contribution of the Wine Industry to the U.S. Economy, 1997," *Wine Business Monthly* 6 (August 1999): 29.

4. Judy Kimsey, "Globalizing the Wine Industry: Shipping to the European Union," *Wine Business Monthly* 5 (November 1998): 1, 13.

5. Eric N. Sims, "A Study of the California Wine Industry and an Analysis of the Effects of the Canadian–United States Free Trade Agreement on the Wine Sector, with a Note on the Impact of the North American Free Trade Agreement on California Wine Exports" (Ph.D. diss., University of Arkansas, 1995); David Scott Shaw, "Firm Export Strategies and Firm Export Performance in the United States Wine Industry: A Longitudinal Study" (Ph.D. diss., Purdue University, 1996); Juan B. Solana Rosillo, "Firm Strategies in International Markets: The Case of International Entry into the United States Wine Industry" (Ph.D. diss., Purdue University, 1997).

6. John Love, "The Long Future of U.S. Wine Value," *Wine Business Monthly* 6 (August 1999): 34–37; Abby Sawyer, "The Wine Industry on Wall Street: As Business Booms an Increasing Number of Wineries Consider Public Stock Offerings," *Wine Business Monthly* 4 (December 1997): 1, 10–14; "Wine Market News," *Wine Business Monthly* 6 (July 1999): 41–47.

7. Gomberg, Fredrikson and Associates, *The Wine Industry's Economic Contribution to Santa Barbara County, 1998 Survey Update: An Assessment of the Industry's Economic Dimensions* (Santa Barbara, Calif.: Santa Barbara Vintners' Association, June 1999), 1.

8. Ibid.

9. Ibid.

10. Ibid., 1, 2.

11. Ibid., 3.

12. Gomberg, Fredrikson and Associates, *The Wine Industry's Economic Contribution to Santa Barbara County, 1999 Survey Update: An Assessement of the Industry's Economic Dimensions* (Santa Barbara, Calif.: Santa Barbara Vintner's Association, 1999), 3.

13. *Business Wire,* "Santa Barbara County's Wine Industry Experiences Tremendous

Growth" (Document ID: FC2001111554000031, 15 November 2001). MKF is a Napa-based winery consulting, tax consulting, market research, accounting, and strategic planning firm.

14. Kathleen Marcks, "Former Olympian Takes on Winemaking Challenge," *Wine Spectator,* 31 August 1996, 15.

15. Lindquist interview.

16. Clendenen interview.

17. Robyn Bullard, "Sons and Daughters," *Wine Spectator,* 30 September 1993, 29–35.

18. Louis S. Freeman, "Combining the Use of Corporation, Partnerships, and Trusts to Minimize the Income and Transfer Tax Impact on Family Businesses and Investments," *Taxes* 62 (December 1979): 857–80.

19. Robert F. Schnier, "A Study of the Will to Survive of the Family-Owned Wineries of California" (Master's thesis, Pepperdine University, 1982).

20. Limited aid for small family farms came with the passage of the 1997 federal budget and increased estate tax exemptions. The new eventual $1.3 million exemption, up from $600,000, did not eliminate estate problems for multimillion-dollar wine businesses. Mark Van De Kamp, "Tax Cut Boosts Family Farms," *Santa Barbara News-Press,* 2 August 1997, sec. B, pp. 1, 2.

21. Mark Van De Kamp, "Report Predicts Boost for Economy," *Santa Barbara News-Press,* 31 July 1997, sec. B, p. 1; Gomberg, Fredrikson and Associates, *The Wine Industry's Economic Contribution to Santa Barbara County: 1996.*

22. White, "State Policy and Public Administration," 97–104. White reached a similar conclusion for the Oregon and Washington wine industries.

23. Gomberg, Fredrikson and Associates, *Wine Industry's Economic Contribution to Santa Barbara County: 1996.*

24. Ibid.; M. L. Hilton, "Out of the Garage and into Haute Cuisine: Boutiques Wines Find Their Place at the Table," *Wine Business Monthly* 6 (January 1999): 34–38; Michael J. Okoniewski, "Robert H. Frank: Resisting a Society's Rage to Spend," *New York Times,* 14 August 1999; Robert H. Frank, *Luxury Fever: Why Money Fails to Satisfy in an Era of Excess* (New York: Free Press, 1999).

25. Gomberg, Fredrikson and Associates, *The Wine Industry's Economic Contribution to Santa Barbara County: 1996,* 7. The report also stated that in 1998 winery tourists spent $10.7 million on wine and $2 million other sales.

26. Laura Madonna, "Making the Consumer Connection: The Importance of Tourism to the Wine Business," *Wine Business Monthly* 6 (May 1999): 1.

27. "Jug Wine Sales Down, Revenues Up," *Wine Business Monthly* 6 (May 1999): 10.

28. Gomberg, Fredrikson and Associates, *The Wine Industry's Economic Contribution to Santa Barbara County: 1996,* 5.

29. Statistical information compiled by the author from "Wine Spectator Buying Guide: Special Report, California Pinot Noir," *Wine Spectator,* 15 September 1999, 158–64.

30. Statistical information compiled by the author from the "Wine Spectator Buying Guide: Special Report, Chardonnay Review," *Wine Spectator,* 30 April 1999, 142–51.

31. Jay Palmer, "The Coming Glut: Why the Wine Industry's Long String of Price Hikes Is About to End," *Baron's Dow Jones Business and Financial Weekly,* 3 August 1998, 25–29.

32. Abigail Sawyer, "Premium Wine Prices Soar with Economy: No Glut at High End of Market," *Wine Business Monthly* 6 (January 1999): 17–18 (1, 14–18).

Epilogue | A Backward Look Forward

1. Keith Scott, "Seeing Steady Increases, U.S. Remains Among Top Wine-Producing and Wine Drinking Nations," *Wine Spectator Online* (http://www.winespectator.com), 12 December 2001. However, Americans still only consume an average of 2 gallons of wine each year, making the United States 34th in per-capita consumption.

2. Ibid. Many predict that China is on the verge of becoming a major player in the global wine industry. See "China's Wine Industry Needs WTO," *Asiaport Daily News,* 28 November 2001.

3. Elizabeth Becker, "Ideal Farms vs. Industrial Farms," *New York Times,* 7 October 2001.

4. Ted Appel, "State's Wine Industry Takes Hit," *Santa Rosa Press Democrat,* 25 January 2002; Ted Appel, "Recession, Imports Rein in Wine Sales," *Santa Rosa Press Democrat,* 31 January 2002.

5. Appel, "Wine Industry Takes Hit."

6. Peter Sinton, "Tough Times in the Wine Trade: Mondavi Cites Recession, Attacks in Slower Sales," *San Francisco Chronicle,* 18 January 2002; Paul Franson, "Many in Wine Business Trying to Ignore Reality," *Napa Valley Register,* 26 December 2001.

7. Michael Doyle, "Wineries in State Endorse Tariffs," *Fresno Bee,* 29 November 2001; Appel, "Recession, Imports"; Peter Sinton, "Cheers! Price Cuts Make This a Good Time to Be a Wine Lover," *San Francisco Chronicle,* 23 December 2001.

8. Stinton, "Cheers!"; Franson, "Many in Wine Business Trying to Ignore Reality."

9. Tim Fish, "In an Uncertain Market, Wine Sellers Report Buyers More Focused on Value," *Wine Spectator Online* (http://www.winespectator.com), 29 November 2001. Costco is one of the nation's largest wine retailers.

10. Stavro Sofios, "Wine Glut Fear After Record Harvest," *News.com* (http://news.com.au), 29 January 2002.

11. Tim Tesconi, "Grape Prices Expected to Sink," *Santa Rosa Press Democrat,* 17 January 2002; Dennis Pollock, "Grape Prices Yield Woe," *Fresno Bee,* 2 January 2002.

12. Quentin Hardy, "A Surplus of Fine Wine Leaves California Vintners Seeing Their Glasses Half Empty," *Forbes,* 7 January 2002.

13. "Wine Oversupply Challenge," *Advertiser* (Australia), 14 November 2001.

14. Tony Baker, "Australia: BRL Hardy Sets Sights on Global Position," *Just Drinks.com* (http://www.just-drinks.com), 7 January 2002.

15. Jeff Quackenbush, "Diago Plans Napa HQ," *North Bay Business Journal,* 2 January 2002.

16. "Sutter Home Deal Collapses," *Wine Spectator Online* (http://www.winespectator.com), 26 November 2001; "Constellation Rumored Buying Trinchero Family Estates," *WineBusiness.com* (http://winebusiness.com), 8 November 2001; Tim Fish, "Constellation Eyes Purchase of Sutter Home," *Wine Spectator Online* (http://www.winespectator.com), 9 November 2001.

17. Hasani Gittens, "Constellation Brands Still Cheery as Boozers Shift Venues, Not Habits," *New York Post,* 2 January 2002; Jessica Wohl, "Constellation: Acquisitions to Lift Growth," *Yahoo! News* (http://dailynews.yahoo.com), 8 January 2002.

18. Tim Moran, "Good News for Wine Lovers Is Bad News for Grape Growers," *Modesto Bee,* 1 February 2002.

19. Fleur Anderson, "Mergers Essential to Remain Big Player," *Sunday Times,* 16 November 2001; Eric Johnston, "Southcorp Gets $540 Cash Injection," *Herald Sun,* 11 December 2001.

20. "Wine Oversupply Challenge," *Advisor* (Australia), 14 November 2001; "World Glut Tipped to Bring Cabernet to NZ," *New Zealand Herald,* 26 December 2001.

21. Alejandro Waters, "Rebuilding Technologically Competitive Industries: Lessons from Chile's and Argentina's Wine Industry Restructuring" (Ph.D. diss., Massachusetts Institute of Technology, 1999), abstract.

22. Abigail Trafford, "Calif. Vintners Put Hopes in Brazil's Labs," *Washington Post,* 2 January 2002.

23. Andrew Bridges, "Vineyard Symbol of Sharpshooter Battle," *Napa Valley Register,* 26 November 2001.

24. Heather Osborn, "Federal Government to Provide $16.5 Million to Combat Pierce's Disease," *St. Helena Star,* 3 December 2001.

25. "Viticulture," *Santa Rosa Press Democrat,* 19 November 2001.

26. "For Use with Portable Cyler and GeneXpert Systems," *Stockhouse USA News* (http://www.stockhouse.com), 30 November 2001.

27. Trafford, "Vintners Put Hopes in Brazil's Labs."

28. Mark Van De Kamp, "Dreaded Bug Found in Wine Country," *Santa Barbara News-Press,* 30 September 2000.

29. "Gallo Research Center Creates Tools to Improve Testing in Winemaking," *Excite News* (http://news.excite.com), 7 November 2001.

30. William Neuman, "The Grapes of Math," *Wired Archive* (http://wired.com), 16 November 2001.

31. Tim Fish, "Sonoma-Cutrer Tests Screw Caps on Top Chardonnay," *Wine Spectator Online* (http://www.winespectator.com), 16 November 2001.

32. "UC Davis Wine Executive Program February 3–6 Blends Business and Science of Winemaking," *Excite* (http://wwwnews.excite.com), 30 November 2001.

33. "Wine Students Travel World for Degree," *Yahoo! News* (http://wwwdailynews.yahoo.com), 26 January 2002.

34. Tamar Kahn, "New Technology to Help Winemakers," *Business Day,* 26 November 2001.

35. James Sterngold, "Davis Seeks Rule to Protect Older Trees in California," *New York Times,* 10 September 2001.

36. Tom Chorneau, "Land Use Rules May Change to Aid Salmon," *Santa Rosa Press Democrat,* 7 November 2001.

37. Tim Tesconi, "Salamander Plan May Hit County Landholders," *Santa Rosa Press Democrat,* 16 November 2001.

38. Michael Doyle, "Celebrated Frog's Future in the Air," *Sacramento Bee,* 25 November 2001.

39. Tim Moran, "Gallo Preserve Settles Violation," *Modesto Bee,* 16 November 2001.

40. Carol Benfell, "Lily May Block Winery Expansion," *Santa Rosa Press Democrat,* 16 November 2001; John Speck, "Sierra Club to Appeal Beringer Winery Approval," *St. Helena Star,* 21 January 2002.

41. Lynn Alley, "California Winegrowers Work Toward Statewide Code on Sustainable Practices," *Wine Spectator Online* (http://www.winespectator.com), 29 November 2001.

42. "Viticulture: Vineyard, Wildlife Workshop," *Santa Rosa Press Democrat,* 26 January 2002.

43. Mark Van De Kamp, "A New Leaf," *Santa Barbara News-Press,* 3 November 1999.

44. Mark Van De Kamp, "Winery Pitches Big New Building," *Santa Barbara News-Press,* 9 December 1999.

45. Mark Van De Kamp, "Fess Parker Woos Lompoc for Winery," *Santa Barbara News-Press,* 24 October 2000; Mark Van De Kamp, "Planners Approve New Inn, Winery," *Santa Barbara News-Press,* 5 February 2000.

46. Mark Van De Kamp, "Marshall Sides with Neighbors on Wine Events," *Santa Barbara News-Press,* 25 May 2000.

47. "To Our Health!" *Santa Barbara News-Press,* 20 June 2001; Mark Van De Kamp, "Vintners Reach out to Public," *Santa Barbara News-Press,* 28 February 2001.

48. Andrea Laura Della Valle, "The Taste of Globalization: The Wine Industry of Ontario (Canada)" (Master's thesis, University of Windsor, Ontario, Canada, 1996), abstract.

49. Phylicia Ann Fauntleroy, "An Economic Analysis of the United States Demand for Distilled Spirits, Wine, and Beer Incorporating Taste Changes Through Demographic Factors, 1960–1981" (Ph.D. diss., American University, 1984), abstract.

50. Rod Phillips, *A Short History of Wine,* (New York: Harper Collins, 2000), 308, 311.

51. Ibid., 314.

52. Becker, "Ideal Farms vs. Industrial Farms."

53. Chris Sanders, "US States Turn to 'Sin' Taxes to Fill Budget Gaps," *Yahoo! News* (http://dailynews.yahoo.com), 24 January 2002.

54. Erin Allday, "Rabbit Ridge to Pay Record Settlement," *Santa Rosa Press Democrat,* 8 November 2001; "ATF Settles Cases Against Rabbit Ridge," *ATF News* (http://www.atf.treas.gov), 9 November 2001.

55. Peter Sinton, "Winemaker Wins Right to Labels," *San Francisco Chronicle,* 7 December 2001.

56. Mark Van De Kamp, "Name-Calling Shaking up Wine World," *Santa Barbara News-Press,* 25 April 2001.

57. Randy Falco, "The Facts on NBC and Alcohol," *Washington Post,* 19 December 2001.

58. Andrew Grossman, "NBC Drinking in Revenue from Hard-Liquor Ads," *Yahoo! News* (http://dailynews.yahoo.com), 7 January 2002.

59. Michael Laris, "Small Wineries Fight Sales Laws," *Washington Post,* 2 January 2002.

60. Frank Jones, *The Save-Your-Heart Wine Guide* (New York: St. Martin's Press, 1996), 3; Suzanne Rostler, "Study Suggests Why Red Wine Does a Heart Good," *Yahoo! News* (http://dailynews.yahoo.com), 7 January 2002.

61. "Study: Alcohol in Moderation May Help Brain," *Yahoo! News* (http://dailynews.yahoo.com), 7 January 2002.

62. "World's Oldest Man Dies at Age 112," *Yahoo! News* (http://dailynews.yahoo.com), 7 January 2002; "World's Oldest Man Dies in Italy, Wine the Secret," *Yahoo! News* (http://dailynews.yahoo.com), 7 January 2002. Todde died on 4 January 2002 just short of his 113th birthday. In an odd coincidence, Italy's oldest woman, 110-year-old Maria Grazia Broccolo, died just a few hours after Todde.

63. "Public Interest Groups Appeal in Alcohol Advertising Case," *C|E|I Competitive Enterprise Institute* (http://www.cei.org), 7 January 2002.

64. John M. Glionna, "Catholics Slam Napa Art Exhibit," *Yahoo! News* (http://dailynews. yahoo.com), 5 January 2002.

65. Margie Mason, "Catholic Group Upset by Exhibit," *Yahoo! News* (http://dailynews.yahoo.com), 6 January 2002.

66. Mark Van De Kamp, "Nothing to Wine About," *Santa Barbara News-Press,* 16 November 2001.

67. Mark Van De Kamp, "Is Santa Barbara County's Booming Wine Industry Aging Gracefully?" *Santa Barbara News-Press,* 3 September 2000.

68. Ibid.

Selected Bibliography

Newspapers

Chicago Tribune, 12 March 1990.

Escondido Daily Times Advocate.

Los Angeles Herald Examiner, 18 May 1989.

Los Angeles Times, 2 April 1972–29 September 1996.

Los Padres Sun, 17 August 1988.

Modesto Bee, 16 November 2001–1 February 2002.

Napa Valley Register, 26 November 2001, 26 December 2001.

New York Times, 23 July 1978–7 October 2001.

Sacramento Bee, 22 March 1989, 25 November 2001.

St. Helena Star, 3 December 2001, 21 January 2002.

San Francisco Chronicle, 7 December 2001–18 January 2002.

Santa Barbara Independent, 19 April 1993–15 May 1997.

Santa Barbara News-Press, 19 June 1988–16 November 2001.

Santa Rosa Press Democrat, 7 November 2001–31 January 2002.

Santa Ynez Valley News, 22 November 1984.

Washington Post, 19 December 2001, 2 January 2002.

Journals

Amerine, Maynard A. "An Introduction to the Pre-Repeal History of Wine." *Agricultural History* 63 (April 1969): 259–68.

———. "The Napa Valley Grape and Wine Industry." *Agricultural History* 49 (January 1975): 289–91.

Atack, Jeremy. "The Agricultural Ladder Revisited." *Agricultural History* 63 (April 1969): 1–25.

Berlow, Rosalind Kent. "The 'Disloyal' Grape: The Agrarian Crisis of Late Fourteenth-Century Burgundy." *Agricultural History* 56 (April 1982): 426–38.

Best, Michael R. "The Mystery of Vintners." *Agricultural History* 50 (April 1976): 362–76.

Breimyer, Harold F. "The Economic Returns of Agricultural Education." *Agricultural History* 60 (spring 1986): 65–72.

Bunce, Richard. "From California Grapes to California Wine: The Transformation of an Industry, 1963–1979." *Contemporary Drug Problems* (spring 1981): 55–74.

Burnham, John C. "New Perspectives on the Prohibition Experiment of the 1920s." *Journal of Social History* 2 (fall 1968): 51–68.

Caire, Helen. "A Brief History of Santa Cruz Island from 1869 to 1937." *Ventura County Historical Society Quarterly* 27 (summer 1982): 3–33.

———. "Santa Cruz Vintage." *Noticias: Quarterly Magazine of the Santa Barbara Historical Society* 35 (spring/summer 1989): 142–51.

Cipolla, Carlo. "European Connoisseurs and California Wines." *Agricultural History* 49, no. 1 (spring 1975): 294–310.

Folwell, Raymond J., and Mark A. Castaldi. "Economies of Size in Wineries and Impacts of Pricing and Product Mix Decisions." *Agribusiness: An International Journal* 3 (fall 1987): 281–92.

Fusonie, Alan E. "John H. Davis: His Contributions to Agricultural Education and Productivity." *Agricultural History* 60 (spring 1986): 97–110.

Geraci, Victor W. "El Cajon, California, 1900." *Journal of San Diego History* 36 (fall 1990): 221–33.

———. "The El Cajon, California, Raisin Industry: An Exercise in Gilded Age Capitalism." *Southern California Quarterly* 74 (winter 1992): 329–54.

———. "The Family Wine-Farm: Vintibusiness Style." *Agricultural History* 74, no. 2 (spring 2000): 419–32.

Jenkinson, Clay. "Thomas Jefferson: Refining the Art of Living." *Wine News* (n.d.): 25–27.

Kaplan, Isadore. "The First Recorded Case of Alcohol Abuse—Noah's Alcoholism." *Maryland Medical Journal* 42, no. 5 (May 1993): 444–45.

Lewis, Carolyn Baker. "Cultural Conservatism and Pioneer Florida Viticulture." *Agricultural History* 53 (July 1979): 622–36.

Luckett, Liz. "Carey Cellars Fit for Future." *Grape Grower* 23 (August 1991): 4–5.

McCormick, R. P. "The Royal Society, the Grape, and New Jersey." *Proceedings of the New Jersey Historical Society* 81 (1963): 75–84.

McGee, Irving. "The Beginnings of California Winegrowing." *Historical Society of Southern California Quarterly* 29 (March 1947): 59–71.

———. "Early California Winegrowers." *California Magazine of the Pacific* 37 (September 1947): 34–37.

———. "Jean Paul Vignes, California's First Professional Winegrower." *Agricultural History* 22 (July 1948): 176–81.

McMurray, Sally. "Who Read the Agricultural Journals?" *Agricultural History* 63 (fall 1989): 1–19.

Olmstead, Alan L. "Induced Innovation in American Agriculture." *Journal of Political Economy* 101 (February 1993): 100–18.

Peele, Stanton. "The Conflict Between Public Health Goals and the Temperance Mentality." *American Journal of Public Health* 83, no. 6 (June 1993): 805–10.

Peters, Gary L. "Trends in California Viticulture." *Geographical Review* 74 (October 1984): 455–76.

Pickleman, Jack. "A Glass a Day Keeps the Doctor . . ." *American Surgeon* 56, no. 7 (July 1990): 395–97.

Renaud, E. B. "Wine, Alcohol, Platelets, and the French Paradox for Coronary Heart Disease." *Lancet* 339, no. 8808 (20 June 1992): 1523–26.

Rossiter, Margaret W. "Graduate Work in the Agricultural Sciences." *Agricultural History* 60 (spring 1986): 37–57.

Samsel, Lynn, Diane I. Hambley, and Raymond A. Marquardt. "Agribusiness' Competitiveness for Venture Capital." *Agribusiness* 7 (July 1991): 401–13.

Spitze, R. G. F. "A Continuing Evolution in U.S. Agricultural Policy." *Agricultural Economics* 77 (1990): 126–39.

Winkler, A. J. "Better Grapes for Wine." *American Journal of Enology* 9 (1958): 202–3.

———. "The Effect of Climatic Regions." *Wine Review* 6 (1938): 14–16.

———. "Varietal Grapes in the Central Coast." *American Journal of Enology and Viticulture* 15 (1964): 204–5.

Winters, Donald L. "The Agricultural Ladder in Southern Agriculture." *Agricultural History* 61 (fall 1987): 36–52.

Magazines

Adair, David. "Defining Organic Wines." *Wines and Vines,* March 1991, 23–24.

Alperstein, Ellen. "Savoring South Australia: Touring the Country's Wine-Producing Region." *Relax: The Travel Magazine for Practicing Physicians,* August 1993, 16–18.

Auf der Heide, Ralph. "The Vineyards." *Santa Barbara Magazine,* winter 1977, 6–14.

Balzer, Robert Lawrence. "California Grand Cru in a Lompoc Barn." *Robert Lawrence Balzer's Private Guide to Food and Wine,* May 1978, 14–15.

Baum, David. "These Golden Vineyards: How Did Santa Barbara Get So Good So Fast?" *Santa Barbara Magazine,* July/August 1992, 30–35.

Berger, Dan. "The BATF Label Fable." *Wine News,* February/March 1992, 10–11.

———. "Crush Preparations: Is 'Modern' Winemaking Re-Inventing the Wheel." *Wine News Monthly,* August 1996, 33–37.

———. "Defining the Legal Limit." *Wine News,* December/January 1993–1994, 12.

———. "Freedom of Speech." *Wine News,* April/May 1992, 9.

Bullard, Robyn. "One Part Chuck Ortman, Three Parts Vineyard." *Wine Spectator,* 15 April 1994, 31.

———. "The Power of the Paradox." *Wine Spectator* (http://www.winespectator.com. archives), 15 March 1994.

———. "Sons and Daughters." *Wine Spectator,* 30 September 1993, 29–35.

Burden, Annette. "Pride of the Valley." *Santa Barbara Magazine,* November/December 1983, 38–47.

Caldwell-Ewart, Carol. "Sanford Winery: Managing Costs Profitably." *Pacific Wine and Vines,* November/December 1993, 40.

"California Wine: Everybody Wants In." *Forbes,* 1 December 1968, 70–77.

Carlson, Cliff. "Case Study: Emergence of 'Escargociants.'" *Wine Business Monthly* 3 (June 1996): 51–52.

Cartiere, Rich. "1995: U.S. Vintners 'Worst Best Year Ever.'" *Wine Business Monthly* 3 (March 1996): 1–2.

Cartiere, Rich, Teri Shore, and Marshall Farrer. "Calif.'s 'Vineyard Royalty' Doubles Holdings." *Wine Business Monthly* 3 (May 1996): 1–6.

"Commission Vote?" *Wines and Vines,* April 1987, 18–19.

Coverdale, Jennifer. "Alcohol and Heroin: Schools Say They Are the Same." *Wine Business Monthly* 3 (June 1996): 1, 4–7.

Elson, John. "A Golden Age for Grapes." *Time,* 10 December 1990, 88–92.

"Ernest Gallo Calls for Action." *California Wine Tasting Monthly,* October 1993, 4.

Farmer, Lyn. "Beringer on the Offensive." *Wine News,* February/March 1993, 7.

———. "The Quirks of Cork." *Wine News,* February/March 1994, 10.

Frons, Marc. "Tasting Wines at Their Scenic Sources." *Business Week,* 15 May 1989, 157.

Gallo, Ernest. "Gallo Jabs at Distillers." *Wine Spectator,* 16–31 July 1984, 5.

Galphin, Bruce. "Santa Barbara Has Joined Winegrowing Major Leagues." *Wine News,* August 1990, 1.

Garrett, Tom. "New Santa Barbara Vintner Plans Rhône Varietals." *Wine Spectator,* 30 April 1996, 13.

Gilster, Paul. "Style and Substance." *Wine Spectator,* 16–22 November 1989.

Gold, Jonathan. "California's New Wave Winemakers Rockin' Vines in the Santa Maria Valley." *Elle,* January 1992, 76.

"Growers Want Separate Commissions." *Wines and Vines,* May 1987, 16.

Hardy, Quentin. "A Surplus of Fine Wine Leaves California Vintners Seeing Their Glasses Half Empty." *Forbes,* 7 January 2002.

Harris, Paula. "Harvest Preparation Case Study: Neutron Probe to Gauge Irrigation Comes of Age." *Wine Business Monthly* 3 (August 1996): 29–32.

———. "Wine's Medicinal Nutritional Roots Traced Back to Stone Age." *Wine Business Monthly* 3 (July 1996): 29–30.

"Harsh New Law in Kentucky Draws Furious Reaction." *Wine Enthusiast,* June 1996, 13.

Harvell, Erik. "Turning Overseas for the Home Market." *Wine Business Monthly* 3 (September 1996): 12–13.

Heimoff, Steve. "Gay Wine Marketing Slowly Follows Beer and Spirits Lead." *Wine Business Monthly* 3 (March 1996): 14–17.

———. "How to Create a New Cult Cabernet from Scratch." *Wine Enthusiast,* June 1996, 51.

Hiaring, Philip. "*Wines and Vines* Revisits Santa Barbara County." *Wines and Vines,* April 1991, 29–32.

Hilton, M. L., Rich Cartiere, and Christian McIntosh. "Capacity and Demand Debate." *Wine Business Monthly* 3 (July 1996): 1, 4, 6.

———. "Vine Grafting Boom Leads to Vineyard Surge." *Wine Business Monthly* 3 (August 1996): 1, 4.

Hinkle, Richard Paul. "Searching for the Holy Grail." *Wines and Vines,* July 1993.

Hochstein, Mort. "Seagram Reveals Its Strategies." *Wine Spectator,* 16–31 July 1984, 4–5.

"Infestations and Tight Money Will Shake out Wine Industry." *California Wine Tasting Monthly,* April 1993, 7.

Irving, Clive. "Juice Valley." *Conde Nast Traveler,* November 1992.

"Kendall-Jackson Petitions BATF." *Wine Business Monthly* 3 (June 1996): 8–9.

Kramer, Matt. "Gone with the Wind?" *Wine Spectator,* 31 July 1996, 31.

———. "Slipperiness at the Smithsonian." *Wine Spectator,* 31 August 1996, 29.

Laube, James. "Hot New Wines from California." *Wine Spectator,* 15 June 1996, 28–50.

———. "Napa Valley's Beringer Vineyards in Play: Investor Group May Pay $300 Million for Wine World." *Wine Spectator,* 15 December 1995, 11.

———. "Richard Sanford Starts Again in Santa Barbara with New Pinot Noir and Chardonnay Vineyards." *Wine Spectator,* 31 March 1996, 14.

———. "Rising Stars of Cabernet: Foxen Breaks out of a Mediocre Pack in Santa Barbara." *Wine Spectator,* 15 November 1992.

———. "Sonoma's Chateau St. Jean Appears Headed to Wine World." *Wine Spectator,* 29 February 1996, 10.

———. "Staking Their Claim in California." *Wine Spectator,* 1–15 June 1984, 18–21.

———. "Trivial Pursuits in California." *Wine Spectator,* 15 December 1995, 25.

———. "Wine World's New Treasure." *Wine Spectator,* 15 May 1996, 25.

Lukacs, Paul. "The Rise of American Wine." *American Heritage,* December 1996, 84–98.

Mansson, Per-Henrik. "The Father of the French Paradox." *Wine Spectator,* 15 March 1994, 45.

Marcks, Kathleen. "Former Olympian Takes on Winemaking Challenge." *Wine Spectator,* 31 August 1996, 15.

Marcus, Kim. "In a Dramatic Shift, New Federal Guidelines Say It's OK to Drink Moderately." *Wine Spectator,* 29 February 1996, 8–9.

———. "New Tests Find Evidence of Wine at the Dawn of Civilization." *Wine Spectator,* 31 July 1996, 8.

Matthews, Thomas. "Britain Raises Safe Drinking Limits." *Wine Spectator,* 29 February 1996, 9.

———. "Onward and Upward," *Wine Spectator,* 30 June 1996, 55–56.

———. "Wine: Prescription for Good Health." *Wine Spectator,* 15 March 1994, 37–44.

Morgan, Jeff. "California's Jed Steele Decides to Put Down Roots." *Wine Spectator,* 15 June 1996, 13.

———. "California's 'Other' Coast." *Wine Spectator,* 15 May 1996, 49–59.

———. "'Mad Rush' to Chile by California and French Vintners." *Wine Spectator,* 31 May 1996, 8–9.

———. "Mondavi Buys Key Santa Barbara Vineyard." *Wine Spectator,* 30 April 1996, 13.

Mead, Jerry. "High Drama in the Wine (Shipping) Biz." *Wine Enthusiast,* 31 July 1996, 30.

"New Tasting Room." *California Wine Tasting Monthly,* April 1993, 7.

"New Wine Commission Gets off to a Fast Start." *Wines and Vines,* July 1987, 13.

O'Hara, Steven. "Afraid to Prescribe Wine." *Wine News,* December/January 1993–1994, 14.

Perdue, Lewis. "It's the Alcohol, Stupid." *Wine Business Monthly* 4 (April 1997): 6, 66–67.

Peterson, Thane. "A Glass of White—Hold the Pesticides." *Business Week,* 14 September 1992, 116.

Pitcher, Steve. "'Signature' Collaborative Offering." *Wine News,* December/January 1993.

"Pour Us Some Blues." *Playboy,* August 1996, 161.

Pryor, Alton. "Tasty Marketing Twist: A Gourmet Wine Tour." *California Farmer,* 11 August 1984, 53.

"Ranch Building Winery with Direct Marketing Approach." *California-Arizona Farm Press,* 26 May 1984, 8.

"Rapid Changes in Wine Commission Legal Dispute." *Wines and Vines,* April 1990, 14.

Rapp, Robert P. "Wineries Boycott Kentucky." *Wine Spectator,* 31 May 1996, 27.

Recio, Maria. "Wine That Lets You Keep Your Head." *Business Week,* 11 November 1991, 184.

Robards, Terry. "History of Wine Repeats Itself: '76 Paris Tasting Recalled at Smithsonian." Edited by Ben Giliberti. *Wine Enthusiast,* July 1996, 8.

Roberts, Larry. "Masters of Wine on First California Tour." *Wine Spectator,* 1–15 June 1981, 19.

Rolens, Lin. "When the Magic Was on Mountain Drive." *Santa Barbara Magazine,* January/February 1992, 40–47.

Shapiro, Laura. "To Your Health." *Newsweek,* 22 January 1996, 52–54.

Shore, Teri. "Cellar Direct Shipping Network." *Wine Business Monthly* 3 (July 1996): 12–15.

Shufer, Jane. "Good Medicine: How Doctors Incorporate Wine In Their Lives." *Wine Spectator,* 15 March 1994, 46–47.

St. Pierre, Brian. "Getting Great Grapes." *Decanter,* 1990, 2–10.

Stepanovich, Mike. "The Roots of Wine." *Wine News,* June/July 1991, 23–24.

Stuertz, Mark. "Texas Looks into 21st Century; California's Hampton Farming Helps Lead the Way into the Future." *Wine Business Monthly* 3 (July 1996): 10.

Stuller, Jay. "Hollywood and Wine: Making the Most of an Image." *Hemispheres*, January 1995, 89–90, 92, 95.

Suckling, James. "An Ongoing Race with the French." *Wine Spectator*, 16–30 November 1983, 4.

———. "Wine Legislation Attempts to Curb Tariff Barriers." *Wine Spectator*, 1–15 June 1983, 2.

"They Will Sell No Wine." *Time*, 29 May 1989, 75.

Thompson, Bob. "Sorting out the Sites." *Decanter*, 1991.

Van Kriedt, Phyllis. "BATF Issues a Landmark Industry Circular." *California Wineletter*, 2 September 1993.

———. "Free Run." *California Wineletter*, 14 August 1992.

———. "Hartzell Explains the Consequences of the 1990 Excise Tax Increase." *California Wineletter*, 2 September 1993.

———. "NASA Joins the Fight Against Phylloxera." *California Wineletter*, 23 April 1993.

———. "A New Wine from Phil Awksira." *California Wineletter*, 14 August 1992.

———. "Phylloxera Update." *California Wineletter*, 7 September 1993.

———. "A Welcome New Focus for AWARE." *California Wineletter*, 24 September 1992.

———. "W.I. Tries to Pull a Fast One." *California Wineletter*, 2 September 1993.

Walker, Larry. "A Napa Valley Quiz Show." *Wine Enthusiast*, June 1996, 55–59.

———. "Wineries Are Trying Organic Techniques." *Wines and Vines*, June 1989, 59–60.

Walter, Gregory S. "Marketing Executive Calls for New Winery Association." *Wine Spectator*, 1–15 November 1983, 24.

Whitten, David. "Fighting Puritans." *Wine Spectator*, 31 March 1996, 36.

"Wine Couponing Now in California." *Wine Spectator*, 1–15 June 1984, 3.

"Wine Industry Continues Battle Against Regs, Taxes." *California Wine Tasting Monthly*, June 1993, 6.

"Wine Industry Fights Health Tax, Opposes Perception of Wine as Sin." *California Wine Tasting Monthly*, April 1993, 5.

Wines and Vines Statistical Survey, 1972–1992.

"Wine Tariff War Could Aid California Vintners." *Advertising Age*, 9 November 1992, 8.

Winters, Mark. "Nouveau Vintners Break Ground in Santa Ynez." *California Law Business*, 17 July 1989, 9.

Books

Adams, Leon D. *The Wines of America.* San Francisco: McGraw-Hill, 1990.

Adlum, John. *A Memoir on the Cultivation of the Vine in America, and the Best Mode of Making Wine.* Washington, D.C.: Davis and Force, 1823.

Amerine, Maynard A., and Maynard A. Joslyn. *Commerical Production of Table Wines.* Berkeley: California Agricultural Experimental Station, College of Agriculture, University of California, 1940.

———. *Table Wines: The Technology of Their Production.* Berkeley: University of California Press, 1951.

Amerine, Maynard A., and H. Phaff. *A Bibliography of Publications by the Faculty, Staff, and Students of the University of California, 1876–1980, on Grapes, Wines, and Related Subjects.* Berkeley: University of California Press, 1986.

Amerine, Maynard A., and Vernon L. Singleton. *Wine: An Introduction.* 2d ed. Berkeley: University of California Press, 1972.

Balzer, Robert L. *California's Best Wines.* Los Angeles: Ward Ritchie Press, 1948.

Bancroft, Hubert Howe. *The Works of Hubert Howe Bancroft.* Vol. 34, *California Pastoral, 1769–1848.* San Francisco: History Company, 1888.

Barron, Cheryll Aimee. *Dreamers of the Valley of Plenty: A Portrait of the Napa Valley.* New York: Scribner, 1995.

Bogue, Allan G. *From Prairie to Corn Belt: Farming on the Illinois and Iowa Prairies in the Nineteenth Century.* Chicago: University of Chicago Press, 1963.

Braconi, Frank. *The U.S. Wine Market: An Economic Marketing and Financial Investigation.* Merrick, N.Y.: Morton Research Corporation, April 1977.

Brownlee, W. Elliot. *Dynamics of Ascent: A History of the American Economy.* 2d ed. New York: Alfred A. Knopf, 1979.

Burnham, John C. *Bad Habits: Drinking, Smoking, Taking Drugs, Gambling, Sexual Misbehavior, and Swearing in American History.* New York: New York University Press, 1993.

Carlson, Vada F. *This Is Our Valley.* Santa Maria, Calif.: Santa Maria Historical Society, 1959.

Carosso, Vincent P. *The California Wine Industry: A Study of the Formative Years.* Berkeley: University of California Press, 1951.

Chiacos, Elias, ed. *Mountain Drive: Santa Barbara's Pioneer Bohemian Community.* Santa Barbara, Calif.: Shoreline Press, 1994.

Conaway, James. *Napa.* Boston: Houghton Mifflin, 1990.

Coombs, Gary B., ed. *Those Were the Days: Landmarks of Old Goleta.* Goleta, Calif.: Institute for American Research, 1986.

Cowan, Robert G. *Ranchos of California: A List of Spanish Concessions, 1775–1822, and Mexican Land Grants, 1822–1846.* Fresno, Calif.: Academy Library Guild, 1956.

Dercierdo, Margarita Arce. *Mediating Conflict in California Fields, 1975–1977.* Oakland, Calif.: Center for Third World Organizing, 1980.

Fay, James S. *California Almanac.* 5th ed. Santa Barbara, Calif.: Pacific Data Resources (ABC-Clio), 1991.

Fisher, M. F. K. *The Story of Wine in California.* Berkeley: University of California Press, 1962.

Fuller, Robert C. *Religion and Wine: A Cultural History of Wine Drinking in the United States.* Knoxville: University of Tennessee Press, 1996.

Gallo, Ernest, and Julio Gallo, with Bruce Henderson. *Ernest and Julio Gallo: Our Story.* New York: Random House, 1994.

Gates, Paul W. *California Ranchos and Farms, 1846–1862, Including the Letters of John Quincy Adams Warren of 1861, Being Largely Devoted to Livestock, Wheat Farming, Fruit Raising, and the Wine Industry.* Madison: State Historical Society of Wisconsin, 1967.

Gavin-Jobson Publication. *The Wine Marketing Handbook.* New York: Gavin-Jobson, 1972, 1980, 1990.

Geraci, Victor W. *Santa Barbara New House: The First Forty Years, 1955–1995.* Santa Barbara, Calif.: Santa Barbara New House, 1995.

Gidney, Charles M. *History of Santa Barbara, San Luis Obispo, and Ventura Counties.* Chicago: Lewis Publishing Co., 1917.

Graham, Otis L. Jr., Robert Bauman, Douglas W. Dodd, Victor W. Geraci, and Fermina Brel Murray. *Stearns Wharf: Surviving Change on the California Coast.* Santa Barbara, Calif.: Graduate Program in Public Historical Studies, University of California, Santa Barbara, 1994.

Graham, Otis L. Jr., Sarah Harper Case, Victor W. Geraci, Susan Goldstein, Richard P. Ryba, and Beverly Schwartzberg. *Aged in Oak: The Story of the Santa Barbara County Wine Industry.* Santa Barbara, Calif.: Cachuma Press, 1998.

Hakluyt, Richard. *The Principal Navigations, Voyages, Traffiques, and Discoveries of the English Nation.* 1589. Vol. 8. Reprint, Glasgow: J. MacLehose and Sons, 1903–1905.

Henretta, James A. *The Origins of American Capitalism: Collected Essays.* Boston: Northeastern University Press, 1991.

Hilgard, Eugene W. *Report of the Professor of Agriculture to the President of the University.* Sacramento: State Printing Office, 1879.

———. *University of California–College of Agriculture Report of the Viticultural Work During the Seasons 1887–1893 with Data Regarding the Crush of 1894–95.* Sacramento: Superintendent of State Printing, 1896.

History of San Luis Obispo County, California. Oakland: Thompson and West, 1883.

Hussmann, George. *Grape Culture and Wine Making in California: A Practical Manual for the Grape Grower and Wine Maker.* San Francisco: Payot, Upham, 1888.

Hyams, E. Dionysus: *A Social History of the Wine Vine.* 2d ed. London: and Jackson, 1987.

Hyatt, Thomas H. *Hyatt's Handbook of Grape Culture; or, Why, Where, When, and How to Plant a Vineyard, Manufacture Wines, etc.* San Francisco: H.H. Bancroft and Company, 1867.

Johnson, Hugh. *Vintage: The Story of California Wine.* New York: Simon and Schuster, 1989.

Jones, Frank. *The Save-Your-Heart Wine Guide.* New York: St. Martin's Press, 1996.

Jones, Idwal. *Vines in the Sun: A Journey Through the California Vineyards.* New York: Ballantine Books, 1949.

Kingsbury, Susan M., ed. *The Records of the Virginia Company of London.* 4 vols. Washington, D.C.: Government Printing Office, 1906–1935.

Kladstrup, Don, and Petie Kladstrup, with J. Kim Munholland. *Wine and War: The French, the Nazis, and the Battle for France's Greatest Treasure.* New York: Broadway Books, 2001.

Kolpan, Steven. *A Sense of Place: An Intimate Portrait of the Niebaum-Copola Winery and the Napa Valley.* New York: Routledge, 1999.

Kramer, Matt. *Making Sense of California Wine.* New York: William Morrow and Company, 1992.

Kulikoff, Allan. *The Agrarian Origins of American Capitalism.* Charlottesville, Va.: University of Virginia Press, 1992.

Lampard, Eric E. *The Rise of the Dairy Industry in Wisconsin, 1820–1920.* Madison: State Historical Society of Wisconsin, 1963.

Lapsley, James T. *Bottled Poetry: Napa Winemaking from Prohibition to the Modern Era.* Berkeley: University of California Press, 1996.

Larsen, John W. *Vineyard Development Financing in California.* San Francisco: Wells Fargo Bank, 1972.

Lemon, James T. *The Best Poor Man's Country: A Geographical Study of Early Southeastern Pennsylvania.* Baltimore: John Hopkins University Press, 1972.

Lukacs, Paul. *American Vintage: The Rise of American Wine.* New York: Houghton Mifflin, 2000.

Mason, Jesse D. *History of Santa Barbara County, California.* Oakland, Calif.: Thompson and West, 1883.

McGinty, Brian. *Strong Wine: The Life and Legend of Agoston Haraszthy.* Stanford, Calif.: Stanford University Press, 1998.

McNutt, Joni G. *In Praise of Wine: An Offering of Hearty Toasts, Quotations, Witticisms, Proverbs, and Poetry Throughout History.* Santa Barbara, Calif.: Capra Press, 1993.

Melville, John. *Guide to California Wines.* Garden City, N.Y.: Doubleday, 1955.

Millner, Cork. *Vintage Valley: The Wineries of Santa Barbara County.* Santa Barbara, Calif.: McNally and Loftin, 1983.

Mondavi, Robert, with Paul Chutkow. *Harvests of Joy: My Passion for Excellence.* New York: Harcourt Brace, 1998.

Murdock, Catherine Gilbert. *Domesticating Drink: Women, Men, and Alcohol in America, 1870–1940.* Baltimore: Johns Hopkins University Press, 1998.

Muscadine, Doris, Maynard A. Amerine, and Bob Thompson, eds. *The University of California/Sotheby Book of California Wine.* Los Angeles: University of California Press, 1984.

Peninou, Ernest P., and Shirlkey S. Greenleaf. *A Directory of California Wine Growers and Winemakers in 1860.* Berkeley: Tamalpais Press, 1967.

Perkins, Edwin J. *The Economy of Colonial America.* New York: Columbia University Press, 1980.

Phillips, Rod. *A Short History of Wine.* New York: Harper Collins, 2000.

Pinney, Thomas. *A History of Wine in America: From the Beginnings to Prohibition.* Los Angeles: University of California Press, 1989.

Pintarich, Paul. *The Boys up North: Dick Erath and the Early Oregon Winemakers.* Portland, Ore.: Wyatt Group, 1997.

Prial, Frank. *Decantations: Reflections on Wine by the New York Wine Critic Frank J. Prial.* New York: St. Martin's Press, 2001.

Robotti, Peter J., and Francis D. Robotti. *Key to Gracious Living: Wine and Spirits.* Englewood Cliffs, N.J.: Prentice Hall, 1972.

Rorabaugh, W. J. *The Alcoholic Republic: An American Tradition.* New York: Oxford University Press, 1979.

Schaefer, Dennis. *Vintage Talk: Conversations with California's New Winemakers.* Santa Barbara, Calif.: Capra Press, 1994.

Schoonmaker, Frank, and Tom Marvel. *The Complete Book of Wine.* New York: Duell, Sloan, and Pearce, 1934.

Schoonmaker, Frank. *Frank Schoonmaker's Encyclopedia of Wine.* New York: Hastings House, 1964.

Smith, Sydney D. *Grapes of Conflict.* Pasadena, Calif.: Hope House, 1987.

Stuller, Jay, and Glen Martin. *Through the Grapevine: The Real Story Behind America's $8 Billion Wine Industry.* New York: Harper-Collins West, 1994.

Sullivan, Charles L. *A Companion to California Wine: An Encyclopedia of Wine and Winemaking from the Mission Period to the Present.* Berkeley: University of California Press, 1998.

———. *Like Modern Edens: Winegrowing in Santa Clara Valley and Santa Cruz Mountains, 1798–1891.* Cupertino, Calif.: California History Center, 1982.

———. *Napa Wine: A History from Mission Days to Present.* San Francisco: Wine Appreciation Guild, 1994.

Tannahill, Reay. *Food in History.* New York: Crown, 1988.

Teiser, Ruth, and Catherine Harroun. *Winemaking in California.* New York: McGraw-Hill, 1983.

Thompson, Bob, ed. *California Wine: Where and How It's Made, the Winemakers . . . Past & Present. A Sunset Pictoral.* Menlo Park, Calif.: Lane Magazine and Book Company, 1973.

Tompkins, Walker A. *Santa Barbara History Makers.* Santa Barbara, Calif.: McNally and Loftin, 1983.

Tyrrell, Ian R. *Sobering Up: From Temperance to Prohibition in Antebellum America, 1800–1860.* Westport, Conn.: Greenwood Press, 1979.

Unwin, Tim. *Wine and the Vine: An Historical Geography of Viticulture and the Wine Trade.* New York: Routledge, 1991.

Wait, Frona Eunice. *Wines and Vines of California, or, A Treatise on the Ethics of Wine Drinking.* 1889. Reprint, Berkeley: Howell-North Books, 1973.

Wetmore, Charles A. *Ampelography of California: A Discussion of Vines Now Known in the State, Together with Comments on Their Adaptability to Certain Locations and Uses.* San Francisco: Merchant Publishing Company, 1884.

Winkler, A. J., et al. *General Viticulture.* Rev. ed. Berkeley: University of California Press, 1974.

Government Publications

Amerine, Maynard A., and A. J. Winkler. *Grape Varieties for Wine Production.* University of California, Berkeley, Division of Agricultural Sciences. Pamphlet no. 154. March 1963.

Blout, Jesse S. *A Brief Economic History of the California Wine-Growing Industry.* San Francisco: Bureau of Markets, California Department of Agriculture, 1943.

Bioletti, Frederic T. *A New Method of Making Dry Red Wine.* Berkeley: Agricultural Experiment Station, 1906.

———. Agricultural Experiment Station, Berkeley, California. "Grape Culture in California: Improved Methods of Wine Making." Sacramento: Superintendent of State Printing, 1908.

———. Agricultural Experiment Station, Berkeley, California. "Grape Culture in California: Its Difficulties; Phylloxera and Resistant Vines; and Other Vine Diseases." Sacramento: Superintendent of State Printing, 1908.

———. Agricultural Experiment Station, Berkeley, California. "Grape Culture in California: Yeasts from California Grapes." Sacramento: Superintendent of State Printing, 1908.

California. Agricultural Experiment Station. State Board of Public Health. Bureau of Food and Drug Inspection. *Regulations Establishing Standards of Identity, Quality, Purity and Sanitation, and Governing the Labeling and Advertising of Wine in the State of California.* Sacramento: California State Printing Office, 1942.

California Agricultural Statistics Service. *California Agriculture: Statistical Review 1986 and 1987.* Sacramento: California Department of Food and Agriculture.

———. *California Grape Acreage 1979, 1981, 1984, 1990.* Sacramento: California Agricultural Statistics Service.

Department of the Treasury. Bureau of Alcohol, Tobacco, and Firearms. Rules and Regulations. "Santa Maria Viticultural Area," 46:150 (5 August 1981): 39811–12.

———. "Santa Ynez Valley Viticultural Area," 48:74 (15 April 1983): 16250–51.

Hoch, Irving, and Nickolas Tryphonopoulos. *A Study of the Economy of Napa County, California.* Giannini Foundation of Agricultural Economics Research Report no. 303. University of California, Davis, Agricultural Experiment Station, August 1969.

Mouton, Kirby S., ed. *The Economics of Small Wineries: The Proceedings of Two Seminars at University of California, Davis, May 1979 and May 1980.* Berkeley: Cooperative Extension, University of California, 1981.

Quayle, H. J. Agricultural Experiment Station Berkeley, California. "The Grape Leaf-Hopper." Sacramento: Superintendent of State Printing, 1908.

Santa Barbara County. Department of Resource Management. *Agricultural Planned Development and Transfer of Development Rights.* Santa Barbara, Calif.: Santa Barbara County Department of Resource Management, September 1985.

University of California. Agricultural Extension Service. *The Climate of Santa Barbara County: Plantclimate Map and Climatological Data.* Santa Barbara, Calif.: University of California Agricultural Extension Service, 1965.

Winkler, A. J. "Grape Growing in California." California Agricultural Extension Service Circular no. 116. November 1950.

Oral Interviews

Adams, Leon. Interview by Ruth Teiser. 1986. In *California Wine Industry Affairs: Recollections and Opinions.* Berkeley: Regional Oral History Office, Bancroft Library, University of California, 1990.

Addis, Craig. Interview by Beverly Schwartzberg. Tape recording, Santa Barbara, Calif., 28 January 1994. Special Collections, University of California, Santa Barbara.

Babcock, Bryan. Interview by Susan Goldstein. Tape recording, Santa Ynez, Calif., 2 February 1994. Special Collections, University of California, Santa Barbara.

Banke, Barbara. Interview by Richard P. Ryba. Tape recording, Santa Maria, Calif., 11 February 1994. Special Collections, University of California, Santa Barbara.

Bedford, Stephan. Interview by Victor W. Geraci. Tape recording, Santa Maria, Calif., 24 February 1994. Special Collections, University of California, Santa Barbara.

Beko, Norman. Interview by Sarah Harper Case. Tape recording, Santa Maria, Calif., 28 January 1994. Special Collections, University of California, Santa Barbara.

Bettencourt, Boyd. Interview by Beverly Schwartzberg. Tape recording, Santa Ynez, Calif., 8 April 1994. Special Collections, University of California, Santa Barbara.

Blewis, Sharon. Interview by Sarah Harper Case. Tape recording, Santa Ynez, Calif., 9 February 1994. Special Collections, University of California, Santa Barbara.

Block, David. Interview by Richard P. Ryba. Tape recording, Santa Ynez, Calif., 28 January 1994. Special Collections, University of California, Santa Barbara.

Brander, C. Frederick. Interview by Beverly Schwartzberg. Tape recording, Santa Ynez, Calif., 16 February 1994. Special Collections, University of California, Santa Barbara.

Brown, Byron Kent. Interview by Richard P. Ryba. Tape recording, Santa Maria, Calif., 14 September 1994. Special Collections, University of California, Santa Barbara.

Brown, Dean. Interview by Victor W. Geraci and Jeff Maiken. Tape recording, Santa Ynez, Calif., 25 October 1995. Special Collections, University of California, Santa Barbara.

Brown, Michael. Interview by Victor W. Geraci. Tape recording, Santa Barbara, Calif., 22 November 1996. Special Collections, University of California, Santa Barbara.

Clendenen, Jim. Interview by Richard P. Ryba. Tape recording, Santa Maria, Calif., 10 February 1994. Special Collections, University of California, Santa Barbara.

Duggan, Sheryl. Inteview by Sarah Harper Case and Victor W. Geraci. Tape recording, Santa Ynez, Calif., 27 January 1994. Special Collections, University of California Santa Barbara.

Firestone, A. Brooks. Interview by Richard P. Ryba. Tape recording, Santa Ynez, Calif., 18 February 1995. Special Collections, University of California, Santa Barbara.

Firestone, Catherine Boulton. Interview by Victor W. Geraci. Tape recording, Santa Ynez, Calif., 3 February 1994. Special Collections, University of California, Santa Barbara.

Haley, Brian. Interview by Susan Goldstein. Tape recording, Santa Barbara, Calif., 1994. Special Collections, University of California, Santa Barbara.

Hampton, Dale. Interview by Victor W. Geraci and Susan Goldstein. Tape recording, Santa Maria, Calif., 10 February 1994. Special Collections, University of California, Santa Barbara.

Hayer, T. Interview by Richard P. Ryba. Tape recording, Santa Ynez, Calif., 29 June 1994. Special Collections, University of California, Santa Barbara.

Hill, Stanley. Interview by Teddy Gasser. Santa Barbara, Calif., 10 January 1987. Collection of the Santa Barbara Historical Society.

Holt, Ed. Interview by Richard P. Ryba. Tape recording, Santa Maria, Calif., 21 April 1995. Special Collections, University of California, Santa Barbara.

Houtz, David, and Margy Houtz. Interview by Sarah Harper Case. Tape recording, Santa Ynez, Calif., 28 January 1994. Special Collections, University of California, Santa Barbara.

Jackson, Jess. Interview by Richard P. Ryba. Tape recording, Santa Maria, Calif., 11 February 1994. Special Collections, University of California, Santa Barbara.

Jessup, Hayley Firestone. Interview by Victor W. Geraci. Tape recording, Santa Ynez, Calif., 3 February 1994. Special Collections, University of California, Santa Barbara.

Johnson, Barry. Interview by Susan Goldstein. Tape recording, Santa Ynez, Calif., 28 January 1994. Special Collections, University of California, Santa Barbara.

Kerr, John. Interview by Sarah Case. Tape recording, Santa Ynez, Calif., 9 February 1994. Special Collections, University of California, Santa Barbara.

Knox, Mel. Interview by Richard P. Ryba. Tape recording, Santa Ynez, Calif., 1 July 1994. Special Collections, University of California, Santa Barbara.

Lafond, Pierre. Interview by Beverly Schwartzberg. Tape recording, Santa Barbara, Calif., 28 January 1994. Special Collections, University of California, Santa Barbara.

Lindquist, Robert. Interview by Sarah Case. Tape recording, Santa Maria, Calif., 24 February 1994. Special Collections, University of California, Santa Barbara.

Longoria, Rick. Interview by Victor W. Geraci. Tape recording, Santa Ynez, Calif., 14 August 1996. Special Collections, University of California, Santa Barbara.

Lucas, Louis. Interview by Richard P. Ryba. Tape recording, Santa Maria, Calif., 29 June 1994. Special Collections, University of California, Santa Barbara.

Maiken, Jeff. Interview by Sarah Case and Victor W. Geraci. Tape recording, Santa Ynez, Calif., 27 January 1994. Special Collections, University of California, Santa Barbara.

Marks, Donna. Interview by Beverly Schwartzberg. Tape recording, Santa Ynez, Calif., 8 March 1994. Special Collections, University of California, Santa Barbara.

McGuire, Bruce. Interview by Beverly Schwartzberg. Tape recording, Santa Barbara, Calif., 28 January 1994. Special Collections, University of California, Santa Barbara.

Miller, Bob. Interview by Richard P. Ryba. Tape recording, Santa Barbara, Calif., 15 September 1994. Special Collections, University of California, Santa Barbara.

Mosby, Gary. Interview by Sarah Case. Tape recording, Santa Ynez, Calif., 24 March 1994. Special Collections, University of California, Santa Barbara.

Mosby, Geraldine. Interview by Susan Goldstein. Tape recording, Santa Ynez, Calif., 28 January 1994. Special Collections, University of California, Santa Barbara.

Murray, Fran. Interview by Susan Goldstein. Tape recording, Santa Ynez, Calif., 16 February 1994. Special Collections, University of California, Santa Barbara.

Murray, Jim. Interview by Susan Goldstein. Tape recording, Santa Ynez, Calif., 16 February 1994. Special Collections, University of California, Santa Barbara.

Newton, Jeff. Interview by Victor W. Geraci. 15 June 1994.

Parker, Fess. Interview by Victor W. Geraci. Tape recording, Santa Ynez, Calif., 17 April 1995. Special Collections, University of California, Santa Barbara.

Pfeiffer, Harold. Interview by Richard P. Ryba. Tape recording, Santa Maria, Calif., 21 April 1995. Special Collections, University of California, Santa Barbara.

Rashid, Laila. Interview by Beverly Schwartzberg. Tape recording, Santa Barbara, Calif., 28 January 1994. Special Collections, University of California, Santa Barbara.

Rice, Fred. Interview by Richard P. Ryba. Tape recording, Santa Ynez, Calif., 28 January 1994. Special Collections, University of California, Santa Barbara.

Sanford, Richard. Interview by Victor W. Geraci and Otis L. Graham Jr. Tape recording, Santa Barbara, Calif., 7 March 1995. Special Collections, University of California, Santa Barbara.

Scott, Doug. Interview by Beverly Schwartzberg. Tape recording, Santa Ynez, Calif., 10 February 1994. Special Collections, University of California, Santa Barbara.

Tanner, Lane. Interview by Susan Goldstein. Tape recording, Santa Maria, Calif., 3 February 1994. Special Collections, University of California, Santa Barbara.

Whitcraft, Chris. Interview by Beverly Schwartzberg. Tape recording, Santa Ynez, Calif., 3 February 1994. Special Collections, University of California, Santa Barbara.

Wilkes, Jeff. Interview by Susan Goldstein. Tape recording, Santa Maria, Calif., 3 March 1994. Special Collections, University of California, Santa Barbara.

Woods, Bob, and Jeanne Woods. Interview by Richard P. Ryba. Tape recording, Santa Maria, Calif., 12 April 1995. Special Collections, University of California, Santa Barbara.

Yager, David. Interview by Sarah Harper Case and Otis L. Graham Jr. Tape recording, Santa Barbara, Calif., 18 January 1995. Special Collections, University of California, Santa Barbara.

Unpublished Material

Brown, Jerry B. "The United Farm Workers Grape Strike and Boycott, 1965–1970." Ph.D. diss., Cornell University Latin American Studies Program, 1972.

Casper, Ellen. "A Social History of Farm Labor in California with Special Emphasis on the United Farm Workers Union and California Rural Legal Assistance." Ph.D. diss., University of California, Santa Barbara, 1984.

Conard, Rebecca Ann. "The Conservation of Local Autonomy: California's Agricultural Land Policies, 1900–1966." Ph.D. diss., University of California, Santa Barbara, 1984.

Curry, James Harold, III. "Agriculture Under Late Capitalism: The Structure and Operation of the California Wine Industry." Ph.D. diss., Cornell University, 1994.

de la Peña, Donald Joseph. "Vineyards in a Regional System of Open Space in the San Francisco Bay Area: Methods of Preserving Selected Areas." Master's thesis, University of California, Berkeley, 1962.

Della Valle, Andrea Laura. "The Taste of Globalization: The Wine Industry of Ontario (Canada)." Master's thesis, University of Windsor (Canada), 1996.

Fauntleroy, Phylicia Ann. "An Economic Analysis of the United States Demand for Distilled Spirits, Wine, and Beer Incorporating Taste Changes Through Demographic Factors, 1960–1981 (Beverage Alcohol)." Ph.D. diss., American University, 1984.

Geraci, Victor W. "Grape Growing to Vintibusiness: A History of the Santa Barbara, California, Regional Wine Industry, 1965–1995." Ph.D. diss., University of California, Santa Barbara, 1997.

———. "The Rise and Fall of the El Cajon, California, Raisin Industry, 1873–1920." Master's thesis, San Diego State University, 1990.

Haley, Brian D. "Aspects and Social Impacts of Size and Organization in the Recently Developed Wine Industry of Santa Barbara County, California." Working paper, University of California, Santa Barbara, Center for Chicano Studies, 1989.

Heien, Dale M. "The Impact of the Alcohol Tax Act of 1990 on California Agriculture." Position paper sponsored by the United Agribusiness League, Irvine, Calif., July 1990.

Heintz, William F. "The Role of Chinese Labor in Viticulture and Winemaking in Nineteenth-Century California." Master's thesis, California State University, Sonoma, 1977.

Hofer, James D. "Cucamonga Wines and Vines: A History of the Cucamonga Pioneer Vineyard Association." Master's thesis, Claremont University, 1983.

Keller, David Stanford. "Vineyard Imageries in the Old Testament Prophets (Imagery)." Ph.D. diss., University of Minnesota, 1995.

Knox, Trevor McTaggart. "The Economic Organization of Winemaking: French Cooperatives and California Corporations in Historical Context." Ph.D. diss., University of Connecticut, 2000.

Levi, Anette Ellery. "Domestic and Foreign Wine Demand in Major Wine Producing and Consuming Nations (Domestic Wine Demand, WineDemand, Demand Analysis)." Ph.D. diss., Washington State University, 1990.

Mink, James V. "The Santa Ynez Valley: A Regional Study in the History of Rural California." Master's thesis, University of California, Los Angeles, 1949.

Poletti, Peter Joseph, Jr. "An Interdisciplinary Study of the Missouri Grape and Wine Industry, 1650 to 1989." Ph.D. diss., Saint Louis University, 1989.

Schnier, Robert F. "A Study of the Will to Survive of the Family-Owned Wineries of California." Master's thesis, Pepperdine University, 1982.

Shaw, David Scott. "Firm Export Strategies and Firm Export Performance in the United States Wine Industry: A Longitudinal Study." Ph.D. diss., Purdue University, 1996.

Sims, Eric N. "A Study of the California Wine Industry and an Analysis of the Effects of the Canadian–United States Free Trade Agreement on the Wine Sector, with a Note on the Impact of the North American Free Trade Agreement on California Wine Exports." Ph.D. diss., University of Arkansas, 1995.

Solana Rosillo, Juan B. "Firm Strategies in International Markets: The Case of International Entry into the United States Wine Industry (Market Entry, International Trade)." Purdue University, 1997.

South Central Farmers Committee. "The Delano Grape Story: From the Growers' View." Delano, Calif., n.d.

Vine, Richard P. "The Negociant-Shipper as the Remote Market Channel for Eastern U.S. Boutique Table Wines (United States)." Ph.D. diss., Mississippi State University, 1984.

Waters, Alejandro. "Rebuilding Technologically Competitive Industries: Lessons From Chile's and Argentina's Wine Industry Restructuring." Ph.D. diss., Massachusetts Institute of Technology, 1999.

White, Anthony Gene. "State Policy and Public Administration Impacts on an Emerging Industry: The Wine Industry in Oregon and Washington." Ph.D. diss., Portland State University, 1993.

Reports

Bank of America. *California Wine Outlook: An Economic Study Prepared by Bank of America.* San Francisco: Bank of America, 1973.

Bank of America National Trust and Savings Association. *Outlook for the California Wine Industry.* San Francisco: Bank of America, 1970.

Gomberg, Fredrikson and Associates. *The Wine Industry's Economic Contribution to Santa Barbara County: Based on the Santa Barbara County Vintners Association 1992 Economic Survey.* San Francisco: Gomberg, Fredrikson and Associates, 1994.

———. *The Wine Industry's Economic Contribution to Santa Barbara County: Based on the Santa Barbara County Vintners Association 1996 Economic Survey.* San Francisco: Gomberg, Fredrikson and Associates, 1997.

Lee, Wendell C. M. *U.S. Viticultural Areas.* San Francisco: Wine Institute Legal Department, 1992.

Pacific Gas and Electric Company. *Finest Dry Wine Grapes: New Tepusquet Vineyard Blessed with Ideal Climate.* N.d.

Stetson Engineers. *Santa Ynez River Water Conservation District Water Resources Management Planning Process, Phase 1, August 31, 1992.*

Index